The Overturned Canoe

Printed in Victoria, Canada

Note for Librarians: a cataloguing record for this book that includes Dewey Classification and US Library of Congress numbers is available from the National Library of Canada. The complete cataloguing record can be obtained from the National Library's online database at: www.nlc-bnc.ca/amicus/index-e.html

ISBN 1-4120-2227-4

TRAFFORD

This book was published on-demand in cooperation with Trafford Publishing.
On-demand publishing is a unique process and service of making a book available for retail sale to the public taking advantage of on-demand manufacturing and Internet marketing. On-demand publishing includes promotions, retail sales, manufacturing, order fulfilment, accounting and collecting royalties on behalf of the author.

Suite 6E, 2333 Government St., Victoria, B.C. V8T 4P4, CANADA

Phone	250-383-6864	Toll-free	1-888-232-4444 (Canada & US)
Fax	250-383-6804	E-mail	sales@trafford.com

Web site www.trafford.com TRAFFORD PUBLISHING IS A DIVISION OF TRAFFORD HOLDINGS LTD.

Trafford Catalogue #04-0055   www.trafford.com/robots/04-0055.html

10   9   8   7   6   5   4   3   2   1

Preface

Thank God, a man can grow! He is not bound
With earthward gaze to creep along the ground:
Though his beginnings be but poor and low...
The fire upon his altars may grow dim,
The torch he lighted may in darkness fail,
And nothing to rekindle it avail-Yet high beyond
his dull horizon's rim.   Florence E.Coates

When I was a snotty nosed kid I got a book called Jonah and the whale given to me. Years later it all became clear what that was all about.

When I looked back at the past I heard the words and views of an immature kid. But as I moved in my memories toward the present, and held my life up toward the light, I think my words and insights grew more into becoming those of an adult. I discovered that I had, like Jonah, at first got it all wrong, stumbling about in the dark, unaware of real possibilities.

As I put more and more birthdays behind me, tried more things, won and lost some battles with myself and others, I had my eyes opened even more to what's real. I guess that's what growing up is all about.

To put some flesh on the bones of this one life lived with others, share with me glimpses of a prairie boy and young man struggling and stumbling to come to terms with adolescence and work, then finding a purpose in life. Get a personal insider's look at a clergy person's life, and listen in as he thinks out loud.

Ken Crassweller,
Lethbridge, Alberta, 2002

To Lesley who teamed with
me in ministry, and to all
families with whom I had
the pleasure to serve,
associate with, and be
supported by.

Ken Crassweller

Lethbridge, December, 2004

CONTENT

Book 1

Book 2

Book 1

All great truths begin as blasphemies   Plutarch

If you really want to hear about it, the first thing you'll probably want to know is where I was born, and what my lousy childhood was like, and how my parents were occupied and all before they had me, and all that David Copperfield kind of crap, but I don't feel like going into .

1

1 Family

You may think that's not worth telling. I disagree. Since we are a part of all who have touched our lives, both they and we are worth talking about. So here it goes.

"Pile of Bones," that's what Regina, Saskatchewan was once called and where my dad and mother got together. My dad suffered hard times like others. He shoveled coal slag off railway cars. He said "to keep the home fires burning." Both mom and dad came to Canada in their teens, my mom, Josephine from Chernovtsy, Buchovina, that's in the Ukraine; dad, Herbert, from Portsmouth, England. Bill, my dad's father, came to Regina with his family because the city didn't have many who knew how to operate street cars. How he came remains a mystery. For a while dad bell-hopped at a Regina hotel before working, "mucking about with coal." After slag shoveling, he bucked the "spare board," getting what hours he could as a street car driver. That's part of our family's story. Still, there was more to tell.

I didn't know about a whole lot of it. It took my mother to put me straight on some things, my dad on others. More than once he threatened to clip my ear or use his belt if I was bad. Other relatives put me straight on other family goings-on, while my mother had the last word on how I got into the world in the year 1935 in Regina. My mother, declared that I, a walking miracle, gingerly stepped into this world feet first, but not after giving my dad conniptions. I would also have had conniptions if my age back then matched my mom and dad's. They were old, almost forty.

Stepping Out of the Womb

In the dark womb where I began
My mother's life made me a man.
Through all the months of human birth
Her beauty fed my common earth.
I cannot see, nor breathe, nor stir,
But through the death of some of her.   2

That fortunate happening from an early age, for my sake, may have caused me to see myself as different from a lot of people. I wanted to test the out-of-womb temperature first, before I had a really good look at what I was getting into.

I've got to hand it to my dad, though, for having the guts to wait it out when the doctor broke the bad news. It was going to be either my mother's life, or mine if my mother, in labour, suffered any longer. He most likely cried out, through his tears, "Doc, just a little longer." So old Doc. Moore waited, and I was born, and my mother lived to be over ninety.

It was the same old Doc who wore glasses with a black, thin ribbon hanging down, glasses that pinched his nose. And it was the same old Doc who once told me, when I was in my teens, that I was just suffering growing pains. That was the time when I was bent over in agony. I can't even imagine the agony my mom must have gone through giving birth to a guy like me.

Tossed out of a warm cosy womb, where the thermostat was set just right, into a noisy place of flashing lights, and a slap on the rump, I began life, not really knowing up from down. So there I was, a walking miracle, and one who, so I was told, began wandering early. That feet-first affair must have been an omen, pointing to the fact that I wouldn't stay put in any one place too long.

Even as a toddler, I caused my mother more than once to scream, "Oh my God!" Once, soon after I got control of my legs, I got myself lost. I didn't think that I was, but everyone else did! During one of my parents' picnics at the Legislative buildings, near the two cannons looking over the flower garden, I wandered off, crossed Albert Street with car horns honking, and tires screeching. They found me somewhere,, unconcerned, gazing at a maze of houses. My mother concluded that I must be ordained to live a charmed life, for I wasn't squashed flat like a bug on the pavement, or picked up by a dog catcher.

Years passed. We continued to live at 863

Robinson Street within the sound of the 12 o'clock brewery whistle, where the spur line railway crews stopped for lunch. Mom gossiped with Mrs. Sparks over the fence. I listened and heard "Isn't it a shame that..." and "My, how could he...!" and other public secrets, so many juicy bits to roll around in my innocence. I remembered watching my Winnipeg Street Grandpa's chickens pecking away, tossing down what wasn't tasty enough, reminding me of my own way of tackling the new. Sometimes I suffered indigestion, and other times satisfaction, but not really grasping any idea of what the meaning was behind so many interesting fresh sensations.

They say that what we do as we get older is, we expand the play pen more, while getting others to notice. My mother's apron strings were targets for getting her attention. She would brush my hands away as she would swat a fly while I tried to bug her to get even with her. Why? Because on the way to the Safeway Store, she often licked her handkerchief to wiped dirt off my face. I never liked that!

I would persist in bugging even more, running a stick along the picket fence to get her goat. But she always won out, adding the stick to her collection destined to warm the kitchen and not my backside. The only piece of wood that both she and I took a liking to was the board that the barber hoisted me up onto to straddle the black leather arms of the chair. The big moment came, though, when I didn't need the board anymore. My barber pumped up the chair so that he could get at me. Then I, elevated to grown-up status, sat right down in that chair, and he asked me "What will it be?" Kenny had arrived. I was a man! The spell was broken though when after squirming, I hopped down from the chair and followed my mom who as usual spat on her handkerchief and...

I didn't have a clue why my mom was so clinging and protective till years later. I found that I had a way of picking up every disease under the sun. Scarlet fever almost did me in. Mumps gave me gopher cheeks. Chicken pox made me look like a raspberry. Measles, two different kinds, German, and Canadian, left me short-sighted, and never able to join the Mounties to fulfil my dream. I somehow always got well and the play pen, my home, yard, and neighborhood expanded even more, beginning with the shopping trips with my mom.

Mom wore a shabby black coat with an imitation fur collar. Her feet were shod in cheap felt fur-trimmed galoshes that tipped to the sides when she walked. That's the way she was when, with me in tow, she routinely headed out toward Simpson's, the tallest building in north end Regina.

We often had to walk on a path deep in snow parallel to a long hedge bordering the grave yard. I'd firmly grip my mom's hand while she pulled me along, and I'd peer through the hedge at the marble monuments. Those walks were scary. But they weren't as scary as when I and other grade eights wildly rode our bikes around the grave, whooping and hollering to fend off our fear, while shining flashlight beams on grave stones and below our chins to make grotesque faces.

Thinking back to Simpson's, I was most fascinated by those metal tubes that clerks filled with mysterious stuff and dropped into pipes that swallowed them up like snakes swallowing mice. It's so sad that many fascinations of youth tarnish when the truth is told. The pipes carried money and messages to different store departments in a big rush, faster than hand-carrying. The time to stop and stare in youth was gradually fading with every new mystery solved.

My mother took me by the hand to many places to fulfil her out-of-house tasks and do lots of visiting with friends and family. But I always felt like someone looking in, or being talked about, a spectator, rather than included in the family of mom, dad, granny and grandpa.

Grandpa and Granny

I never knew much about either side of the family. I really never thought to ask. Despite my mind being elsewhere, I did overhear a family legend that kind of answered my question about how my mom's family landed in Canada, of all places, since they mostly spoke another tongue. Some gypsies, apparently, whispered in my grandpa's ear that there was a war coming and he had better make tracks and get his family and himself out of the country. My grandpa worked as an "artisan plasterer" of church buildings and such. He and his family escaped capture. Others didn't. I once saw a picture in mom's family album of a soldier in an old-fashioned uniform and a big handle bar mustache like my grandpa's. It wasn't him, though. Mom said that man and his wife, also in the picture, disappeared in Romania. The fellow wore a sword and looked quite capable. I guess that didn't help. Luckily grampa, granny, my mom and two sisters, and one other brother did get out in time. Otherwise, I wouldn't be here!

That was a long time before I came on the scene. My grandpa's life sure changed over the years. He once had a small farm. In the end he just had a big two storey house on Winnipeg Street. On Sundays, dad, mom, and I would drive over to grandpa's and granny's house. On the way my dad would mumble under his breath about those, "Damn farmers. They can't drive worth a..! " as he passed the odd pickup truck, with the driver looking for something. I wasn't too sure about my dad at that point.

Grandpa's place always got me squirming in my seat, while I tried to pay heed to my mom saying, "A little boy should be seen but not heard." But I always had so many questions to ask about the many living things moving about in the shadows of the house and yard. Grandpa kept canaries singing in his basement and chickens cackling in his yard. He didn't have a cow though. Yet he did have a manure pile out back that gave blue bottle flies a place to buzz. My grandpa, who looked a little like Stalin, except for his coke bottle glasses, never did look the part of a farmer. He mostly wore a white shirt, braces, black pants, slippers, and always held a long black cigarette holder to smoke roll-your-owns in.

Granny had a sweet smile and looked upon me and dad with proud pleasure, whereas grandpa frowned. He didn't seem to have a job. Yet Granny always did. She got out of the house more, scrubbing floors, cleaning offices, and attending the Ukrainian Church, that strange place down the street with the onion domes on top.

Some in the family said that granny eventually died of a broken heart. "Life hadn't been easy for her," they said. Uncle Joe, like a shadow in the night, came and went, never giving us the time of the day. He just staggered up the stairs to his room, gripping the bannister; so uncertain was he on his feet. He must have been a worry! Granny put up with a lot. The last hours of her life were spent lying helpless on the kitchen floor, grandpa unable to help her up. Yet, she had her moments, despite the "old tyrant."

On our Sunday visits granny would slip in and out of her summer kitchen where a big, friendly, hot monster of a stove and deep fryer kept her supplied with poppy seed buns, iced "pigs ears" pastries, and other goodies. She would load us up with so much to take home, looking so pleased with herself. I hated to look otherwise, either. Yet, I couldn't help but frown and strain to understand my mom talking to granny and grandpa in their old country native tongue. Now and then I would hear my dad in his English accent quietly get the odd word in edgewise. I'd prick up my ears when I heard the words "duck" or "goose."

Back home an old single shot, twelve gauge shotgun with the name "Dread Naught" marked on the blue steel near the wood stock, often seemed to invite me to lift it out of its dark corner of the basement. Then I'd pretend that I was one of the "big shot" doctors or lawyers that brought ducks, geese, and other game birds to granny and grandpa's to clean and pluck at 25 or 50 cents each. The closest I got for a long time to a good hunt was watching my mom and dad accepting game birds at our door. Mom and dad had taken over the business and plucked canvas backs, mallards-but not teals, nor mud hens, but sometimes pheasants and geese. Dad got a big thumb from plucking hundreds of birds. Sometimes the birds came in really "gamey," that is, they were really "high," in fact, rotten! I bet they could have walked in under their own steam even when full of lead. The odd time the rich guys at the door with their bloody birds would give the family a few birds as gifts, but we wouldn't accept the rotten ones. I grew up spitting pellets while often finishing off a whole duck myself, just as my dad did. He was really good at spitting lead, too. Who knows, how much lead I missed and is still lurking around in my gut.

My English Granddad

Often when the smell of pastry or duck wafted through mom's kitchen, my other granddad showed up. He'd drive up in his big black Buick. It had a square top, and blinds with tassels to pull down for privacy. Granddad would wink at me and there it was, it never failed, a shiny quarter, all mine! His bushy mustache turned up at the corners when he smiled. His bald head shone in the sunlight. I thought a lot of him, though I really only knew about him from photo albums and what I was told. Granddad was once a Marine and sailed on one of the first British submarines.

He was a bit of a free spirit, who owned little more than his railway man's watch, a few campaign medals, a conductor's metal change-maker, a shot-gun or two, and, for a while, his car. He liked to hunt and garden. When visiting he always pestered mom to let him wash dishes. In the end he met his death, not in war, but by falling off a small bridge and landing face down in a shallow pool of water out in Victoria.

Leaving this earth in such an undignified way in his nineties, was very unbecoming of that ramrod old British marine. I learned that later in his married life he and my grandmother separated to live out their own lives as they saw fit. Granddad's full life included making his beloved "spotted dick" (suet pudding). He knew just how to wrap the doughy mixture with raisins in cloth, steam it, and served it up with butter and syrup. I liked my granddad, not just for the great dishes he served up, not because he always gave me a quarter, but for his style. He had class!

I couldn't say that for my grandmother, his wife. I never really knew her, other than what my mom told me about her "running a brothel with her girls' help." But I never believed that, and the old photo album showing my family roots didn't prove that to be true either.

Mother and Dad

My mom once told me that she ran away from home because her father wanted to marry her off to an old rich farmer. No way was she going to do that, even if she were the oldest girl! Finding herself in Regina, she waitressed in a Greek restaurant where the "handsome, wealthy Greek owner" proposed to her. But she married my dad instead. How come? Well, the car barns, the home of Regina's streetcars, were just across the street from where Josephine worked after the Greek affair. My dad used to sit at the counter in that cafe. He took a liking to this farm girl, and she took a liking to him, for he was a fine-looking man with an English accent.

The Spoilt Brat

By the time I came on the scene a pattern was in place where the burden of the home fell upon mom's shoulders. Self taught for the most part, she arrived in Canada at age 14. Her living for her family began soon after she married and continued till her death. I remember when dad joined the Veteran Guards in WWII and left her with my sister Pat, and me. (Brother Norm, and sister Blanche were away). Mom helped make ends meet by following in granny's footsteps. She "scrubbed floors" for Dr. McAllister and for Mrs. Lovering, a school teacher at Scott Collegiate. She wore pressure bandages because she said she had water on the knees "because of scrubbing."

My sister Pat, who no doubt felt I was a little brat, had to put lunch on the table at noon. Often when mom came home late in the day or late in the evening she would bring some "treats." Those were castoffs (clothes) from her boss's daughters, and the sandwiches and dainties, leftovers from their tea parties.

To show appreciation, I think that's what it was, I saved up some of my money from selling coloured plaster cast roses, horses, and dogs from door to door to buy my mother some figurines. I started a real collection of those for her: a collie, boxer, and a spaniel. I tried to get them all about the same size so they would line up well on the window ledge in the front room by the radio. Mother would thank me by wrapping her arms around me. I'd try to do the same to her, but couldn't reach all the way around. Her corset slats and ties reminded me of my hockey equipment, and that I'd better get ready for a game.

Mom was someone I thought about enough to give her little gifts, but she was also someone with whom I often grew impatient. Yet she was a good mom sometimes! When I was a kid, she slaved over the hot stove. She loved to cook and bake, bran muffins loaded with raisins, corn fritters, and granny's kind of food. She was Ukrainian. Always it was "Eat, eat! Finish it up. There is more!" I liked that! Not so much, though, when she'd say,

"Clean up your plate. Don't waste it. There are children starving all over the world you know."

Then there were only four of us in the house. Yet most of the time, I could get all the attention. The house was my kingdom. My routines for tugging at my mom's heart strings usually worked. I gained a really neat way of descending from my attic bedroom. I'd bump down the narrow stairs on my rump. When that didn't work and my mom displeased me, I'd run screaming out of the house shouting,

I won't come back ever again!"

I guess my parents got tired of that. They knew I never meant it. So they stopped coming after me. The back screen door would slam shut, and I'd hide behind the garage, peeking out now and then. But the doors stayed shut. I felt ignored. After that I would roar out the back door, sneak in through the front veranda door, and quietly go up to my room, sniffling, and whimpering, feeling really powerless. But still I tried to keep up the crying bit to get attention whenever I could.

Even in the higher grades at Kitchener school I could turn the tears on and off at will. At home, I'd cry even louder, stop, and listen from my attic room to hear whether my mom was coming to say,

"What's the matter, dear?" None of my friends were around, so I didn't have to drop my routine. It was disappointing, though when my mom caught on. I thought it was a quite good act for a time, till she'd just go out and hang the clothes on the line.

Crying never even paid off any more. Once when a wild storm blew my tent up against some barbed wire, making it tear, outside our summer cottage, I cried and stomped around right in front of Flashy, my friend at the time. He seemed concerned. Yet, mom wasn't. So I got even madder. Giving her the benefit of the doubt, it could have been that, as usual, the lightning and thunder frightened her and so she disappeared. I knew where she was, on her hands and knees praying. She always did that when it stormed. She'd pull down the blinds, turn off the radio, stay away from anything metal, and I wouldn't see her again till all was quiet outside.

My sisters, Pat and Blanche, especially Pat, used to say that I never thought about anyone else but myself. She'd say that I always got my own way. Maybe it was because by the time my parents got around to me, being the last kid in the litter, that they were just too tired to fight with me. Then again, I wondered if it was because they saw me as a pleasant, last minute surprise. Maybe they thought, considering the way I came into this world, that I had gone through so much and deserved a break.

For a long time I thought of myself as number one. I guess that showed that I was completely insensitive to the fact that my mother worked her fingers to the bone, and wore the skin off her knees scrubbing floors. She did that to pay off the loans at Household Finance and People's Credit Jewelers so that I could have a new balloon tire bike for Christmas, and for my birthday, a black onyx ring. It had my initial and a small diamond in it, a ring just like my dad's.

I got so that I felt guilty, yet annoyed, especially at the constant nagging by my mom. That was one of many reasons I believed back then, that caused me to leave home before finishing my grade twelve. It wasn't until years later that I thought it was the only way she knew how to show that she cared. What made it harder, too, was I felt that she was always trying to buy my love. I think my sisters thought the same

My Dad and Me

Then there was my dad. My dad was someone whom I never heard much from at home. When he was in the house he was often not to be disturbed, especially when either sleeping on the front room couch, or in his chair, ears glued to a hockey or football game on the radio. Other times he'd mope when he was worried. When not at work and doing that, he was out in the garage, or hunting, fishing, at the Legion, or watching sports first hand. It was either the Regina Caps, Pats, or the Saskatchewan Roughriders. For a while the excitement, even around the house, reached a screaming pitch for Glen Dobbs, the Roughrider quarterback. Even our car licence plate sported a sticker proudly reading "Dobberville." If my dad had his way he would have renamed Regina for sure. I wish he could have got as excited about some things that I did. But I wouldn't want my name changed! I guess he maybe didn't praise me because I was never on a team that had a really winning streak. Regina's hockey and football teams did.

Things seemed to rumble along okay, according to dad, until Regina suffered a big loss. The car barns burned down and there went most of the streetcars and buses. It turned out not so bad, though, when our city inherited a stable of old orange street cars from Winnipeg, the home of the Blue Bombers. What do you think of that, the home of a rival team got us out of a scrape?

The Regina Transit system seemed never off my dad's mind, nor that of my friend's dad, who also drove streetcars. The difference between my dad and my friend, Bob Andrew's dad was, that his dad was an artist. Bob once snuck his dad's collection of coloured pencils out to show me. I had something better to show him, though. Sometimes my dad's uniform jacket hung on a chair. I was proud of my dad. He had five (or was it six) shiny gold metal bits sewn on his sleeve, like a metal watch bracelet, each standing for five years of service. Imagine anyone working that long for the city! Bob's dad only had fifteen!

Dad, then, was my hero. I felt great when I could stay up till he came home late from work and he let me sit up at the table with him. Mom would serve up some canned shrimps or kippers, and I'd get to have some, too. We two men would eat together! My dad always sat with his shirt off, underwear showing, and his braces down around his pant pockets, one foot on the rung of his chair, saying little or nothing. He'd break off a piece of bread, and knife a bit of butter on each bit as he ate it, sometimes also a bit of cheese or jam. He never ever buttered or spread jam over a whole piece of bread at any one time. I was never sure why he did that. Could it have been that he was just the kind of dad that did one thing at a time, finish it, then go onto the next chore? He was very orderly in what he did, maybe because he got trained that way in an English boys' school, or in the army.

When dad came home from the army he still worked shifts. I missed him. A friend down the street got to be with his dad more than I did with mine. Sometimes he'd share his dad with me. His dad had a bunch of saws, and plywood in his basement. But his dad didn't say much either, though he did help us make things. We had to be careful with the power saws; still they were faster than the hand held coping saws that I had to use at the Regina downtown Crafts Centre. At the Centre digging deep into the mucky clay barrel was also fun. I'd make things, dry them, and bring them home as gifts for mom. But dad wasn't there to say, "Hey, that's great!" So my friend's dad down the street would do in a pinch.

I didn't always need a substitute dad. My dad would from time to time take notice of me. Though as I said, he never spoke to me much, seldom about war, and hardly ever on fishing or hunting trips. Oh yes, he'd mumble some instructions on how to put a squirming minnow on a hook, net a fish from a boat, and keep quiet lest the fish hear me. I often wondered what it would be like to be a fish swimming deep in the dark waters below our boat, getting that much attention.

I never did go anywhere with my dad underwater, but I did on top. Dad would sometimes take me duck hunting with him, when his old cronies weren't available. I saw a picture of them once. They proudly displayed their hunting gear and dead ducks with wrung necks. Written on the picture's back was, "The three musty steers." My dad didn't like being indoors that much, at least not in our house, so it wasn't surprising that I got to do more with him outdoors than within. The worst of hunting with dad was I didn't have a gun, and our Springer Spaniel dog died. "He was no damn good anyway!" said my dad. That left me as the retriever. I used a rubber dingy that I bought with my own money from the Army and

Navy store to go fetch dead ducks. More than once
my dad would shout and point,

"There it is." More than once I'd reach down
among the reeds and display a dripping, maggot-
covered corpse. Dad told me that often hunters never
found some ducks that they wounded, and so they
left them to die in agony. I thought maybe my dad
remembered the way it was for some of his WW1
buddies that he or others couldn't get to where they
lay dying, tangled up in barbed wire, and not simply
in the reeds.

Hunting with my dad wasn't that much fun at all,
even when sitting on the car running board, drinking
tea fortified with lots of milk and sugar, eating
sandwiches, and sadly accepting the silence of dad's
company.

That's about the way it was when fishing too. First
we had to net shiners for bait. I'd walk out from the
shore pulling one end of the net while my dad held
the other and shouted, "Just a little further, son." I'd
sweep out in a circle in deep water up to my neck,
then back into the shallow water with the net forming
a hammock with one side dragging the bottom. On
the shore we'd spread the net on the sand. Green
slimy weeds, cray fish shells, and stones were mixed
in with shiners, suckers, stickle back, tiny pickerel,
pike and perch that frantically flipped their tails
about and gasped for air. They seemed as helpless
as I did when trying to please dad. He seldom smiled
at me.

Once, something shook my faith in my dad's true
blue honesty. After dragging the net, besides the

usual assortment of minnows and debris, we found, a big jack fish thrashing about. To my surprise and moral indignation, dad quickly covered the fish, ran with it to the car and hid it in the trunk.

"Don't say anything to anyone about how we caught it, you hear!"

Dad's fishing licence wasn't for netting.

The worst I heard or saw before that from my dad was "God damn!" especially when he hit his thumb or caught his hand in a trap trying to catch the rats in our back garden. I got a rude awakening finding out that about my dad. Would you believe it? My dad wasn't perfect!

I got the message that my dad liked doing things his way. I needed an imagination to keep my mind from feeling guilty in not wanting to help him. If he wasn't fishing, he was labouring in or around the cottage. One day the results of his efforts caught my attention. Clearing away brush at the back of the cottage and digging a new hole for our biffy, he turned up a coconut-shaped thing. It looked very much like part of a human skull, maybe from a scalped person. Dad often seemed to discover things, but never shared their secrets with me. He never even talked to me about sex. Figuring out for myself was no fun. So I waited around some, thinking dad would tell me something. He didn't. So I did my usual disappearing act, since dad didn't seem to want me hanging about to help him solve any grownups' mysteries.

The other side of this growing up was thinking about dark holes. Why? Back-houses had holes and some of us kids used to talk about our fear of falling into them. The grease pits in the filling station garages could also cause a guy to break out into a cold sweat; and the ones in the streetcar barns, well that's where my dad would lead me from bright sunlight into dark shadows; scary, especially when my dad told me to watch where I was walking or I'd fall in. The blinding light each one-eyed street car made as it rattled toward me always made me grab dad's hand. Eventually we'd stop and step out of the darkness into the light and laughter of the motormen's lunch room. There it never failed, dad would show me off to the men and let me feed the coke machine. It was among dad's kind that I first tasted Coca Cola. Things got even better than that. Mom would give me dad's lunch on Saturdays. I'd wait on Dewdney Avenue for his streetcar to come along, and hop in. Then I'd sit proudly right behind him. I'd watch him turn a handle to speed up or slow down, open the door with another lever, greet passengers, make change, give out transfers, and finally get to the end of the line to turn around. After he punched the time clock, and had a pee, (me too), he'd let me change the sign telling people where his streetcar was going. Then we'd eat lunch together. Then same as always, he never spoke much, yet that didn't matter for I was with my dad at work.

The odd time I think I even pleased him. I got the chance to do that a couple of times. Once I drew a picture he asked me to do, of a little boy peeing in the snow to make the words "Merry Christmas," for a Christmas card! The other time was when I showed him how to do long division. He only had his grade eight, but I knew he must have had fun in school in England. A brownish photo of a football team dressed in striped jerseys with dad in it hung on the veranda wall. All his teammates looked so serious with their arms crossed in front of them. They looked like winners but are all dead now.

I wanted to find out more about my dad as time passed. When my folks were out, I often snooped around in my dad's bureau drawers, once even pocketing his precision railway man's watch. After, I snuck it out to show my friends and accidentally dropped it in the water. Scared, I took the back off and filled its innards with oil. In that way I hoped it wouldn't rust. I never told my dad about that and he never spoke to me about it, either. Nor did he say anything to me about the many times I took his two revolvers out of his drawer, spun them around like the cowboys did on the Roxie Theater screen. I always put them back carefully under his long underwear and near the red arm band with the black letters reading "Special Police." Just to touch and handle my dad's things, including his collection of union cards, was as good as the hug that I never got from him. I never knew if he loved me or not. He never said so.

Yet I still respected him, even more when he broke down the bathroom door to get at me where I was hiding. I had given my mom a bad time, shouting and hollering at her, when I was in my teens. She phoned him at work, saying that she couldn't do anything with me. He rushed home, and though I was bigger than he was, he gave me a thrashing, beating me with his fists, while I cowered all rolled up in a ball in the bathroom corner, covering my head with my hands. I never forgot that, and the bathroom door lock never got fixed, a reminder of the fact that I'd better watch myself.

Pat and Gord

Speaking of locks, I believe that I might have been one of those latch key kids who were always getting in trouble, and didn't know it. You heard already that my sister Pat was left to make lunch Monday to Friday. She was to look after "Kenny," that kid who often raided her room, read her green-covered diary, and made a pest of himself, especially when her boy friend came to call. Gord was courting Pat. Once he gave me a whole bunch of NHL hockey crests and some Brill Cream. I suspected that to be the beginning of a good thing. Believing that Pat and Gord wanted to neck, I'd stand my ground in their presence, like a bell hop waiting for a tip before I'd leave. Gord's gifts of hand-painted ties, fishing tackle, a ball glove, hockey sticks, and more, became mine, either because he wanted to get rid of me, or because he didn't have a kid brother. On the other hand, maybe it was just because he was a generous guy. I think that was it!

Once, Gord even got me to make a poster for the sports store window where he worked. It was to advertise fishing tackle. Imagine, a real artist's commission. Caught up with the idea that he really recognized my great talent, I never even thought that it was just to help me feel better about myself. I was at an awkward age and no great shakes at team sports.

A person never knows how, sometimes, that what seems really nothing to the giver, leaves a lasting good impression on the getter. I remember when I was just small and my sister Pat got down on her lanky legs and bony knees and helped me with my road building, which I had going in the dirt by the back porch. She actually pushed a few toy cars down the road we had built together, and she did it for me, for me! She did have to make lunch, yes, but play cars? No!

Sometimes, as a kid, I really saw some good in my sister. So when mom would stay up late waiting for Pat to come home, and shout and scream at her, calling her a "hussy" or a "tramp" for staying out so late, I feared that Pat would really feel bad inside. I surprised myself for feeling for her. She didn't deserve that treatment.

Somewhere back in my memory, I remember my oldest sister, Blanche, hearing the same stuff from mom. Her boyfriend had an old car. Blanche and Ted spent a lot of time in that car. In the end I don't think Blanche wanted to hack the shouting and hollering or mom's nagging and harping. So she left home. Did Ted and Blanche elope? I can't remember.

The Uncles

Uncles and aunts seemed to have a better foothold in the house than us kids. One of my uncles stayed with us for a while. He belonged to the Salvation Army, but got a job driving streetcars and buses. He worked the spare board, going in for work when and as he was needed. My dad helped him get that job. My uncle would wash his hair and comb it over the kitchen sink, since we didn't have a sink in our bathroom. He had dandruff. I often wondered how it never got on the plates and in our food. Maybe it was because he also slapped Brill cream on his hair, and that's why his hair didn't fall out in the sink. Good advert for Brill cream! Uncles stayed over with us even at the cottage we rented before we got the one on the hill.

That was the time when my sunburned body looked and felt like a boiled lobster, at least my back did. I ended up with the habit of sleeping on my stomach ever after. Anyway, one uncle was a barber. He said he was going to swim across the lake. It was a long way. He started out with many of us watching. I never saw him again till, we, in the family, noticed him drive off in his car. I never did find out whether he accomplished that great feat or not. He looked really rested up and dry to me.

My Uncle John, one of my mom's brothers, was sure different from that guy. He looked like the movie star Clark Gable. Every time he came to visit he had a camera in his hand. We'd gather by the front steps to "smile and say cheese." He insisted. His camera wasn't just one of those department store black boxes. His was the real thing with a bellows and complex mechanism. I liked Uncle John, but I didn't like standing around much. Most of the time my mind wandered. Since we were posing near the caragana bushes, running along the city wooden sidewalk, I'd think of the good things a guy could make with the caragana pods. I could make whistles and boats to float in the gutters after a cloud burst. I liked Uncle John because he gave me a chance to day dream about things. Though his pictures were all right, too; that is if I hadn't been able at the last minute to spoil one with a silly face when everyone else was putting on the dog.

I never got to know Uncle Joe. My brother Norman did. Joe was a regular customer at places on South Railway Street where Norm, then a policeman, pounded the beat. That wasn't a nice end of town!

Uncle Frank, who lived down east and worked in a steel mill, was supposed to be the one that I looked like most. I heard he had round shoulders, wore glasses and was "easy going."

2 Beyond the Playpen

I didn't know those uncles that well, partly because I didn't know whether they were patient and understanding or not, like my Aunt Milly, one of my mom's sisters. Her second husband, George, was kind, like her. Her first husband was a nice guy also, but he got killed working in a brewery. Anyway, George, Milly, their friend Wally and his wife met many Saturday nights at our house to play cards with mom and dad and other adults. It was a ritual reserved for grownups. They decorated the card table with open Drewery beer bottles, and surrounded it with a halo of blue smoke. It became an ongoing irresistible attraction to me. I didn't wear glasses yet, and thought everything I saw was supposed to be fuzzy and foggy, like the smoke, filled room. Though I could barely see over the top of the card table for many card-table-years, the grownups challenged me to entertain as part of the Saturday ritual.

Find the bird, the train, the car, and more things on the Drewery beer bottle label. As I grew older and got bored with that, I began to understand a little of the mystery of their rituals, the meaning of the red, blue, and white plastic chips, and the different games, seven-up (not the drink), twenty-one, rummoli, canasta, even poker, and of course rummy. Then one day, I really arrived. They let me sit in, and gave me some of those magical chips. I thought it was too bad, though, that my mom got mad at me for winning a few hands of rummy and proudly showing off all the chips that I won. It wasn't long before I wore out my welcome, although Aunt Milly and George, Wally, and his wife never said so. Dad said nothing; Mom said a lot. So I left, wreaking my vengeance (I got those words from a movie).

I drained the dregs from the beer bottles left unattended in the kitchen, often filling a glass. That, like the Saturday card games, also became a sort of ritual. I didn't really care for the taste, but just doing it was exciting, especially since I never got caught. I never got tight either. That word often puzzled me. I knew it meant drunk. Still, I heard it more than once on the radio, "The security was tight," the news reporter said. Eventually I did get the idea. It had to do with keeping people out who didn't belong. I guess you could say my mom tried to keep security tight around the card table at home.

I remember some year later in my teens that when I, out of sight of my vigilant mom, hung out with the guys. Playing cards with Aunt Milly and George, mom and dad was tolerable, but it was more hair raising with the guys. We'd sometimes get really hot under the collar, especially when we played canasta, or black jack. It would have been fun playing strip poker, especially with the opposite sex, but that never happened. Thinking about it caused me to feel I was maturing. But back when Milly and George and Wally came over, and I drained the dregs of beer bottles, my playpen never reached much further than the house, yard and street.

Mom locked our veranda door on Robinson Street with a skeleton key. It always stayed inside the key hole. A yellow dusty see-through curtain hung on the door on an imitation brass rod. Geraniums, red, and pink spread themselves out on the window ledges. A Winnipeg couch (why Winnipeg, and not Regina, I'll never know), and a wardrobe kept company with the sociable flowers. I'd snoop or hide in the wardrobe when I wanted to be scarce. Maybe locking the front door wasn't necessary. Who would be interested in what the veranda had to offer? The back porch was different. Mom left milk bottles there with money for Vic, our milkman friend. She locked the door leading from the porch into the kitchen when we were out, and hid the key under a paper on the shelf behind the milk bottles. Before she went to bed, she'd slide a knife between the door frame with the handle reaching a bit across the door. More security.

No grass grew under my mom's feet. Josie, as her sister Millie called her, kept us kids secure and well fed. She always said she wanted to fill us up, especially me. She did! Somehow in time I made the connection between being loved and full of food. Yet I never caught on to the connection between food and the fact that many kids called me "fatso" and were right in their estimation. How could it be otherwise? I found it so easy to respond to my mom's urging to "eat up."

Whereas my diet contained a lot of different stuff, the furnace in our basement was only a glutton for coal. It liked the hard shiny stuff! But now and then, we shoveled in that dusty soft lignite that crumbled and made a mess. No matter what kind of coal that we used, it sure did make a lot of work. Where the toilet took care of what the body couldn't use, I had to cart out pails of ashes up the stairs, adding the kitchen stove ashes to the load. But before that I had to scrape out the stove with a hoe-like tool, running it along under the stove grate. A guy had to be careful lugging the ashes out. Some glowing hot coals could spill and probably burn the stairs, the house, or the back alley fence. It sure felt good that my parents trusted me with such an important job where so much could go wrong, but did it have to be such a pain?

I still liked the kitchen though, even if it did remind me of work. That place was the source of wonderful cooking smells, including baked beans and molasses. But it was even more than that. I'd come in stiff with frozen clothes after hockey, building a snow man, making a fort, or digging a snow cave. I remember the smell of wet clothes steaming while I stood by the stove or propped my feet up on the oven door. I remember the Watkins man bringing tins of powdered custard puddings, and mom's red hot liniment.

It was in the kitchen that I first got to compare good and bad smells and shy away from the bad ones. There I learned to follow my nose to sources of the most delectable. It's amazing how a person loses a real sense of smell over time. But when I was a kid, my sense of smell was incredible! While visiting friends and neighbors, my "sniffer" could find the source of stuff I liked. Sometimes it would even be on the roof of a back porch.

A really nice hefty farm girl, (at least that's what mom called her) moved in across the street with her three brothers, and her mom and dad. She seemed really comfortable talking to boys, especially if her brothers weren't around. A few of us guys from the neighborhood would visit her place, more often when only her little brother, our friend was home. When he talked, you had to dodge the spit. But his sister didn't spit. We liked her. She showed us how to make marshmallows from scratch. She also made fudge and we helped her reach up on the roof to cool it off. The more we praised her, the more fudge she made. I got her recipe for fudge. Lots of times, when my parents were out, I'd gather pots and pans around me, mix up a whole batch, a couple of pans full. But no matter what I did, by adding more Roger's Corn Syrup, vanilla, it seldom hardened. I'd raid the cupboards of peanut butter, molasses. But, still, only goo, even when I put it out on the back porch to cool, after I'd boiled the dickens out of it.

Sometimes when mom and dad were out I'd get caught up in listening to a radio mystery. Then the fudge on the stove would burn cinder black, leaving a mess for my mom to clean up and get mad about. When it didn't burn, I could at least spoon the sticky mess out of the pan. Sometimes I'd even try to make toffee out of it, like those hard Macintosh toffee bars I'd buy at the store. People said toffee pulls were always fun. For me toffee was just second hand fudge, flavored with what came off my grubby hands. It sounded like I never had much luck making fudge, but come to think of it, sometimes I did get lucky. I hadn't a clue why. But the fudge did get hard like peanut brittle. The only thing was, when I used a pie plate with one of those thin metal arms that you could crank around the bottom of the pan to free the fudge, it wouldn't work. I'd smear a little lard on the pan. No dice!

3 My Private Space

I am open to receive with every breath I breathe. 1

Despite it all, I often did enjoy not having mom and dad around, especially when I took over the kitchen for food experiments, or when I holed up in my attic room. Sure, it was lonely sometimes, but it felt safe and I didn't have to be nice to anyone. My attic room wall slanted inward with the top closer to my head than the bottom when I lay in bed. It was a little awkward hanging the near naked girl pin ups on the walls, but I managed. Beside my bed was a small table on which I kept my collection of sayings and poems. That table was better than the cloth-covered apple boxes that once shared the room with me. That was when a curtain divided my room into two parts. My oldest sister, Blanche, and her kids slept on one side and me on the other. She did that because her husband, Ted, was down east in the air force.

My bed was my private domain and good for hiding things. Sometimes my mom would find all sort of embarrassing things, and books like "Tobacco Road." That was more exciting than my pin ups. Growing older you gain and lose some. I no longer got a few cents from the tooth fairy. The guys would have laughed themselves silly if I had, as they would if I still played along with the idea of Santa Claus. I didn't find it embarrassing though to leave National Geographic Magazines around. They were educational, even though my purpose was to admire the half naked ladies. I never lost interest in the Geographic, but I found "True Murder Mystery" magazines about real criminals exciting. I'd read them most nights, using a flashlight under the covers. They weren't as scary as the radio mystery programs, maybe because I usually had in my hand a loaded double decker sandwich for a bedtime snack. Food was kind of soothing and kept my attention divided between magazine and the sandwich.

The first thing I remember liking that liked me back
was food. 2

You might think that food was my big interest. But
that's not true. More exciting to me than food and
murder mysteries was art. Art books with paintings by
Modigliani, Picasso, and Chagall got me wanting to
paint. There were also the drawings in some
magazines by a guy, I think his name started with
"Archabash..." He used to draw pictures of machines
so that they looked like strange people or animals.
Every time I'd look at a tap in the bathtub, the knobs
looked like eyes, and the nozzle like a nose.
Sometimes the grilles of some cars looked like teeth
and the headlights like eyes. I got so that I could tell
a lot of the artists' works without even looking at
their signatures, Besides, most of them you couldn't
read anyway. Someone once said, I think it was my
art teacher at Scott Collegiate, that artists have styles
of their own. Maybe that's why I could recognize
them. Some of my friends could tell the makes and
models of cars, in fact, it got to be a game for them. I
felt out of place because I couldn't. Yet I could surely
beat them if they ever asked me about artists. But
they never did.
    I did feel, though, that I could compete well with
them at drawing. Though at least one of my teachers
said I just never knew when to stop when I had a
picture on the go. Just when it seemed right to my
teachers, I'd want to do some more with it, fix this or
that. According to them I spoiled it. I guess it was
kind of like it was with me and food. I just never

knew when enough was enough.

    I let people know what I could do in art. But there was something that I always kept a secret. It wasn't anything I could show anyone even if I wanted to prove it. For a lot of years, I was puzzled and even marveled a bit at a gift that I thought might be mine. Other kids never talked about having it, so I thought it must be something special that I had and they didn't. It was a gift that I was also a little afraid of having. It was like this. Some event would take place with me involved. When it did, and after, I felt strongly that I had pictured it happening in my mind long before it ever did, weeks, months, sometimes even a year or more before. I found it scary, especially if it wasn't nice. So when a thought would come to me, a "premonition," that I didn't want to have happen, I'd try to rid it from my mind. If that didn't work, I'd try making it a pleasant future happening like a dream with a good ending (It didn't have to be in technicolour). Then I'd be safe, and so would anyone else in the picture, from what was to come. When I got older, I tried to think of good things that I wanted to have happen by painting pictures of those events in my mind, showing lots of details. Then I got afraid that, just as I did with my drawings, I'd not know when to stop.

    My premonitions could happen anywhere. Those weren't messages that I got from the radio, although there were two radios in the house. Mom turned on the one in the kitchen in the morning and off late at night. It was set at CKCK on the radio dial and mostly, it seemed with Johnny Esau spouting off sports. The other radio, shaped like an arched church window with its lit-up electric eye, dominated the small front room. When you glanced left, coming home late, walking by the side window, you couldn't see who was sitting by it because the lamp stopped you seeing further into the room. But you could bet your bottom dollar if there was hockey on the radio, my dad, as usual, would have his ear "glued" to it. If it was soap opera, it would be mom; a mystery, it would be me, biting my nails. I was always happy that the lamp light reflecting off the window glass shut out anyone lurking in the shadows outside as I listened to "Who knows what's lurking in the hearts of men? The shadow knows!" or "For whom the Bell Tolls." I wasn't too much for soaps, especially Ma Perkins. It seemed its stories went on forever. You could miss a whole bunch of days, get back to it, and having missed very little, easily pick up where you left off. Ma's son, Shuffle, would still be just shuffling along.

As the only child left at home, there were times when, feeling very lonely, I'd get quite philosophical. That's a word I looked up in the dictionary. It was mostly when I listened to "Gilmore's Album" on the radio. It was then I'd recite Gilmore's opening remarks

Isn't it strange that princes and kings, and clowns that caper by sawdust rings and common folk like you and me are builders of eternity? each is given a bag of tools. . .e'er life has flown to build a stumbling block or a stepping stone.   3

I never really put my finger on when I stopped
dropping in on the radio mysteries, or Lux Radio
Theater. All I know is that I started becoming, as I
said, more philosophical about things. Maybe it was
because my body started to change and my voice got
deeper. But, before it did, my sister Pat teased me
about my soprano voice that started to sound like a
screen door that needed oiling. One day after it
settled down, I heard a strange sound coming out of
a kid movie actor. When he talked his voice sounded
like the slow vibrations of a base fiddle, but even
lower. I never heard anyone else turn those sounds
into words. So, curious about whether I could do it
too, I practiced, and practiced until I could. Someone
told me I was merely relaxing my "vocal cords " so
they'd vibrate like loose rubber bands. I was proud of
being able to do that, but again, no one paid much
attention to my great accomplishment, so in time I
lost that gift. Speaking of gifts:
Christmas
Christmases aroused my curiosity, too, for different
reasons. There were the Christmas gifts I'd find under
the tree, that is, if I hadn't already found them hidden
away before Christmas when I did my annual
snooping tour. Every year the gifts were much the
same. Black, they were breeches like the RCMP wore,
yet different, no yellow line. Mrs. Zimmerman made
them from my dad's discarded street railway uniform
pants. Wearing my dad's altered hand-me-downs
gave me a feeling that my dad had in a way given
me a personal gift. He didn't give me my moccasins
though. Mom did. They were white leather and good

for sliding while holding onto the back of moving delivery wagons.

I still liked Christmas just the same, even though it was supposed to be for kids. The car barn's staff put on Christmas parties or "Christmas Trees " as they called them. One of my dad's old cronies did the honours as the master of ceremonies. He did a good job of calling out our names so each of us could go up and get a Christmas gift and bag of candy from a very happy Santa smelling of beer.

The car barn's Christmas Tree master of ceremonies was also a good auctioneer. During the big feed and party right after my sister Pat's wedding, I wondered what all the racket in the basement was about. What did I find? There was this pretty lady sitting on top of mom's wringer-washing machine that some characters were auctioning off. I never did find out whether she went with the washer till next day. She didn't, and neither did the washer. It was still in the basement, but in the veranda flaked out on the couch, and elsewhere throughout the house, was a bunch of dad's old cronies. It looked like their wives had given up on them and gone home alone.

Speaking of wives, I often wondered whether my American Aunt Jean, who once lived in Flin Flon, married more than once. That question matched that of how old she really was. In the end for me it never mattered much. I liked her. She was a WAC in the army. That didn't matter much, either. She, not having any kids of her own, sent me lots of gifts at Christmas and on my birthday. Uncle Wiggly books, a big metal army truck with a USA star on its hood, and a canvas top that you could put on or take off just by pulling some wires out of slots. I was always sure that Aunt Jean wouldn't let me down at Christmas, just as I was sure that the tube-like package under the tree was Tinker Toys.

The Kaleidoscope

But one Christmas was different! I got a cardboard tube alright, but when I unwrapped the parcel, I grasped something very different from tinker toys. It was covered with metallic paper, and had a little window on one end to look through and another at the other end to let light in. What was it? My mother shouted from the kitchen. "Hold it up to the light and look." I did. Surprise! Brilliant coloured snowflake- like things, and as I shook the tube, they changed, transforming themselves into other colourful incredible patterns. Looking back now, it seems that, unlike the ever changing computer screen savers, I had an immediate chance to make a difference in what I saw.

"What's it called?" I asked my mom.

"A Kaleidoscope. Magic!"

But it lost its spell when I broke it open only to find bits of colored glass, like people, all different, who lost contact with each other, places and events fading into memory. Yet I remembered, and was a bit disappointed.

Christmases came and went, and so did the gifts. The only annoying thing was that my mom would always cut out and keep the wrapping paper and labels so we would know who to give thanks to, and I would whisper under my breath, "And how much to spend on gifts for them next year."

Some of the labels had "From Santa." I wasn't supposed to know who that person was. So I couldn't really thank him or her for my Christmas stocking. But then, when I was small, I'd shout, "Thank you Santa" as I hopped up on mom and dad's bed, waving my stocking in the air. They and I knew whom I was thanking for the stocking and stuff. As I got older, each stocking got bigger, filled with life saver rolls, a Japanese orange or two, candies looking like red and white barber poles, and sometimes a package of assorted postage stamps for my album.

One other good thing, I felt safer scoffing the edibles from the stockings than Halloween candy, especially apples. My friends and I would bring home pillow sacks full of our loot. But a guy had to be careful what you pigged out on. There could be razor blades in the apples. You just would never know.

Besides eating, it didn't take much to amuse me. That's what some people said about me. While at loose ends at home, down with some disease, I made elevators from Eddy match boxes. They had sliding drawers full of matches that you could dump out. The outside cover became the elevator shaft, the drawer, the elevator. A guy could also get all sorts of useful cardboard things, some by sending away for them. There were the cardboard periscopes. The parts came flat with square mirrors and easy to read instructions for quick assembly. A person could look around corners without being seen. I couldn't understand why no one was impressed when I poked out behind something with only my periscope showing.

The Unexpected

It took a lot to get people's attention. I know I wasn't too successful. But one thing did. The living room was just big enough for a sofa, chair, radio, table, a few other things, and a stove made from what looked like two shallow metal drums, one above the other. The top one had a stove pipe coming out of it that went up through the attic. Neither I, nor the sofa, nor the chair, not even the radio got much attention.

But one day the stove sure did! Choking smoke filled the room, huge rubber boots and rubber coats with men inside them came charging in, scattering soot-filled hot pipes, sparks, and part of the stove all over the room. Mom and dad sent me packing outside, but I got an inkling of what happened when I was let back inside. Back in the attic room I peered down through the hole where the pipes had passed through on their way to the roof. I wondered how it felt to be a chimney pipe crashing to the floor below, coughing up soot.

I knew how I felt. I heard years later that one fireman, seeing me shaking all over, suggested putting a bell on me.

What really happened? I guessed it was a chimney fire! I'd hate to see what a real fire was like!

Nosing About

It seems when you're a kid, nobody will give you a straight answer. You had to find out things for yourself. In the veranda on a low shelf were some books. Someone had scribbled in them and cut bits and pieces from them. They were books on the first war, of soldiers knee deep in mud trenches, of killings, of tin-helmeted men clinging to horses, trying to free guns mired in the muck and mud, of old-looking tanks, double winged airplanes with wire holding the wings together. They were upstairs in the house.

Down stairs was different. I stood on a chair in the basement. I reached up, and felt around in the nooks and crannies between the rafters. Stuffed in those dark corners were spider webs and cocoons. But there was more, old-fashioned stuff. Mr. Owen, who owned the house before us, left behind three silver medals with no ribbons attached. One was round and blackened. When rubbed with Silvo polish it showed some figures in strange clothes, and around the outside were the words "Watch and Be Sober." I guess it meant that the missionaries to India, that I saw pictures of in one book in the veranda, were to stay away from booze. That may be because the others in the pictures had beards and turbans. I was starting to think about different people, like the Germans, and "Royalty " that I read about. They were different but were okay, too. I just didn't understand why being that way was so bad. So, wanting to see how it felt to be different like them, I made paper hats to look like those worn by royalty who held their hands on swords by their sides. Eventually I finally decided that worrying about being different was a waste of time. I had better things to do.

I'd count and shuffle my bubble gum and Lipton

tea cards, and gloat over the ship and aircraft cards that I got from smokers. That's what I often did in the house when I wasn't busy doing other things. Outside, I'd lick honey from the caragana bush pods, hide under the back steps, or toss about my Flash Gordon swept-back wing plane. It was the one which I didn't like much because it wasn't like the kind I saw landing and taking off at the airport. Playing around the house, and satisfying my curiosity about what there was to do, only lasted so long. I was glad when I was able to "get out from under foot," as mom often said.

4 Trying Things Out

We learn simply by the exposure of living. Much that passes for education is not education at all but ritual. The fact is that we are being educated when we know it least.

1

There was this rain barrel by my dad's garage door. It looked like a big beer keg, though I never saw a real one. I was told ours was supposed to hold rain water for the garden because rain water was soft. But it felt like any other water I poured through my hands. Anyway most of the time our barrel held rusty looking water with little bugs rowing across it. Sometimes it kept company with blue bottle flies, beetles, and other crusty creatures. Down deep I could see the stuff I tossed in: pennies, and metal slugs, like the kind guys put in candy machines. I had fun with that barrel, sometimes inviting my friends over to enjoy it. Tin cans leaned on their sides, floated for a while, then with a little help sank to the bottom, just like those that we threw into Joe's Creek and pop shot at with our Beebee guns.

Besides the rain barrel, I often hung around by myself out on a field. It was on the next street over. I played in the dirt and caught grasshoppers. It wasn't because sometimes kids teased me by calling out "Grasshopper" for my last name that I tore the legs off the hoppers. Farmers said they were a nuisance. That could be true, for the hoppers would spit tobacco juice at me. The locusts, (I think that's what they were) didn't spit. Nevertheless, I was scared of those dusty looking grasshoppers' cousins. Their legs were prickly in my hands when I squeezed them tight. Often when I got bored with trying to help the farmers get rid of the grasshoppers and their relatives, I'd search out ant hills. They were even more interesting. I would stir a stick deep into one and watch the ants scurry about. Sometimes I'd find their eggs that they were trying to carry to safety. I learned how to take two window panes, sandwich them, leaving space between for dirt to build an ant colony. Watching them make tunnels was fun, though I never found a queen anywhere to keep the whole business going. That was always sad. I wondered if those hard-working ants knew that they weren't getting anywhere?

It was also a sad day for me when my dad would find out that I had been poking around with his tools-those that I took out in the garden to play around with. Sometimes they would disappear and show up all rusty in the spring. "They are no damn good now," dad would tell mom. I thought it was just because they didn't look new and shiny anymore. Sharing the back yard with dad was sometimes a real pain. It seemed that as long as I stayed out of his garden, unless he wanted me there, I was okay. Lots of times he did want me there. I was to pick potato bugs and drown them in coal oil. Then I was safe from frowns and growls.

His garage was a different story. It was off limits, period! That is, except when he wasn't around and I could sneak in and play dad. Then, after using his stuff, I'd carefully put it back exactly as I thought I had found it, including getting the gears on the car back where they belonged. I wasn't good at that and I often got an ear full indirectly from mom. Dad wasn't much for lecturing. Somehow, I usually got the message that dad looked at his garage as something holy and sacred. I wondered how many other fathers felt the same way. Imagine, almost holy. I whispered the word to myself when I felt I should be careful how I walked and talked in special places like the movie theaters, and other dads' garages. My dad made me think I wasn't welcome there unless he got in the car to go to granny's on Sundays. Then I had the privilege of being a man by opening the garage door and pulling it shut after, locking it by dropping a wooden bar down into the slots. But there was more to the neighborhood than my dad's holy garage.

Fourth Avenue, Retallick and Robinson Streets had gravel roads. In the summer the ditches on Fourth avenue would glow with bright yellow dandelions. We made dandelion chains, and held dandelions under other people's chins to see if they liked butter.

From a distance we'd watch some people pick buckets-full to make wine. I never got to taste their stuff, but they said, "It was really smooth!" Fourth avenue was busy. Besides delivery trucks, there were lots of motorcycles, and once even an older boy who would jump up out of the ditch and chase the cars like a dog.

I never kept company with cars, but people told me that I was good company for my mom. Lots of times when I was small and she wasn't working, we'd go out together to the library on ten block Robinson St. I sat and looked at books full of pictures pasted in them. When I got a little older, I got books with words. One story I liked was about a boy who was lost in the woods with nothing, no clothes, no food. He kept alive using his smarts and getting everything he needed from the land. I think it was called "Cache Lake Country." I took that book out a lot. More than once I also took a book out that showed pictures of how things worked. I used to copy those diagrams and print names beside the parts.

After mom started taking me to the library, I lost a bit of interest in colouring books, plasticine, Chinese checkers, snakes and ladders, and bingo. Yet I still liked the smell of the colouring book paper.

I even, for a while, lost interest in the girls I used to skip rope with. Reading was more like it! I still liked cereal boxes that had "press and cut out" little buildings, a church, school, and stores, to make a small town. I dreamed that I'd live in a peaceful town like that one day. I had some other books of cutouts that I put together to make war ships, tanks, and

planes. Somehow they attracted me. But I couldn't understand that, since I didn't like fighting.
Was there something the matter with me and my family? Were we different, or was it just me? I found the answer in the strangest place.

I was digging around in the garbage of my mother's minister. I don't know why. I and another guy did it. Maybe it was because I was just curious; or maybe it was because of what one of my other friends said,

"Ken, you should be a preacher one day, you're always preaching at us." Anyway, I found stuff in that garbage like beer bottle caps, food wrappers, exactly like the stuff we threw out at home. Hey, he wasn't much different from us living on Robinson Street, even though he lived on Dewdney. There was supposed to be a "better class of people" living there.

"Keeping up with the Jones" to impress was supposed to be good, so I thought that I'd try it. You could always scrounge wood from somewhere. Once I got an old square butter box with tongue and grooved corners. I nailed it to a long board, and put a couple of cross pieces front and back. I put a bolt through the long board to make the front one turn and used big spikes to attach four wheels from a carriage. I promised to give my cousin a ride first thing when it was finished. It was, and I did. I pushed my butter box bug with my cousin visiting from Hamilton. The tin can lights stayed on the front, but the wheels fell off. I just didn't seem to get it right. It was the same when I tried making tin can telephones. They didn't work either. I tried building stilts. The blocks stayed on, but I didn't. It seemed the other guys could get things right, like the Scouts who were older than I was. Maybe that's because some built racing go-carts using real bicycle wheels. Their wheels never fell off. But I only had a three wheel tricycle and I couldn't take those. My dad would give me heck if I did. So I didn't.

My dad sure got mad sometimes! I mentioned his Springer Spaniel dog died. Here's how. Dad was going to make him into a bird dog. Something bad happened though! Someone found Prince. He was shivering in pain with blood and foam dribbling from the side of his mouth. One of the bread trucks had hit him. Someone had left the door of Prince's pen open and skittish Prince leaped over the back gate to become a goner! Damn!

Someone else died in our neighborhood. Bob Stewart, the kid across the street who once ate mustard sandwiches and was a sea cadet looked good in the coffin in his uniform.

Lots of us kids did things together. Bob didn't. But we did. We'd make slings and arrows. We'd use them for fighting or for shooting them high in the air. Sometimes they'd disappear, and we'd wonder if they hit anyone. We'd take a piece of inner tube. If we were lucky it was from a bike. Sometimes we had to settle for a car inner tube from the dump. We'd cut a piece about a foot long, tie a string loop at the end of the rubber and attach the other end of the rubber to a stick handle. There always seemed to be somebody ripping old cedar shingles off a roof. The shingle strips were thin and fragile on one end, and, at the other, thick enough to make a notch. We'd slip the string loop over the notched shingle arrow head that was part of the shaft, just like slipping a halter and bit over a horse' head. Then our weapon would be loaded. Nothing to it, pull back, stretch the rubber and let fly a shingle arrow up into the sky. When it reached its highest point, it would dive like a Nazi Stuka bomber. Only it would bounce on hitting the ground. Sometimes we'd steal some matches and light the arrows. It was fun, reminding us of the fire arrows shot by Indians in the cowboy movies we'd see at the Roxy Theater. If we weren't Indians, we were definitely cowboys.

The cowboys used guns. We had cap guns. Still it was even more fun to take a hammer to the cap strips, or even better still, get some fire crackers and let them off under tin cans. We'd get the caps and fire crackers at the corner store.

Sometimes I'd need more than all that stuff. I'd sneak all kinds of things out of the house, like old silk stockings for kite tails. I suppose they made better Halloween masks when you pulled them over your face. Naturally a guy had to wash the salty leg sweat out of them first. Sometimes you'd find them rolled up and left in the bathroom corner.

There was more to do outside, most of the time, than indoors. The wooden side walk boards hid money and other lost treasures. Sometimes we'd pry up some of the boards with a crow bar. The boards, like railway ties, crossed the long wooden spans of sidewalk that stretched up and down Robinson,

Cameron, and Rae streets. Lots of things turned up
when we scratched around in the dirt under the
boards. Of course we'd have to brush aside the
spiders and other bugs. Once I found a silver baby
spoon, a part of a bicycle, and some pennies, even
fire crackers with their fuses still in them. There was
only one problem with prying up boards. Sometimes
the spikes wouldn't go in right when we tried to put
the boards back the way we found them. Often an
older person would come along then and give us
hell. Rakes did the same. When a guy stepped on the
rake the handle would slap him in the face, like
getting hit with a hockey stick.

Boards with nails in them could be dangerous.
They were always around to step on. Once I got a
nail right through my foot near my big toe, not like
Jesus on the cross though! The hole wasn't even as
big as the ones under my arms when I had boils and
got the pus cores out with my mom's poultices.
"Those were supposed to draw the poisons out," she
said. Rusty nails could be trouble when we played
around houses that were just torn down. A guy could
really feel a nail going in through a running shoe. It
even hurt more when he'd have to try to get the
blood showing up out of the hole in his foot to
prevent blood poisoning. Other body parts could be
trouble too. Often I'd fall and make a mess of my
knee, elbow, or hand. I'd be afraid to look. Then it
wasn't so bad. But when I did, and would see the
bloody torn skin and flesh, then it hurt, it really did!

The odd time my friends and I would choose safer
things to do. We'd save our cloth handkerchiefs to

make parachutes instead of cleaning our noses with them. Although a little camouflage never hurt. After tying bits of string to each handkerchief corner, bringing the strings together at their ends, we'd tie on heavy bolts. The bolts were the parachutists. We could get the chutes airborne by first folding them like they do real parachutes, and pitching them up like balls, or by just hanging onto the center of the handkerchief chutes and swinging them around before letting go. Climbing onto a garage roof to do that made it even better.

You never know what a guy finds when he elevates himself. Once I discovered an old Triumph motorcycle leaning against one of my friend's back yard garage. Often I'd stop by, get on it. Then I'd imagine that I was wearing goggles, a helmet, and riding it like beat all, letting the wind rush by my face. I'd always flip the light switch to see where I was going. That's as far as I went. It had no engine.

But, I could do something even better and more in touch with the real world, I thought. A guy could make a good arrow-like plane. He could toss it about in the school classroom, have it stick into the ceiling hot air register, or have it catch the wind by throwing it out the classroom window on a dare. Then again, a guy could toss it out his attic window like I often did.

Better still, there was a kind of aerobatic plane that I made from paper. I learned how from Grandpa Forgie, the old man, once a baker, who sat on his stoop next door. I was proud of how the plane could fly. When a guy held it properly before launching it into the air, he could make it turn in circles, causing him to get dizzy following it in flight. To throw it properly he'd have to hold it by the nose, two fingers on the top, thumb below, and nose facing him. Then he'd give it a flip when he released it into flight with a wide swing of the arm. He could fly it inside a building too, maybe better because the wind currents weren't as strong. A little draft from a door or window would help. The plane was sure different from any paper dart that I had ever made. It had a triangle shape. A pilot could also cut the tail to look like a real plane. He could cut into the trailing edges of the wings to form ailerons so it would turn steeper. I learned those words at air cadets.

Darts, of course, were swifter than that specially designed paper plane. They could go faster and straighter and made better weapons, especially if a guy folded them over and over to make them really lean. But Grandpa Forgie's design could do the loop-the-loop.

One other neat thing Grandpa Forgie taught some of us boys was a design for a good water bomb to drop off stair wells on people below. We'd make paper ball-like shapes with holes in the middle to fill with water; then when we'd hit our targets, Splat!

Grandpa Forgie was a real good friend with a quiet sense of humor. He liked us neighborhood kids. His stoop was a heavy piece of timber that he sat on and sunned himself in the summer. He had retired but still kept an eye on how things were going in his bakery next door. We'd gather around him and play on the bakery's driveway. Here we also learned how to make good kites as well as those paper planes and water bombs.

During the time Buzz Beurling, the war hero, flew over the city, the girl across the street, the one next door, and some of us neighborhood guys thought it would be nice to copy a show seen at the summer exhibition. Sally Rand performed there almost bare naked. The little girl next door did a dance like her on a stage we built from boards and things. It seemed like a good idea, but for some weeks after, we weren't allowed to play with each other. At that time the grownups seemed to know something we didn't know that made it wrong. Later, when I reached about thirteen, I knew why. So did the other kids. The days of discovery were soon at hand when conversation and such became more risky. But we didn't get too much direction. As kids, seemingly trapped in childhood, and with little learning in grown up stuff, we had to swim about in our own rain barrels. Then, I felt like one of the minnows that I'd bring up from the beach in pails, fish like shiners, stickle backs, suckers, all different just like people. They had nowhere to go but swim around till they went white belly up, just like "puberty," which at times, seemed just as limiting.

We never let the barriers that grown-ups set up stop us from testing out what we could do. We even rafted in the spring after climbing over high fences into warehouse property. It was near the company that made grave head stones. That's where we found the best wood and stuff to build rafts. It was fun. Grandpa Forgie didn't teach us rafting though.

I talked about Grandpa Forgie a lot. He had two

sons, John and Huey who, with their dad, owned and operated the bakery next door to us. Grandpa Forgie started his business out of his home, baked and carried a basket, delivering from door to door. Later his son, John, joined him delivering the baked goods, first by horse and wagon. Eventually they got a truck, then more trucks. Around five in the morning, a person could hear Huey, the baker, whistling tunes through the shop's window, open summer and winter. That window was within spitting distance of our bathroom window. Though I never tried spitting to prove it. Huey sounded good enough to join a chorus of sparrows, especially when accompanied by the clinking of the bread-wrapping machine. He was real good to me. I would often visit him first thing in the morning and return with a small loaf of fresh bread right out of the oven made from left over dough. The sound of the bread-wrapping machine was my cue to go and get it.

We didn't always live next door to Forgie's bakery. Someone in the family told me that I started out in life living on Cameron Street, in a house my mom and dad lost when they couldn't make the payments in hard times. I think before that my family lived near the tracks on Retallick Street. I do remember on my way to school the stand pipes and taps on some street corners. In winter ice would build up around those taps making it really slippery to get water.

Sometimes I'd leave the guys and go over to Bob Cameron's. He even lived on Cameron Street. I 'd go there to see his stained glass window that made rainbow colours dance around the toffee coloured stair rail.

Bob didn't save stamps, but I did. One Christmas my Aunt Jean sent me a stamp album. I searched the house for envelopes with stamps on them, soaked them off in the kitchen sink and glued them into the album. Later I found out how to use cellophane hinges. I ended up with a lot of ruined stamps. South Railway Street, where the "Ladies of the Night " hung out, also had a store where I'd buy packages of stamps. It was close to the hotel where my dad once worked. I also bought stamps through the mail "on approval." I could send back the ones I didn't want to keep. The problem was, which to buy? I couldn't recognize or even pronounce a lot of the countries' names. My hobby lurched along through the school years in fits and starts, with a growing collection of bags of identical stamps stuck to torn bits of paper.

A couple of bright boys lived across Fourth Avenue and down one house. They were skinny. with dry and scaly skins. But they sure could play the clarinets. The younger one also had a great match folder collection. I, also aspiring to great heights, found out his secret and joined him in digging through hotel dumpsters. We sifted through half-eaten food, and other crap to find real match folder treasures. Sometimes the finds would have to be left behind because they were too sticky and gooey. Often I'd pick folders off the street. They were more than likely sopping with dirty water. Sometimes the print ran, but as my collection grew I found my efforts worth it. If the matches inside the folders were still good, I'd fan them apart and light them to cause a swoosh before I blew them out. Success! Why! I had folders from the USA, with seltzer bottles and side views of dancing girls' legs, and even folders from night clubs and restaurants, including one from Drumheller Coal company, and lots of duplicates for trade. There was no end to the kaleidoscope of characters appearing on my match folders!

I also tried collecting butterflies. I caught those white garden ones, and kept them in a jar till the jar clouded up. They died, and when I screwed the lid off, the inside stank. I had put lettuce in the jars. But the butterflies hadn't touch the food. Butterflies seemed to like it better in the garden. Once I caught a Monarch butterfly. Yet when I picked it up, it flapped about and my holding it caused it to tear its wings. It looked too moth-eaten to mount so that dampened my zeal for collecting things with wings.

I gave up on stamps and butterflies. Bikes were more fun! Bob Andrews was always fixing his second hand bike. He often took the greasy guts, bearings, and little V shaped pieces out of the back wheel hub. Sometimes he'd be short a few bearings lost in the dirt. I didn't have to do that fixing bit, but I often did anyway. One Christmas, I had nagged my mom for a balloon tire bike, and she bought me one. It was good for jumping curbs and sidewalks. Sometimes I'd turn the handles the other way around like steer horns. My bike had white walls like my dad's Maroon Mercury car, the gem that he put on blocks when he went to join the Veteran Guards. My friends and I came up with all sorts of names for our bikes. Some weren't for public use. Yet, John, a really smart guy in school used, to say "wheatnannycabibby " when he was talking about this or that. Each guy wanted to out do the other with a fancy sounding name like that. I came up with one. I called my bike "Homer Gahalmamier Dishwasher Junior." I never really knew how to spell it, but I could shout it out really loud when crashing through bushes, or bumping into fences off the bike trail near the Legislative buildings. I felt proud coming up with a name nobody else had and one that nobody poked fun at.

Promotion to a two wheeler made me feel a little sad though. I missed the good old days. Back then I often attached a red wagon to the back of my tricycle to pull my friends to the corner store for black jaw breakers, and cards to collect inside packages of gum. I liked them better than the cards I got from tea packages and cereal boxes. They only had ships, fish or other sea animals. The bubble gum cards had the baseball players.

But one thing better about my two wheeler was that I could stick a card with a clothes' pin on the front wheel forks. It hit the wheel as it turned to make my bike sound like it had a motor. Sometimes I'd turn the bike over so it balanced on its seat. Then I'd pour water in the fender wheel wells and crank to make water spray as though from a water wheel.

I got a little tired of that kid stuff, though, just as I had tired of playing the part of Poncho from the radio program Cisco Kid. Mom bought me a black Poncho hat with a cord that went around my chin. Up and down the block I used to ride imagining myself in western movies. It didn't occur to me that no one else was sporting such a hat or even cared to own one.

As neighborhood kids we didn't own the same things, but we did a lot of things together. At nights a bunch of us boys and girls gathered under the street light. There moths, attracted to the light fluttered about while we also strutted our stuff across from Mrs. Sparks. She did a lot of peering out from behind her curtains at us. Often she reported back to our parents what we were up to. Mr. Sparks never did. He took off to the beach to fish! He wasn't the kind of guy to squeal on us. We'd play the cigarette game, kick the can, and sometimes, when we got tired, raided gardens. Raiding gardens seemed an okay thing to do. All excited, we'd grab a bunch of carrots and run for the open door of the garage behind Peter Head's place. Peter was always on the run, and was always trying to catch his breath. He had asthma. When Peter's mother called, in an English accent, "Pee... tah" We'd whisper,

"You're not here, Peter, you're not here. Stay with us and we'll grab some more carrots."

He did and we did! Another night we crouched behind some garbage cans and again heard Peter's mother shout out, "Peet... ah, are you in the gar-rage ?" She always said garage that way. That night we were doing our usual shopping for carrots, pulling some up and putting them back when they were too small, when the lady who owned the garden charged out of her house and shouted out to us guys hiding in the shadows, " Just ask, I'll give you all the carrots you want, but don't do that, please!" She said it so nicely, we never raided her garden again. It was great to be asked nicely.

I never did steal too much. Other kids did. I tried once, though. I took a red plastic helicopter from Woolworths, hiding it in my jacket. I got it home, and after twirling the rotor blade a few times, buried it in the back yard. Another time, on a dare, I crept into McGavin's bakery truck garage, grabbed a roll of wrapping tape off the bench, hopped on my bike and waved it happily in the air as I rode up to my friends. That tape went into the garbage right after. Proving to my friends that I was okay was hard work.

5   A Taste of School

My spelling is Wobbly. It's good spelling but it Wobbles, and the letters get in the wrong places.   1

Once upon a time, I didn't want to go to kindergarten. But my mom took me and I stayed. Some kids played really close to each other. I stayed by myself in the corner watching them for a long time. In grade one, our teacher gave out the readers. I got one. The cover was blue with some red on it. It smelled of glue, and felt a bit sticky from the sweat on my hands. Teacher showed us how to take the new reader, open it in the middle, smooth down the pages, then open some more pages on one side of the middle and then the other. That way we wouldn't break the spine. Imagine even a book has a backbone! I put my nose close to the pages. I liked the smell and never forgot it. It didn't smell the same as colouring books. I always got colouring books for Christmas, with crayons. The crayons weren't as hard as those at school. The school's were "crayolas."

Only thing better than the smell of the books and crayons was my teacher's smells. She sure was a good reading teacher. When we did well, she gave us each a jelly bean. Black ones were the best. She kept them in her right-hand desk drawer. Once when she was out of the room my friend and I snitched a couple, black ones, of course!

Teacher's black marks weren't much fun though. I could never get above sixty's in most subjects, mostly fifty's and some "F's." When report cards were handed out, I would always get out of the classroom fast so no one would ask me what I got. I felt the same way when the only valentines I ever got were from my teachers. My art marks were different. Those were high. So were my attendance marks, except when hunting season came around and my dad would take me out of school.

I often felt good about my dad rescuing me from school. He got me away from a lot I didn't enjoy in the least. I did like some people. But some, I had mixed feelings about: the vice-principal for one. Our concrete playroom was small and dusty and our playground was covered with melted glass and cinders, the stuff from our school furnace. Our bony knees hurt a lot when wrestling inside or out. However, our backsides felt even worse the many times when, the vice-principal, roaming the playroom, didn't take a liking to our behavior. He would generously whip his chalk board pointer across whatever parts of our anatomy were handy. Howls, or shouts of "What the... ?" would answer his efforts. Nevertheless our vice-principal who hurt us, still kept in my good books when he taught art. True, he kept up to his old tricks, but we did too.

One favorite dirty trick at Kitchener was to get kids to hold their breath till they passed out, or, better still, make them sit cross-legged around a swing pole. Just before recess ended, we'd push them down so they couldn't get up. Then we'd leave them there to be late, and have the teacher send someone out to set them free.

I felt safer while the vice-principal was around than I did with our beautiful grade seven teacher. She stomped her feet, and cried more than once right in front of us after she'd come back to the classroom, having stepped out. Before she left she'd always say, "Just for but a moment." I didn't like those "Just for a moment times." Chalk flew and I'd duck! I wasn't very accurate at returning fire. Most of the time I'd hear the chalk whizzing by my ears and see it splat on the blackboard, thank goodness.

Even when our beautiful teacher sat in the room things could get wild. One guy who bullied, just for fun, would sometimes have a fit, roll around on the floor and vibrate. Someone would shout, "Don't let him swallow his tongue! " Once, two girls even went for each other's throats when they didn't agree about something. The two hit the floor kicking, clawing like cats, and pulling hair.

Classrooms could also get wild even when others

taught us. One substitute teacher, who filled in for our principal in grade eight, tried her best to keep order by strutting around the classroom whirling her strap about to put the fear of God into us. But it only made some of us laugh, which of course made it worse for Bob, Montany, and me. Montany was the guy who wore big clod hopper boots, and had to check his smokes in daily with our principal, Mr. Paul.

If it wasn't for art and my dad's rescue missions from time to time, I don't know if I could have survived the classroom battle field. Art, of course, was my happiest class period. Sometimes we'd go down the street and draw houses. Other times we'd make paper mache masks at Halloween, turkeys, pumpkins for Thanksgiving, shamrocks, pigs, and leprechauns for St. Patrick's day. Then there was all the Christmas stuff. That was great!

> No one can make you feel inferior without your consent   2

The days I skipped school with dad were a break from teasing. For I could only take so much of being called "fatso," or "chink," being sat on, rapped on the forehead with sharp knuckles at recess, and called "four eyes" because I wore glasses. When I fought back, they called me a bully, shouting out, "Why don't you pick on someone your own size?" I was big! When I didn't fight back, they called me a "sissy," and "chicken." Sometimes one or two guys would say during class time,

"You're in for it! Wait till we get you after school!"

62

or "If we see you again you're dead!" Hearing that I always had a hard time keeping my ear tuned to what the teacher was saying the rest of the day.

Still, I was the second best drawer in the class. The big sloppy guy who always drew worms' eye views, including the worm and stuff near the ground did better. He and another kid from Britain used to wrestle and included me. Usually I found myself buried under the two during recesses. But I didn't mind it so much with those two. I felt I had something in common with them. The one liked Art, and I did too. The other was British, like my dad.

Maybe I would have had an easier time with some of the others who didn't like Art and weren't British, if I hadn't worn glasses. I held off being called "four eyes" for a long time by cheating when taking eye tests from the school nurse. When I couldn't read the smaller letters with my right eye, I'd peek around the cardboard she gave me to cover my good eye. It wasn't fun being called names, especially when a guy didn't even really know why. Some kids even called me "pigeon chested." I couldn't understand why, anymore than why I was always the last picked to be on a ball team. I suppose it might have been because the ball crossing the plate looked like a foggy blur. It was ridiculous, I thought, for some helpful teacher to say,

"Watch the ball, not the bat!" I could see the bat, but the ball, that was something else!

When I first got my glasses, my cousins Marilyn and Loreen came over to our house. I had those damn things on, but took them off quickly. Mom got mad at me, and Aunt Millie said, I looked okay. I wasn't sure! I guess that's why I liked the movie Hans Christian Anderson with Danny Kaye in it. He seemed to understand what ugly ducklings felt like.

It took me some years before I would listen and accept this advice:

Cure yourself of the condition of bothering about how you look to other people. Concern yourself only with how you appear to God, with the idea that God has of you.   3

Those glasses were a real mill stone around my face. I had to admit one thing though. Before I wore them, I thought the real world was all foggy, and people were kind of fuzzy-like. Wow! When I first put them on, I couldn't believe it! People and things had sharp edges and behinds and also fronts, like 3 D.

How was I to know that many years later, after I had prayed that I wouldn't need glasses anymore, that someone would invent contact lenses? The first ones I wore were "ventiles" that covered a big part of my eyes. They breathed through little vents around the outsides of the lens. They were hard though, and I often scratched my cornea, causing me lots of pain.

Wearing glasses, I often felt ill done by until I saw little Eddy. He was a kid at Kitchener that had to be pushed everywhere and lifted up into grownups arms to get him to hockey games, which he loved. Eddy's thin face, neck, and body flopped around and made me feel awkward in his presence. Though, I liked it when he smiled. His eyes, shining through his glasses, did all the talking. But it must have been really hard for an older guy like Eddy to have someone else wipe his bum for him. But, little Eddy had one thing going for him. He did love to watch sports.

Mr. Pickard, our school principal, let a lot of us guys play pick up hockey during P.T.(Physical Training) periods. Little Eddy watched.

Then Mr. Paul came along. He became our new school principal. He was tall and skinny, wore glasses, and braces to hold up his pants, had thin hair slicked down, and sported a mustache. Mr. Paul reminded me of Ichabod Crane with braces. But I never told him that. Once he shared something that I didn't like. At a parent teacher interview he told my mom, out of my hearing, that I'd make a good fashion designer. I guess it was because I often looked confused in class. When I heard that second hand from mom, I said, "No way! An artist maybe, fashion designer, yuck!"

Mr. Paul did something else that displeased me and the other guys. Instead of hockey at recess, he made us do P.T. in the dusty hall. He would jump up and down, throw his legs and arms to the sides, tire us out, and bore us to tears. Then it got worse. Some of us held off learning our times tables. It was like a shoot out in the OK corral! But he turned out to be the fastest gun in the west! He made us sit in the hall during recess, and sometimes even after school till we learned them, even the twelve-times table! Mr. Powell was the one who once said, "The lazy person makes more work for himself."
Oh, so right he was, and his words of wisdom echoed through all my years, burning in my ears.

There was a lot that I wanted to forget, despite the wisdom our strict, yet wise, principal offered us. At his school during lunch or recesses when we weren't learning times tables, the tripping, punching, sometimes even kicking went on, just for fun mind you. But I, for one, only felt safe when I stood in lines, boys in one, girls in the other. Then it was only shoving and clipping persons in the back of the neck, which wasn't so bad. Still, weapons were needed when not in line. Most favoured paper clips, stolen from the teachers' desk drawers, along with elastic bands. Those were on the top ten list, rather than chalk, as the choice of lethal weapons in the classroom. Where paper clips were really worth ducking from was when people in the back seats let fly. Pea shooters made from clothes pins were also useful weapons on the playground. Eventually, out of the need for self defense, I contributed to the stock pile of weapons, and also reluctantly became a user. At the time I didn't twig to the message

Poor David! He had never had any armour put on him. His metal was on the inside, not on the outside.   4

Despite all the grubby Kitchener school nitty gritty, lo and behold, a surprise! Back in grade six, two strangers stepped gingerly into our classroom and gave each of us kids a Gideon New Testament. That's what it was called. One man said, as he gave each of us one,

"In the front of your little red-covered book is a place where you may commit yourself to Christ." I did that after school on the way down the alley to the corner store for licorice. I wrote my name and date in The book. Though I still wasn't sure who Christ was. I had read the word Jesus in the Sunday School papers full of people in night gowns that I took home from St. Andrew's United Church on Dewdney Avenue. But I didn't really look at anything else but the pictures which puzzled me.

My mom told me that the man dressed up in what looked like a Batman outfit, who waved his arms about and shouted a lot, was a minister. His name was Harry Joyce. I didn't learn much from him. They sent us down to the basement before he stopped flapping about, at least I suppose he stopped flapping later in the morning. He did say "Jesus" a lot, but not the way it was used in our neighborhood. Around home, I only heard it from my dad a few times when he hit his thumb with the hammer. That's when he added "Christ" to "Jesus." Though he seldom said it when he would come home from the Legion with a red nose, and a smelly breath. I guess he was in a better mood than when he worked in the garage at the bottom of the garden.

I never came home with a red nose, not ever! Yet, I did come home with a brush cut. I was told that was the thing to have in grade eight and in high school. My dad reminded me that I'd lose my hair soon enough from wearing a uniform hat. That was his firm belief. I wondered if he knew something I didn't know.

6   Hormones and Adrenalin Rushes

A man who has not passed through the inferno of his passions has never overcome them. [1]

There were lots of boys in the north end where I lived that I stayed away from. I never delivered papers until I was older because the guys at the paper shack had initiations where they beat the crap out of new boys, using their paper bags. Hanging around the playground wasn't quite as bad, though the playground did have lethal weapons. They differed from Kitchener school's. Swings , when let go at quite a height, could knock a person cold, especially when an unsuspecting person's noggin was targeted. Swings were also great for pumping up high then jumping off to skin knees. Teeter totters were good, too, for giving bumps when a partner sat on the high end. Also, if you got off fast when your partner was on the top end, and you were on the bottom, your partner would land hard. It wasn't all hurts though. Some summer nights, we roasted potatoes crispy and black in the red-hot coals of a bonfire. The playground supervisor allowed that.

Our playground came alive even more in the winter. The outdoor skating and hockey rinks got hours of use. Snow banks formed walls around the big rink, great for putting on skates. Even though it wasn't lit at night, lights from a second, boarded hockey rink, shone enough for us to play games like pom pom pull away and crack the whip. In crack the whip the person on the end of the swinging line of kids and grown-ups could really pick up speed before letting go to hit the snow bank with a thump.

A guy who dug graves in the summer supervised the hockey rink shack. In the summer he shoveled deep, in the winter he shoveled shallow. There was always lots of snow to clear. In the hockey shack stood a pot bellied stove, glowing red hot. There was always the smell of burning hockey stick wood and tape. Skates gouged the floor planks. Players nudged each other for a place to sit to tie their skates. Toques would fly, or be pulled over eyes as we bent over. When I was small, I skated to the rinks on icy streets. My skates wobbled by the time I got there. I could tie skates two ways, one, the way you tied shoes, criss-crossed. The other I learned in grade eight was better. I'd tie my skates so that the laces looked "parallel," like railway track ties. That way the skates clung better to my feet. But one kid, a high scorer, never even laced his skates up much at all. They looked like they would fall off his feet any minute, but they never did. I learned to do some of the things that he did, like skating backwards, forwards, spinning, and taking corners by crossing one foot over the other.

None of that helped me though. For a little guy called Forsyth would stare me in the eye as he came rushing toward me with the puck. He'd sneer, bob his head to the side, fake to the left, and go to the right, leaving me standing flat footed and looking stupid. I never did figure him out. So with guys like that around I thought I'd play goal instead. I tried. For some reason or another, my knee kept giving out on me. Someone called it a trick knee, but I didn't find anything tricky about it. It was just a damn nuisance! That blacking out on the ice and waking up to find guys staring down at me was just too embarrassing. Not all my time was spent at the rink. Flashy was a guy a year ahead of me in school who went to the YMCA a lot. He knew stuff that I didn't, not only about the painted lead soldiers and molds for pouring them that he owned, but about sex and stuff that I hadn't a clue about. He said that he learned some of it from older guys at the "Y."

Before, like the kids in Golden's "Lord of the Flies," I lived like a good healthy animal, pushing my luck with my parents' discipline, and connecting with the spirit of Frankie Lane's songs,

"My Heart Goes Where the Wild Goose Goes," and "Ghost Riders in the Sky," both of which stirred my soul, and made shivers run up and down my back. Now the fun of the chase! Sampling and experimenting with everything from adolescent sex to communing with nature was bringing more to think about. Life was losing its lustre and was getting very serious.

There was one girl in grade eight that I liked. Her nickname was "Carrots." She had red hair. Her real name was Kathleen. She played a violin. One day I asked her to meet me by the Met Theater after her violin lessons. She was as shy as I was. We had a pop together, and that was that. I never went out drinking with her again.

Some of us guys were curious about dancing. There was a class one evening a week at Kitchener. We hung around outside for the longest time before we got up nerve to go in. The lady dance teacher, whom we never saw before, wore a slinky black dress and thin, pointed-heel shoes. She smelled really nice. We weren't sure that she could dance with those pointed heels, let alone shift back and forth. But she did, moving her hips and smiling. I felt all squiggly inside. She had a dance partner to demonstrate the steps. He was young like us and a nifty dancer. She tried to teach us how to do the fox trot and waltz, and, using some black plastic castanets, showed us a Spanish dance. The girls did most of the dancing, but then she paired us off. Then we sweated it out. The girls didn't have a problem, but some of us sure did! My feet kept stepping on girls' toes. There and then I decided to hold dance lessons off for another time.

While one person hesitates because he feels inferior, the other is busy making mistakes and becoming superior.   2

Doug, Bob, his friend Roger, and I, and a few others would get rides out to Joe's Creek with our skis. Doug's dad would drive. Sometimes he'd even pull us on our skis over the ice in his car. Like the rest of the guys, I graduated from no ski boots and one strap per ski, to spring bindings. Eventually Bob introduced us to micro-bindings and proper ski boots. He seemed always ahead of the game in learning new things and wasn't afraid of getting hurt. It wasn't surprising that he mastered down hill maneuvers and stops long before I even got up nerve to try them. It took some guts for me to ski the ice-covered steep hills near Joe's Creek. But I never risked, as my friend Bob did, in doing Christies and spinning to a stop, skis spread in a V, at the foot of the hill. Instead, I played it safe, straight down, straight up. Nevertheless it was great being out together, us Limeys and Swedes, Norsekys, and Ruskys, as we called ourselves.

When I wasn't swimming or skiing, or on my side of the tracks in North End Regina, I'd be out at the Isted's, across the tracks. Lots of his friends hung out there. In his yard was a small tar papered house, a backhouse, and machine shed. Bob's father, a milkman with Palm Dairies, would bring home left over dairy products, and Alma, Bob's mom would make big sticky cinnamon buns for all to eat. She would also listen to our gripes about school teachers. Sometimes we'd listen to old records. I took a liking to a song with these words

You ask me why I'm a hobo, and why I sleep in a ditch,
It's not because I'm lonely, no, I just don't want to be rich.
Oh, I could make a million, and eat till I get fat, But then I'd
lose my girlish form, and Oh I wouldn't want that.. . 3

I'd sing that song over and over to friends, and I didn't understand why they weren't the least bit interested in hearing it more than once. I also liked some poems that we took in grade eight. Bob memorized "The Rhyme of the Ancient Mariner."

Then there was the one that started

    I see the lights of the village gleaming through the rain and the mist, and a feeling of sadness comes o'er me that my soul cannot resist.   4

    That poem really used to get to me, like one summer: I felt that kind of sadness right down to my toe nails when I had to stay in town during July and August. Dad needed the car for work, he said, and mom didn't drive. So, instead of going to Regina Beach as I usually did, I stayed in sweltering hot Regina. I found that summer wasn't completely lost though. True, it was really hot, but Bob and I spent many hours at the public outdoor pool, often swimming laps. When tired, Bob would dive off the high and low boards. I couldn't dive, so I'd do cannon balls and see how big a splash I could make. Great fun, especially if I could douse the sun bathers.

    Pools empty of people looked green and ripple free. The pool near our playground was fenced off. Before the pool opened for us, we'd often prop our bikes up against the fence and watch divers on the spring board. We assumed that they were life guards. One day we were talking about someone who wasn't supposed to be in the pool during off hours. I heard that he drowned. I was glad that I had someone like Bob to swim with and was okay with pool rules. That drowned kid could have been me! Bob's body and mine were smooth and streamlined in the water. We looked like a couple of brown seals. If we were swimming at the YMCA it would be bare naked and after a swim we'd most likely be doing jumping jacks and skipping and stuff as part of the YMCA Junior Leaders Corp.

That summer we just lazed about in "adolescent ecstasy." Sometimes the pool got so packed that we just suntanned. Often we had to step over bodies of all shapes and sizes; some looked half baked, others like pink pigs, only redder. Once I almost stumbled over a guy whose skin was all leathery and dry. His face was even wrinkled when he squinted. It made his face look like a turtle's.

Bob and I did other things together. He was a good friend, once he even stopping me from bleeding like a stuck pig. At the time I thought I would have bled to death. He stopped the blood gushing from a gash in my finger, the result of me showing off with a knife. It happened when we had cross country skied to the Lumsden Ski Club shack. The club had a ski tow, but when we got there it wasn't going. Anyway, we lit a fire and sat there talking the night away. That was when I cut myself. That deep scar reminds me of our deep friendship at the time.

I also looked upon Bob's dad as a friend. I thought it would have been great to have a dad like him. His name was Vic. Usually a Dodge Desoto car was parked in Vic's backyard, with him under it. I know, because more than once I saw his shoes sticking out from underneath. In fact, years later, when I stopped in Regina with my wife and visited the Isted's, I couldn't believe it. There was a car, feet sticking out, and when I asked,

"Is that you Vic?" out he slid feet first, and looking

up at me asked,

"Is that you Ken?"

Vic was a lot younger than my dad. He arm-wrestled with Bob and Bob's brother Allen, played ball, and did his Palm Dairy milk deliveries on the run. Vic and Alma had moved in from a small town called Ogema They lived happily in modest surroundings with their kids Bob, Allen, and Arlene. They carried water from a well on a neighbor's property, and the kids walked a long way to school and to work across railway tracks.

It was fun out at the Isted's. There was open prairie to charge about on bikes or on foot. Sometimes, I blew my baritone horn, and Bob blew his trombone. We'd start our squawks in the house, and soon we'd get the usual invitation to blast away outdoors. At night there was the drive-in theatre nearby across the field. There we'd often get close to the fence, in reach of the car speakers, cover ourselves with blankets, lay belly to the ground, propped up on elbows, and enjoy movies. Many nights I'd ride home scared in the dark down the old Grand Trunk railway embankment. The tracks were long gone.

Near the embankment was a deserted mink ranch, and large cages too tempting to leave. That was the beginning of my friend Roy's and my rabbit farm located at his place across the field, over the tracks, and down by the railway roundhouse. One night Roy and I persuaded Bob and some other guys to help us drag a few of those cages to Roy's place. It was a dark night in early spring when the ground was still frozen. Somehow we made it without being caught. We had bought some Angora rabbits, plain white ones, and two Belgian Hares. We thought we had it made by feeding the rabbits saved up lawn cuttings, hay, carrots, and stuff, But one bitter cold morning, we discovered them dead, frozen stiff! That was disappointing since we had carted those rabbits from way over on Winnipeg Street, half way across town, and spent my paper carrier money to buy them.

My religion consists of a humble admiration of the illimitable superior spirit who reveals himself in the slight details we are able to perceive with our frail and feeble mind.   5

   A happier surprise came, when, one day as I was riding to Isted's, I noticed a giant hamburger-shaped rock that, if I spread my arms out wide, they would barely touch its sides. Curious, I had a good look at it. Wonder of wonders! It looked just like a hamburger bun all right, ready to open up to put the mustard and ketchup in. Only it was grey. I borrowed my dad's crow bar and pried it open. It was incredible. The inside shone with shell-like rainbow colours. It was like a clam, only huge! Bob said he'd talk to the museum about it. He knew someone there. We thought we'd found an amazing thing, only to hear, " So what's new." A little later, when I gazed at that giant petrified mollusk, the rainbow shell colours, exposed to the air and light, faded to become dull and chalky. Another of life's many disappointments!
   That disappointment didn't defeat me. There was

still the creek to swim in. Some said it wasn't too sanitary since the blobs floating by were supposed to have come from the city sewage plant. Moreover, it, like some of the dug outs we swam in, gave up the odd dead body, mostly cats with skeleton faces and leering teeth.

The guys I hung out with weren't into conformity, fads, idols and materialism stuff like some others I knew. Dead cats, drowned gophers, and getting hit with Beebee- gun shot during gun fights while climbing the old refinery tower, was more our style. Sometimes Bob, Al, a few other guys and myself would play war. Plastic goggles found in some cereal boxes protected our eyes. They'd fit snugly to our faces with an elastic band. The abandoned refinery tower's circular stairs provided shooting platforms for us to fire away at each other with our Beebee guns. That was okay if we didn't get too close to each other. We'd climb the tower and other bits of machinery and play hide and seek. The Beebees would really sting. So we were careful to miss a lot. I always did find Beebee guns interesting. I'd pour a little oil down the barrel, then fire it off. I liked the smell when it was fired. I had always tried to kill a lot of gophers for their tails, but had very little success. I had heard the tails were worth a few cents each. Cats, birds, and tin cans set up on fences were my usual targets.

Besides playing around with BeeBee guns, some of us across the tracks from the Isteds got into the business of gathering old cigarette butts and sneaking cigarette papers. Once we even invested in a V master cigarette maker; though most of the time we couldn't get enough tobacco from the butts, so we used crunched up dried leaves.

Bob wasn't a cigarette maker, nor was he a hunter like his younger brother Al. A couple of times when Bob was courting his girl friend, Red, I'd ride with Al on his motorcycle to shoot birds. As the only kid at home, I longed for the company of a brother or two like Bob or Al. Yet my birth brother, though a bit of a stranger to me, did touch my life.

7 The War Years

Who live under the shadow of war,
What can I do that matters?   1

When I was a kid, I wondered what I could do when my dad and brother were away. The answer came. When the war was on, I'd take a few cents each week to school. My teacher had a big picture of a soldier in his underwear. He needed dressing. Each bit of money that we as a class came up with would buy a piece of his uniform or "kit." Still, we never bought him a gun. We also brought money to pay for a Red Cross membership card and a small tin badge with a red cross on it. We would wear it at meetings, usually Friday afternoon when we weren't watching National Film Board black and white movies in the auditorium.

I wasn't happy when my dad was away in the army. I never heard from him and didn't get to read his letters to Mom. During those years Norman, my

brother, who served in the Governor General Horse Guards, was but a faint memory. My memory was jogged only when I thumbed through the family photo albums and saw pictures of Norm in shorts, standing in front of a barracks' door that had a light above his head. In a couple of pictures he was holding a gun and had a gas mask covering his face. I got a bit of a clearer picture of who Norm was seeing the photo of him standing proudly at ease with my dad, and granddad, two in khaki brown, and Grandpa, "old Bill," in Legion tam and tie.

Just as I had tried to get closer to my dad by poking around in his stuff at home, I tried to get closer to my brother by doing the same. I wore Norm's skull cap made by turning a fedora inside out and serrating the edges, and coveted his Scout first class hat badge, Scout hat, and other stuff. It wasn't till after the war that I heard from my sister-in-law that Norm felt there was nothing to come home to. All his stuff was gone. When I got older I felt bad about that.

After the war, I had wondered as a kid why Norm didn't want to go with my dad to kill ducks and other birds. It didn't occur to me that he had seen enough killing. He never shared his feelings about the war with any of us in the family.

Somehow, permission was never given to share or take seriously feelings of family members. So Norm's feelings of loss stayed buried for sometime until they surfaced. Al, Norm's wife, told me about some of his traumatic moments, such as the time when Norm and an army buddy stopped their lorries at a bridge to discuss the odds of hitting a land mine, possibly planted either on the bridge or in the water. Norm chose the bridge, the most likely mined bit according to his friend, who chose to cross the stream. Norm lived. His friend got blown to pieces. Like my dad, who said little about WW1, Norm never shared the pain with me that he carried from WW2, other than to say one thing that I'll not forget. Once, near his death, most likely brought on from heavy smoking and diet, he said this about the war,

"We were kids. We got so that we didn't really care about tomorrow. We loved and lived for the day."

When I think back to what Norm must have gone through, I'd had it pretty easy. As just a kid of 17, in battle he faced fear daily. The biggest thing I ever had to face as a kid was keeping my nose clean (keeping out of trouble) at school, and avoiding the gangs hanging around at Chees's cafe on Fifth Avenue. They were some of the guys who kicked my bike spokes in while I visited the library.

I remember at night when I was eight or nine and Norm was overseas fighting, I'd go to bed with my Dagwood double and triple deck sandwiches of onions, tomatoes, and stuff and I'd pray "Kill all the bad guys." I wanted my dad and brother home with me!

To do my part, I also cut out "Life" magazine pictures of army tanks, planes, guns, lots of war stuff, and pasted them in scrap books to show battle scenes.

For years after WW2 I wanted to join the military

so I could really feel like I was one with the three men, my granddad, dad, and brother, whose picture was taken by the guns at the Legislative buildings. I believed, no chance though, since I thought my feet were flat, and my eyes were crappy. Still, my prayers were answered later in life. I never did have flat feet and I could see with glasses. I still had an urge to join the army but I was too chicken to apply, believing I'd fail the physical with my eyes. Rejection would have been hard to take. Besides, by then I was starting to hunch that war was wrong because of what it did to people. My conviction became rock solid when I read in a newspaper about young kids in a town in Europe playing soccer, using a human skull as a substitute for a ball.

Thinking back to the nineteen forties, I wonder if my dad felt that way about war. He didn't, on the surface, seem to have any second thoughts back then of joining up to become a corporal in the Veteran. Guards. Despite his horrible WW1 experiences he insisted in getting back into uniform. He was too old for overseas but that didn't stop him. He put his maroon Mercury car up on blocks and went away. He ended up guarding German prisoners of war with his friend Mr. Stevens,. and Mr. Hibbs. My dad had lots of friends. I often wondered how many were German prisoners. I also wondered whether his bosses picked him to guard Germans because they thought he had a German last name. Once, when my dad was on leave he brought me, as a surprise, two models of German submarines and a Christopher Columbus-type sailing ship model.

Many of those that he guarded were sub crews.
Dad's gifts, made by crew members, were intricately
made to scale. The submarine models, just like the
real thing, had fins, rudders, propellers and more.
That is, until I floated them in the water at the beach
and shot at them with my Beebee gun. What I didn't
wreck soon disintegrated in the water. The glue gave
way, and even the fine toothpick decks parted
company, along with the conning tower details. It
was too bad that I didn't value them. I just couldn't,
feeling that those who made them kept me from my
dad. I guess I was just jealous that the prisoners saw
more of my dad than I and the family did, while
waiting in Regina.

When my dad was away, I would proudly show my
friends his old ball glove. It was black, worn, frayed,
and without a pocket. It hung ceremoniously on a
nail in the veranda across from mom's geranium
plants. I was also proud of the spurs from my dad's
WW1 days. He was in the Horse Artillery back then. I
found other treasures. Hidden among the cobwebs
and rafters downstairs in our home were some
1920's spats, and in my dad's bedroom dresser,
besides his railway man's watch, and two revolvers,
some medals from the First World War.

They reminded me that grandpa William and my
dad Herbert served "King and country " in the
artillery. That even surprised them. Before he left
home, grandpa forbade my dad to join up. He was
too young. Besides, Herbert was to stay home and
look after his mother. But Herbert paid no heed, and
did join up. And what happened? When the new

recruits were all assembled, the sergeant shouted out "Crassweller! " and two, not one, answered,

"Here Sir!" Grandpa turned around quickly to see where the other "Here Sir!" had come from, saw Herbert, and shouted,

"You get home this instant and look after your mother like I told you. Do you hear? Do what you are told!"

Both father and son escaped death, despite seeing gun-pulling horses ground into putrid carcasses, and buddies, wounded, mangled, and still others not making it home.

My dad never spoke about seeing all that slaughter, nor did my brother Norm speak about what he saw. It must have been awful. I never did see my dad or brother enough during WW2 to listen in on what they had to say to each other about the fighting. Even when they were home I got the idea that it was a no-no to ask them about it. Yet, they did seem to pay some attention to me. Once both he and my brother Norm got leave at the same time. Their willingness to help me finish building a model was great, at least at first. I was just putting the finishing touches on it after having struggled with balsa strips and paper. I was looking forward to flying it by winding its elastic band tightly by turning the prop many times. Before I got to fly it, dad and Norman decide that it needed a paint job. A can of grey house paint would do. It did, making it so heavy that the puny elastic band wouldn't power it off the ground. So there it sat on the shelf, a reminder of my dad's and brother's affection for me.

Better times ahead. Dad and Norman sat in the front room. Each in turn, at my asking drew pictures of guns and other weapons that they used. I was thrilled. I remembered, before Norman went to war, he had made some drawings of army tents with flags on them. But guns were even better! Maybe!

8 Back to Nature

There is in the child the intuitive awareness of a belonging to the "whole," The "feeling" fades as the child grows older. The wind is symbolic of God; the story is a concert of life-birth, and death, and climaxes with the death of the grandmother.   1

Scouts

Mr. Setchel, our Scout leader, lived across the street from the Scout shack. I used to get to Scout meetings early. I'd hang around outside, often freezing my butt off till someone unlocked the door. Every week I looked forward to seeing the stuff in glass display cases or hanging on the walls. Miniature horses in full harness, wagons, flags, badges, all were a feast for young eyes. At Scout meetings we played games. Most guys liked the game of "black out." Two teams, one at each end of the room would crawl in the pitch dark toward the opponent's chair. Under the chairs, one at each end of the room, was a flashlight. The idea was to turn your enemies' light on before he got yours, or before someone from the other team touched you and shouted "Got yah!" If you beat the other guy to the draw by shouting first, then he was out of the game. Each team could guard its flashlight but couldn't reach under the chair. The opponents had to have a chance. When a kid shouted "Got yah " the lights would go on to see who was out. When a guy was "out" and couldn't keep playing, most of the others would feel sorry for him. It was nice when guys felt sorry for me, because I knew then that they cared.

Once I had a chance to show I cared. There was this fat kid. His name was Franky. He had tagged along with a bunch of us guys who went out camping without the scoutmaster. Franky used to get himself in an awful flap over nothing; teasing was nothing! Anyway that day he went nuts, fell on his chubby knees, and frantically clawed away at the dirt. His nose ran, his eyes ran, and the guys shouted, "Ah forget it!" and they ran off to hike or swim. That left me to handle him. I finally calmed him down. When we got back to the Scout shack Franky went home, and we never saw him again. I wonder how the poor devil made out.

We camped a lot. Some weekends a handful of us guys would hike out to Joe's Creek. It ran by a farm yard. Turds from the down stream sewage plant and other crap got caught in the weeds. That's why we boiled the water we drank. We also washed our metal dishes in that creek. However, it wasn't any good for washing the mess kits that we got from the Army Navy store. We used sand for them. But we found more black sludge than sand. Sometimes we wondered what it would be like camping by those crystal mountain streams pictured on B.C. calendars.

Boggy Creek used to be another good place to go. We biked there. Sometimes we'd lay flat on a hill with our sweaty shirts around our waists, looking up at the clouds. We'd count the different shapes of animals, birds, people, and the like. At night we'd do the same. Only then we'd look up and gaze at stars. Sometimes a guy could see the red and orange glow of grass fires on the horizon. Wow! More WOW when we'd stop looking at cloud shapes and stars and examine our scars, "war wounds," and birth marks. I got interested in the birth mark on my arm that looked like a pig; then again it could be mistaken for a buffalo; yet, not as easily, for there were no more buffalo around to compare it to, where I hung out on the prairie.

> Freedom's just another word for nothin' left to lose, Nothin' ain't worth nothin', but it's free. 2

Overnighters offered elbow room! We'd be free of walls, grownups, and Scout patrol leaders pushing us around. Some of us would devise all sorts of ways to see in the dark. We'd catch fire flies and put them in a glass jar, with the lid on of course. Other times we borrowed our dad's flashlights. Those were the best. A third choice was to make candle lanterns out of tin cans, using a dad's tin snips. The odd time a guy could get the use of one of those bike lanterns, but batteries were hard to get, and most times the lights were bolted to the bike handle bars. Of course in a pinch, a person could turn a bike over, and flip the generator to touch the whirling wheel. If I did that my arm would be sore by morning from cranking the pedal, that is if we wanted to read all night.

However, that wasn't likely. We talked a lot and didn't need a light to do that.

When our Scoutmaster came along, we'd sleep in army bell tents. Those were the kind that we could roll the walls up in the daytime to get rid of the stinks by letting the wind blow through. Back at the Scout shack, we had a kind of camp fire. It was a bunch of logs, with some tin inside that spun around over some red and black stuff. When we turned off the lights, the light from that danced around the walls of the shack and fell briefly on our faces.

We did a lot of knot tying. I didn't always get the reef knot right. I'd have the cross over going the wrong way. If I did it right, it wouldn't slip; neither would the bow line. That was the easiest for me to tie. I remembered the rabbit coming out of the hole, running around the tree, and back down the hole. It seemed to make sense. I never knew why the sheep shank was called that. It didn't look like a sheep. It was for shortening a rope. That was enough to know.

One guy named Glen Sage, who did know a lot, came back from a Scout Jamboree in Europe. He impressed us by singing "Strodala, Strodala pumpa, pumpa" and stuff like that. At the jamboree he even learned to twirl a rope like a cowboy. He also knew how to do the Scout pace, run some steps, walk some steps, then do it all over again. That way a guy wouldn't easily tire out getting somewhere. Glen was a guy that showed he would never tire.

"Good times were had by all," as the saying goes, until one day Mr. Setchel died. We didn't know why. His wife gave me and my friend Doug each one of her husband's real Mountie hats, better than the floppy ones we wore. We felt honored, like when we started our Scout promise, "On my honour." I wondered whether I could live up to Mr. Setchel's high expectations after he'd gone.

A guy came to lead, but we couldn't take him seriously. Anyway, we remembered all the things Mr. Setchel had done: like getting us working at fixing toys at Christmas and giving us one toy to take home; the Scout camps at his cottage; and giving us bacon and eggs to cook when we burnt our first batch black enough to throw out.

When I got bigger, I passed by the Scout shack. It seemed to have shrunk, like the size of the house I grew up in on eight block Robinson St. Yet the memories were still huge, big like my mom's dog, Skippy. He was a black and white terrier that was fixed. He got fatter and fatter, about a foot wide in the middle, and his legs seemed to grow shorter and shorter. Sometimes we even had to pry him out from behind the stove, his favourite sleeping spot. After he did his business outside, we had to help him up the stairs, and lift him up into the house. It wasn't fun for him, nor for us. When he was younger and thinner my dad tried to give him away. He drove him way across the city, but Skippy somehow kept finding his way back, dodging traffic and mean kids all the way home. So we kept him.

I never had that yearning to come home when I left. I wasn't sure whether mom or dad really would have wanted me back. Yet I do remember my dad saying, when I left, that my room would always be there if I wanted it. I wonder if Skippy knew that his space behind the stove would always be there for him. Maybe that's why he kept coming back.

Regina Beach

Our cottage overlooked the lake. We could see up and down for miles and across the lake to an old tower that was all that was left of a rich family's estate. During the day a person could easily tell the direction of the wind by the white caps. When it was raining or very windy my cousins Loreen and Marilyn and I, who were often together during summer holidays, would stay indoors. We'd play X's and O's, hangman, checkers, monopoly, and listen to the Blue Bird records on the crank-up gramophone, (the one where you took needles out of a metal tin with the sliding top). Sometimes we'd visit the Corner Cupboard, even when it rained. Polly, the talking parrot lived there. As we pointed, the lady owner reached into big glass candy jars to sell us jaw breakers, jelly babies, and other treats.

Taste was only one of our five senses that we satisfied. The juices of life were without number. We took buttons from mom's sewing basket, threaded two pieces of thick thread through the two holes. When done right by pulling the ends, we could get a button spinning to make a loud humming noise. Touch the table or wall and the button would climb that wall or run along the table. Yo Yo's joined the other stuff in our pockets. Some grownups went around town showing what one could do with a Yo Yo, such as make it sleep, rock the cradle, or go around the world. I tried making Yo Yo's from Tinker

Toys, but they couldn't do any tricks. A guy could enter contests and buy string from the store, but flour bag string worked okay. The gold and silver Yo-Yo's were really something! I once owned one at the Beach.

The Beach was my school away from school. There I learned all sorts of interesting things. I learned that a doctor, whose cottage was down the way, had a sheep's stomach. I learned how to find the best golf balls, how to use the old-fashioned wood handled golf clubs, and how to run backwards up a hill. I learned a lot, especially when I wasn't too lazy, like the neighbor's dog at the beach. Once he sat on a cactus and just stayed there with his rump pressed against the prickles. He howled and howled, reminding me of the words of one song

The hound dog's howling all forlorn, too lazy to get up, he's sitting on a thorn. Life gets tedious, don't it.   3

It sure didn't make much sense what that old dog did. Though, I guess, it didn't make any more sense when I often took minnows home in a pail, and as usual found them floating with their white bellies up. They were really a sorry sight. I just couldn't get them to multiply! I wanted to take some home to Regina because I never got to carry goldfish home in plastic bags from the pet shop like some other kids did.

Still, I did better than any minnow, even though it could swim better than I could! There wasn't a chance of me being dropped into a pail and later ending up on some fisherman's hook as bait like those poor suckers. Not only that, but I was free to swim about

when I wanted to. Well, almost free to do that, except
I'd have to wait a half hour after eating before going
in. That's what grownups always told me. So I'd lay
on the sand, just itching to charge down into water.
Then I'd splash a bunch of "timid types" toe testing
that water, and kick my feet like whirling propellers
out to the raft. There a guy could easily look down
into the girls' halter bathing suit tops. Also you could
follow them up the ladder and get a good view of
their bottoms.

Sometimes a bunch of us guys showed the girls
what we could do, like hold one arm up high, then
slowly sink while holding our noses with the other
hand. It sure impressed the girls when we popped up
beside them after a long time under water. They
were scared that we had drowned. We could have, I
guess, if we swam at the point where the undertow
pulled at a guy's legs. Yet the water between the
shore and the raft was okay. Not too many drowned
there. The raft was quite a way from the sandy
beach. On the beach we built sand castles, horsed
around, wrestled, threw sand at each other, ran up to
the booth for dixie cups, pop, and stuff, and charged
back to flop on our blankets and wave to the girls.
Once I even swam across the lake with my friend
John rowing a boat beside me,

I felt really grown-up being able to handle myself
so well in the water. I remembered when I was really
small. My cousin and I, or the kids on the block,
would put on bathing suits. We'd dodge broken glass
and side walk slivers, and scream, wave our arms,
and dance around like maniacs with our mouths

gaping wide while trying to catch rain drops on our tongues. Sometimes we'd even hose ourselves down with water as cold as that at the beach. Some of us had black heavy rain coats. But they weren't much use when we were having fun, especially when we wore bathing suits.

There were a lot of different kinds of bathing suits. Some were of black, heavy, itchy wool. Others had string tied up the sides, and others felt velvety and silky. Taking off a wet bathing suit in the beach changing room was yucky. Once I had to gingerly stepped around some vomit that flies were feasting on. Sometimes when I would see a flabby, beer belly man changing, I'd pull up my pants and quickly get the hell out of there.

The toilets on the beach reeked of piss. Still there was lime dropped down those holes, newspaper to read or use, and a latch on the door through which light slinked in between the boards. Sitting in there you could see the shadows or parts of bodies of people walking. You could hear them talking, saying things they wouldn't if they knew a person was contemplating life in the can nearby.

Lying in the hot sand after a dip in the cold water left gritty bits between my toes, on my legs, and even inside my bathing suit (sometimes called "trunks"). At the water's edge, I often tried balancing like a crane on one foot to slip on my runners. After, I'd charge up the beach to the grass by the garbage barrels. Water would slop around in my runners making a slurping sound. Sometimes if I dug deep enough through the slimy burger wrappers, and other sticky stuff, I'd find a few bottles to exchange for a drink or a torpedo all-day sucker.

On the way home up the hill, I often risked frying my ear like crispy bacon on a sizzling hot railway track. I'd drop to my knees to touch my ear to the track to hear whether a train was coming. That was a good move, especially if I happened to be starting across the railway trestle. The climb up the hill wasn't too bad, even when lugging an inner tube, or clinging tightly to a pail of water, carrying it from the tap by the castle. That was a mighty big cottage! It was big enough to house lots of people. Yet, it wasn't as impressive to me as the sand castles washed away by the small rollers caused by motor boats, or the wild thrashing about of guys wrestling in the sand.

The Beach offered all kinds of mysteries and worrisome moments. Buried in shrubs near the sidewalk leading to the big wharf, lay an old, abandoned rusty metal boat. The story was that some tough guys once used it for "rum running" during "prohibition" times. I poked around in the dictionary to find out what that word meant. I did that with the same kind of persistence that some small trees did when poking their way through parts of that lonely old boat. They reminded me of the stubborn plants pushing through cracks in cement. Nature's persistence never failed to amaze me! Nor did human persistence that aroused my curiosity and caused me to seek answers.

One evening a terrible storm made the lake lose its temper. That night, I watched some bigger guys hammer off the padlock on the boat rental shed, grab some oars, jump down off the dock into a boat, and laughing and whooping, row off into the raging darkness. The next day I heard that the police were dragging the lake for some bodies. I never found out if the night before ended up a tragedy.

Stepping on things and getting surprised happened often. Once walking out in the water at Long Point, along the shore from Regina Beach, I thought my toe touched a crayfish. There were lots of the orange crusty shells with feelers and pinchers washed up on the sand. Yet this was different. My cousins and I made a big discovery under water, a partial set of false teeth. We wondered if a grown-up could possibly swim about without noticing one part of his or her choppers was missing.

I knew that Mr. and Mrs. Atkinson, could, because they were right at home in the water. They even taught me to do the breast stroke. At first I felt like a turtle flaying my arms and legs around. Yet they let me trust them, and in time, my new kick made me feel like a big bull frog.

Aunt Nora, my dad's sister, was nice, too. She had a round hunched back. Her husband, Bert, was a very polite little fellow with a cookie mustache. He never took me fishing, but she did, lots of times. Often the lake was like glass, the sun hot, and her sandwiches scrumptious. She never moped like my dad did, or ever got angry. My mother told me that Bert's brother, who lived at the hotel, was a "Pansy." I never knew why she called him that. He wore a bathing cap and lay on the beach a lot by himself. Still, so did many people. I never knew either whether he danced with women or not since the "Ark," the floating dance hall by the tracks, was pulled up on the shore like a beached whale. It never hosted dances ever again.

What did outlast the "Ark" though was Butler's Fish and Chip shop. The smell of fish and chips with salt and vinegar greeted my nose through many summers. With others I'd climb a bunch of steps, shifting about to avoid bumping the many people sitting necking, flirting, teasing, or just kibitzing around. I remember standing on tip toes when I was little, looking over the open window to place my order. Eventually over the years I found that I could read the cardboard signs plastered all over the walls around the hot stove and fryers. Mr. Butler must have been a philosopher or something to have all those sayings there. I, too, was becoming a collector of sayings, since I was finding that there was more to life than fish and chips, false teeth, and wet bathing trunks.

9 High School Days

All the world's a stage. And all the men and women merely players: And one man in his time plays many parts, His acts being seven ages, At first the infant, mewing and puking in the nurse's arms. And then the whining school boy, with his satchel, And shining morning face, creeping like a snail unwillingly to school...   1

I survived grade eight and left most of the guys in my class behind to find jobs. Grade nine at Scott

Collegiate felt scary and worse! We washed sidewalks with tooth brushes while trying to bend down in tight skirts, and do other embarrassing things. But I soon found that after "freshy week," that school was okay, and it wasn't long before I felt that I belonged. The only thing I had to be wary of was the principal. We only got to know him as someone to stay away from. "Here comes the bull" was a warning cry that the principal was on the prowl through the halls and boys' wash rooms.

Not all guys felt that way. Ed, for one, was from a small town where his dad once ran a hotel. Even though Ed was a bit cross-eyed, he sure had confidence. Boy, could he play hockey! His house was near to mine, so I got rides to school in his jeep.

I felt that art could get me friends, and often I told guys, "Everybody needs to be good at something." I guess I was just fishing for compliments, but they never seemed to come. When Doug, a friend, kept getting better marks than me, and telling me about what he had read, I often told him not to believe everything that he read. My response went over like a lead balloon, and I wondered whether I wasn't just jealous.

Where I didn't have that much success with books, I got some fun out of doing cartoons and things for the school year book inside and out. Also Bob, my friend, asked me to do a poster advertising the photography club. I asked him for a photograph of his little sister standing, and one of a camera. With those I made him a poster. It included a girl's body with a camera for her head.

Sports were usually fun, all except gym. I just couldn't get my body to do what Foo, the gym teacher wanted me to do. He was a well-coordinated skinny guy with glasses. A bunch of guys that he paid a lot of attention to could vault, swing on the rings, tumble and get their pictures in the sports section of the year book. Where they could do all that, my efforts brought me only embarrassment and grief, even though I never skipped the classes and never forgot my gym shorts and runners. Foo must have thought that showed that I keenly wanted to do gym. But I feared the rings!

One day he lost his patience with me, got me up on the rings, and started pushing me. I swayed back and forth like a limp pendulum. Awkward and tensed up from fear I swung up and reached the point parallel to the floor. Just at that moment I let go, landing on my back. When I came to, a bunch of faces stared down at me. Foo bent over me and asked,

"Can you wiggle your toes, and move your fingers?"

I thought, that was a ridiculous question, It was my back that was killing me! Messing up in gym, I thought I'd try out for the football team to play on the line. In practices we did stops and starts, pushups, running on the spot, hitting the ground, up and at it again. Doing what the coaches and helpers wanted me to do, tired me right out. I finally had enough when my trick knee gave out on me. I had tried to pivot on the line, got hit on an angle, my cleats dug into the ground, and I blacked out. I remembered the same thing happening when I played goal in hockey. So I had the biscuit, no more of that!

I began to believe everyone has a disability that could cramp his or her style. Sometimes I'd get crystal-like things in front of my eyes. It took me a few years to figure that was a warning sign that a whacking big headache would follow. Before I twigged to that, the only thing I could do was go home, lay quietly in my bedroom with the blinds pulled, and try to sleep. Eventually, when a crystalline screen began having its way, warning of a migraine coming on, I found that an Anacin would stop it in its tracks a half an hour later. Then I'd just have a faint reminder of the unwelcome visitor.

Gym floors, a trick knee, and migraines never robbed me of my feel for art and music. I had never forgotten my grade three teacher, Mrs. Mahan teaching us the song

I've got rings on my fingers, bells on my toes, elephants to ride upon, my wild Irish Rose...   2

I never quite figured out what the song was getting at, but it didn't matter. I liked the words and tune. I even tried to read the words and sing them backwards. Yet it would always lose something in the singing. Besides, while singing in the school glee club, I got to play a baritone horn in the band. However, neither my mom nor dad ever came to hear me play at a band concert. Yet, I understand why they wouldn't come and hear me. Mr. Cowan had me practice in the room off the auditorium stage, where I'd be far away from everyone's hearing except his. Hearing me honking away in my attic room at home wasn't a treat either at first. Our neighbors must have got indigestion from hearing me search for the right notes while puffing and belching into the brass mouth piece.

Everyone liked Mr. Cowan. He didn't mind the bleeps, and burps I made on the horn. He did have one problem, though. I saw him always holding a handkerchief when he touched an instrument that he demonstrated. I think he did that because his fingers sweated acid. He was very hygienic. We all had to dip the metal mouthpieces in alcohol to sterilize them for the next guys who would use them.

I still took band in grade ten but was put in another class. Our home room was in the basement in the old part of the building. I didn't know at the time that room was for guys who weren't "academically inclined." I think that was the word for it. The class was made up of characters. There was Savage and his friend Bush. Once Bush and Savage changed desks. Bush sat behind Savage. The teacher said,

"I've heard of a Savage hiding behind a Bush, but never a Bush hiding behind a Savage."

There was also the son of the chief of police, who once got me to go along with him to his church Sunday school, and whom I heard held wild parties when his parents were out. He, too, joined our class. It was interesting, though; even more so, because out of that all-male class came another police chief; that was Savage, and a high ranking police officer, that was Bush. Out of that class also came at least one

NHL hockey player. Then there was Chick. He was an older guy with rope burns on his body from amateur wrestling, and Robert, who even while in school, was a disc jockey at a local radio station. Guys like those, along with others made up the gang that gathered in our basement home room.

It was in that class that I got my first public speaking experience. Mr. Philpot, our English teacher, made each of us make a speech. I spoke about fun at air cadet camp. I got lots of laughs that I hadn't planned on, especially when I used hand actions to describe pumping the fire extinguishers unlawfully in the dorms, "pump, pump, squirt, squirt," I shouted loudly. The guys were practically rolling in the aisle. Even Mr. Philpot looked like he was holding back a smile. I didn't think I wanted to be a comedian! I was both hurt and pleased, but I had no idea what was so funny. In my high school years at Scott, I met up with many teachers. They differed as chalk from cheese. A social studies teacher taught us by using diagrams on the board. He labeled them. I liked his style, and copied them out very carefully. The only problem was, when I looked back at them to study what they meant, I often forgot what he had said. No one told me I should take notes and no one taught me how to study. Years later I learned that

"SQ3R" method (Survey, Question, Read, Recite, Review)
3

I never knew whether that social studies teacher used that study method. Though I do know that he ate Sen, Sen. I guess it was for his breath. I don't think he had to worry about that, he never went beyond his desk that he usually perched on if he wasn't making diagrams on the board. Mr. Spears, our home room teacher, taught us grade nine English, and Art. His parents owned a hardware store in Regina, and he wrote out our report cards in green ink. He sure liked green!

The French teacher turned me off French. I felt I had to duck, not only her remarks, but also her. I felt I needed to be wary about being hit on the head. I guess I was gun shy from ducking flying objects in grade eight. I had always found it hard to memorize anything. So blaming that teacher could have been an excuse for fearing the necessary memory work.

I found most school work hard to do. However, one day I got a lift when I was goofing off, skipping a class, and hiding in the stairwell with Tom (His dad worked for the Prairie Farm Rehabilitation Act outfit.) Tom taught me "The House that Jack Built" in old English. To my surprise I could recite it word for word in no time. Being able to recite made me think I wasn't so dumb after all. I had a scrap book full of sayings that I liked and that helped me when I said them aloud, especially when I was feeling down. Also "The House that Jack Built " in old English gave me a real lift when I found I could get my tongue around these words

This is the domiciliary edifice erected by Jon. This is the agricultural produce that was deposited in the domiciliary. .. This is the noxious vermin that destroyed the agricultural that . . .This is the feline domestic animal that bothered the noxious that . This is the canine quadruped that worried the feline domestic that . . . This is the bovine animal with the distorted features that elevated the canine that . . . This is the fair but disconsolated spinster who elacticated the bovine animal who . . .This is the love sick slain who offered his tender oscillations to the fair but disconsolate spinster . . . This is the ecclesiastical functionary who united in menial bonds the love sick swain to the fair but disconsolate spinster that... 4

Reciting that poem could sure take a long time when each time I added a new line. I also included all those that came before. I was getting good at reciting poetry, but I was still happier with my art.

But then one day, I woke up to how things really were. No longer did I enjoy bugging my home room teacher Mr. McDougall, an air force vet. It wasn't even fun any more slouching at the back of the science room playing ventriloquist with Bill, booing noises to infuriate "Dugie," and to even cause such anger that he smashed his glasses on the lab table's gas jet. No longer was it fun just to attend the classes I liked, shops, music, and art, having dropped all the other courses. No longer was it fun to sit day dreaming in the Physics class, gazing out the window to watch a horse showing that he knew where his driver's customers were, while his bread man boss ran in and out of yards, leaving the old nag to pull the wagon ahead.

No longer was it good playing the martyr having a trick knee, and reciting how I became air born from the gym rings, landing on my back on the hardwood floor. So, feeling down on school I waited for someone, a teacher, a friend, parent, anyone to say, "Come on, we want you to stay. Don't drop out."

They didn't. So I did. Had someone followed up with a phone call even after I dropped out, like Mr. Cowan, the music teacher whom I liked, it might have made a difference. He found a place for me in his class and got me a horn solo in the school production. Had he asked "why?" Had my mother or dad shown up at a concert to see and hear me play; my art teacher who got me space for my cartoons of school staff in the year book two years running told me that I was needed, maybe I would have stayed on. Had "Mo" the school trumpet player hero said, "Hey, you can't quit, you're part of our group," or had "Chick" the wrestler, who had quit and come back to high school, or the guy who did disk jockeying, or the air cadet officer, Mr. Winters, said, "Don't do it." Well, just maybe, I wouldn't have quit. But they didn't! Silence, the kind I heard from my dad. That was it! So then what to do? I had started grade twelve only to quit half way through. What good was that?

I rode out to Isted's. There was Bob lying by the wall bordering his house. He was fast asleep with a crystal set that he had built in his hand. I wasn't surprised at his ingenuity. He had built a photo enlarger from an old bellows camera on a stand that he had welded. To take his pictures, he used an old timer of a camera that he had bought from a local pawn shop. His only new purchases were photography magazines. I liked thumbing through those to admire the artistic merit of females found there. Damn it! Why couldn't I be like Bob? He had his homemade gadgets that he had devised, morals that kept him from swearing. He had a mother who gave up trying to get him to clear out from under his bed what looked like a car wrecking yard. He seemed to have his life altogether, while I was still wondering, unlike Bob, whether

Man is (but) a useless passion   5

10 Flying Low

Air Cadets

While at air cadets, I met another sharp character like Bob. His name was John. He was among a handful of guys that I found out attended Albert School, when I attended Kitchener. John was kind of the leader. The guys phoned him to decide what we were going to do in the evenings. He played a cello, tennis, and knew a lot about stuff from his English mother and his dad who worked as a refrigeration man. You had to be smart to do that! Orin Green, another guy in the group lived near the library. His mother read books, lots of books. She had to clear the kitchen table of them to see its top. We played canasta, and other card games at the Green's. Orin's dad was a railway switchman. Sometimes he'd come home feeling very happy from a drink or two. Once he tried swinging his leg over one of our heads while a guy ducked and almost fell off the chair. Orin's dad was lots of fun!

The most deep thinking that I did back then was when John, the smart one, and I would walk home together from air cadets. We'd stop at a corner before we'd each go our own way, look intensely up at the sky, at each other, and tried to fathom the mystery of the stars and the meaning of the universe. Our talks got very philosophical. I wonder what John is doing now. I had heard that he became a physicist. Back then he was just John, an intelligent guy whom I met in air cadets.

Unlike John I didn't learn much at air cadets, even though I did eventually get promoted from a leading aircraftman to a corporal. I didn't rise further in the ranks. I think it was because my posture wasn't good, and I didn't have too many friends, remembering what my dad had always told me:

"Keep your mouth shut and do your work, then you'll be all right." Since he never rose higher than a corporal in the army, I wondered about his advice. We'd march a lot, go upstairs in the armory, have a coke, sit in a classroom and try to understand some kind of dead reckoning instrument that had a wheel to turn. I took a book home that explained it all, but my efforts got no more attention than the wedge that I wore, which I never thought much more about once I put it on.

Once a year we'd be called to attention, then stand at ease to hear that another tag day had come around. We were to report to the armory on Saturday, pick up our boxes and tags, and get assigned to a certain part of Regina, to collect as much money as possible. The one collecting the most money would win "flips." That meant get rides in an aircraft. I got to do the warehouse district. I went into every office there from desk to desk holding out my box for money and giving a little sales pitch. At the end of the day I handed in a full box, thirty-seven dollars. I was announced a winner. I never did earn more stripes in cadets, but I sure proved that I could raise money for "flips."

Often when asleep, I'd dream of flying. But to get airborne I had to run faster and faster. The faster I ran, the higher I flew. Did you ever dream that? Some say I did because my primeval ancestors were birds. Yet the closest I got to flying free, were those "flips," riding in a Beechcraft Expediter. It had a fast take off and landing speed. So much so, that I once read about some Indian kids getting killed in one on the way home from just outside Winnipeg. I liked flying despite all that I heard about crashes. But, unlike a bunch of my friends who were able to get their wings by learning on Tiger Moths, I was out of luck because of poor eye sight.

I was always fond of throwing balsa wood gliders and flying elastic-band-driven, hand built planes. I'd bet myself that they would stay up until I counted to at least twenty-five. Some did. When I got into grade nine and joined air cadets, I had wanted to fly a real plane. I felt really bad when those friends of mine, Bob, and John, and a whole bunch more, did earn their wings while in cadets.

I did get to join the air cadets' precision squad, though. We got to wear white belts, hat flashes, and white gloves, and march by numbers instead by shouted commands. Bob from Cameron Street never did get into the squad. He marched with both arms going the same way instead of alternating. He just couldn't get it right!

I had something else going for me. I'd spit on my boots to make them shine better and use my dad's metal cloth protector under my buttons. That gave me an edge, I thought, over some other guys who didn't know the secrets. I was glad that my dad served in the army, as his dad did, and his dad, before him no doubt.

Putting shellac on the buttons after you had shined them was out! That was cheating! However, the work that I did to look smart paid off. Our precision squad was chosen as an honour guard at the Regina city hall when the Princess Elizabeth and Prince Phillip were visiting Canada. She walked by us up the city hall steps, while we stood at attention in line on the sidewalk. That was great! The only thing was, all I saw really was a hat and coat go by. I think her hat had a feather. Standing ram rod straight and looking directly ahead, I only got a glimpse of that hat. I didn't think it compared in any way to her jeweled crown that I had seen in pictures.

One other good thing as an air cadet, besides getting a glimpse of the Princess, was getting to attend free camps at Gimli, Manitoba, and Abbotsford, B.C. We rode on rickety trains pulled by steam engines belching smoke. Black porters kindly made up our beds, and warned us not to open the windows because the soot would dirty our sheets. We did, and the soot did. When we first arrived, we were issued cotton summer uniforms, some too big, others too small. At camp we "frenched" other guys' beds, and removed the coiled spring clips so guys would fall through between the wires. We fought with fire extinguishers, slid down fire escape chutes, and during the day pleased our officers by doing what we were told. I didn't know many guys at camp. So one day I got the bright idea of polishing all their boots in the barracks when they were asleep. They'd be surprised when they woke up. Somehow I'd let the cat out of the bag that I did that, and I imagined they'd be pleased. I only finished a couple of pair, my own and the guy's in the bunk above me before an officer came through to do a bed check. He ordered me back to bed. I must admit I wasn't too disappointed. It was a crazy idea.

We marched on the hot tarmac, watched movies on air force subjects, played Borden balls, drank cokes, ate ice cream bars, lined up for meals, and helped in the kitchen. Sometimes we'd even bus it to a beach to swim. In BC the bus rides were a bit scary, around sharp turns, along deep gorges. To keep up our courage, being prairie kids not used to mountain driving, we'd sing, "Ninety-nine bottles of beer on the wall."

Now and then we'd get rides on aircraft. We also got to shoot twenty-two bore rifles that weighed the same as army 303's. They gave us ten or twelve rounds each time and we had to hand back the same number of empty shells when we left the rifle range.

At one of the Abbotsford camps, Barry, whose nick name was "Red," and I crawled under the fence, took a well-worn path, and hitch hiked through the evening and into the night to Bellingham, Washington and back by early morning. Along the way we ate apples right off the trees and kept to the

108

side roads. We were tired the next day.

One time my Aunt Jean, who had been in the army during the war, visited our camp. She said she knew the O.C. and could get Barry and me out on special leave to take a trip across the border into the States. We never told her that we had just been down there already. She took us to an officer's mess somewhere and introduced us to some big wigs. We had to wait outside first. She seemed to know a lot of the guys. We drove in her neat car to Seattle where she showed us where she worked. We rode on freeways and overpasses at high speeds. Aunt Jean really impressed not only me, but my friend Barry. My mom, Aunt Jean's oldest sister, had told me that Jean had a "checkered career," whatever that meant. I didn't care. I thought my aunt was all right!

I wasn't sure about Barry though. One day some guys came around to our barracks picking kids for positions as cadet MP's to stand at the gates of the camp. They got special privileges. They asked me if I'd be one. Not wanting to desert Barry and move into another barracks, I said "No." They then turned to him, and to my amazement, he said, "Yes." I became angry, and wondered if it would have been different, had I heard and heeded this advice back then

Don't rely on the broken reed of human support. 1

After camp our friendship still stayed intact. We visited each other's homes, and listened to records. I remember he had a little brother whom he affectionately called "punk," and a mom and a dad who owned and operated a locksmith shop on South Railway Street in Regina. I wonder where Barry is now and what he is doing?

Back then I also had other friends whom I had met at air cadets. Sometimes I got a chance with some of them to cruise around in Dean's car, even with girls in the back, especially when swinging around the park's "lover's lane." We only had more fun when we would go out of town to amateur nights. We'd sit in the back seats, smoke cigars, and do a bit of hooting and teasing when the acts came on, especially the tap dancing. Sometimes we'd get back to Regina early in the morning and catch holy hell from our parents who didn't get much sleep waiting up for us. That is about as wild as I dared get, for a very good reason!

Someone once said that some kids start out in their mother's wombs smoking cigars and carving their initials on their mom's womb linings. I knew I had not been one of those. That's no doubt because, trouble I didn't need. My brother Norm, who became a police officer after the war, threatened me in my teens saying, "God help you if I ever see your name appearing on the police blotter." My dad hammered home the same message.

There was no question though about the fact that I was straining at the bit, wanting to break free from my mother's apron strings, and my father's and brother's reminder to "keep the family's good name!"

I never dated any girls in high school. I felt I looked too fat and none would be interested in me. It did puzzle me though, that girls usually surrounded one fat boy who seemed kind of soft and girl-like. He

was in the typing class that didn't interest me as a
place to find girls. Mom always used to say to me,

"Never mind. One day you'll have a foozy hanging
around your neck." I didn't know what to say to her
about that, but I felt that it wouldn't be such a bad
idea.

I had a lot hanging around my neck at the time,
worry, for one thing. It was about then that I began
struggling with whether I should quit school or not. I
thought back to all the different part time jobs that I
had. None of them appealed to me as a life long
career. My thoughts flashed back to grade eight days,
and then on through my high school years.

11 Job Tasting

Life is something to do when you can't get to sleep.   1

Delivering Groceries

As I grew more, through teenage "grit and bear" it
times, I felt the challenges tested my mental strength,
and pushed my staying power to the limit. Finishing
grade eight, I began delivering groceries by bike for
Mrs. Cawsey. I also had the job of feeding her cat
with a can of Irish stew each day. It lived in the store
basement where it belonged. Right after school and
Saturday mornings Mrs. Cawsey would give me
orders to deliver. She'd do that while staring at the
weigh scale and popping grapes and other good bits
into her gob (That's English for mouth).

She often insisted that I pedal one of the orders

way down town. When I got there, I had to climb a slippery metal fire escape, while balancing the box, and clinging to the rail. I'd get through that ordeal okay. But I didn't relish the idea of riding back to the store in deep icy ruts. That was never any fun, anymore than when I was chosen as meat by a passing dog who left his teeth marks in my leg. Mrs. Cawsey, a good old practical Maritimer, poured turpentine into my ankle wound and sent me off with the next delivery.

Reality confronted me then, and later. From an apartment above the store, a woman showed up with her young husband. She was all swollen in front. He looked pleased, and I wondered what they had been up to. My mom and dad hadn't told me anything about that. Their whispers from their bedroom in our small house I assumed were just their talking about me and my latest comings and goings.

Paper Route

That new revelation about life didn't knock me off my stride, but it did rouse my adventurous spirit. So I left Cawsey's before I had a chance to get one of those heavy balloon-tired bikes with a sign plate on the cross bar. On to the next. I took on my friend Bob's discarded six a.m. down town paper route. What freedom! What fear! Walking often down the middle of deserted Eleventh Ave, normally one of the busiest Regina streets, I'd dip into dark alleys and doorways, climb dimly lit stairs, fold and throw papers, and run back to the safety of the middle of the street. Those early morning excursions reminded me at the time of the way I was living my young life.

Pin setting

Bob didn't get me the next job when I started high school. I got it talking to a guy, who lived next door to a teacher. I didn't have anyone like he had, especially a teacher who taught him things: like how to look at stars through telescopes, and catch moths by smearing guck on the sides of Wascana Park trees. Anyway, I joined him down at Vic Alleys setting pins. In time I took pride in grasping three pins in one hand, two in the other, jump down into either pit to set the pins up, then quickly leap back onto my perch that straddled two lanes. Five pins were great. Ten pins, murder! It seemed necessary, for some reason, that each time the bowler wanted his or her own ball back. Flying ten pins hurt more than fives. My coke bottle filled with water sometimes took a hit, and often, just as I had finished my regular shift, Vic or another boss, would send me back to set up the tens. Ten pins didn't sit well with one of my fellow pin setters one night. He just about got his leg taken off with a ball when he was trying to set up. Recently from Germany with little English, he strode out onto the hardwood alley, and with curses in German, bounced the ball back at the bowler. That night I was so tired and sad in losing my neighbor pin setter that I fell exhausted on my bed, still clothed in sweat grimy jeans smelling of smoke. I now knew why my friend who got me the job pin setting always stunk from B.O. I wonder whether my brother and I had the same smell since he also once set pins for Vic.

Warehouse Work

The second last summer job that I got before

stepping out permanently into the hard cruel world was with the Saskatchewan Power Commission Warehouse. We had to roll big wooden spools of wire around, and carry metal parts about with no idea how they were used. But that didn't matter to us. We punched the time clock, and did what the regular full time workers sometimes did, found a place to hide from the boss until coffee time.

Digging Ditches

The next summer, still thinking of "throwing in the towel" at school, I got a job digging ditches and mowing lawns at the Legislative buildings. The boss would drive by in his truck and dirt would fly. When his truck disappeared around the corner, the shovels would stop, or slow down until he rounded the corner again. However, there was one old guy who just kept digging and didn't get into the rhythm of truck and shovel, shovel and truck. The guys teased him till they found out from one of the regular workers that the man couldn't talk back. The Nazis had tortured him during the war. He had lost his tongue and hair except for some fuzz on top. He just kept his head down, his old rubber boots on the spade, and kept digging the trench. It ran along side the hedge by Albert Street near the bridge across the man-made Wascana Lake.

The bridge, with the figures of Queen Victoria on its pillars, was the same bridge which another immigrant crossed many times while operating a street car. That was my immigrant dad. Now I, a second generation Canadian, had to get out in the world and earn my keep by the sweat of my brow.

114

Would I be in the same space as all those kaleidoscope characters that I met growing up to be a man? What would it be? I wasn't sure, despite the message conveyed by the spading, rubber booted man that echoed

Our main business is not to see what lies dimly at a distance, but to do what lies clearly at hand.   2

Sorting

Maybe I'd apply at the Post Office to become a mail sorter. Once I had worked there during Christmas rush and found that I was good at putting mail in the right slots. It was almost second nature to me. Then again, I wondered if I should answer the Provincial Government advertisement for psychiatric nurses in training? On second thought, maybe I should become a Conservation Officer. The Government's advert looked interesting. But I didn't apply.

Maybe I'd go trapping up north. Perhaps Allen, Bob's brother with whom I had once motorcycled cross country hunting on his bike, would go with me. I wrote to the Department of Natural Resources in La Ronge and got a nice letter back. It said that all the trap lines up there were "Registered" and reserved for the Indians. So that left me with nothing else to do but throw away the books that I had collected on trapping and go to my dad for help since nothing else seemed to be panning out.

Climbing Telephone Poles

"Dad, what to do?"

"Climb telephone poles with Sask. Tel.?"

"Could you get me on there? " "We'll see."

My dad was a man of few words. We all knew that. But being a good CCFer, and union member, it happened. He had pull. Just as he had helped get my brother on the police force, first to wash and drive the "Black Maria, " pick up drunks, and pound the beat, so dad got me on with Sask. Tel. first climbing poles as an apprentice lineman. I was all set to trot, to put on the climbing spurs. Bouncing around in the back of a truck, miles and miles of stringing wire with a long pole with a hook and its four-letter name soon humbled me.

Eventually I did get my climbing belt and spurs. Soon after, the foreman ordered me to climb over, around and through wires to perch on the very top of one pole after another. That helped a bit in ridding me of fear. But it also made me feel damn silly and put me in my place in the pecking order of things. "Old Doc," " Shaky Jake" and others on the construction gang tolerated my clumsiness in slinging cross arms and tying in insulators. Yet they also made me feel at home as we stopped at one hotel after another. They would shoot pool, hit the bar, while I ate liver and onion suppers, and earn my nick name "Candy " by pigging out on chocolate bars. While buying me those, they bet among themselves on how many it would take to make me sick. But the bars didn't. Neither did the two cigar brands "Crooks,"dipped in rum, soaked in wine, and "White Owls " that I smoked while climbing. I claimed that cigars kept me warm. If truth be told, what they really did, was help keep my mind off my fear of falling off tall corner poles, and hard-as-iron tamaracks.

The rhythm of up one pole, down and on to another, while peering ahead to the next town, poking its head just above the horizon, made on-the road-life tolerable. Now, in looking back, I remember feeling the spirit of the prairie that W.O. Mitchell shared in his book, "Who Has Seen the Wind."

Yet there were also unpleasant encounters. Little kids in town would sometimes peer up at me with the kind of glint in their eyes as if they were about to pelt me from their sling shots. Once I heard one little voice shout,

"You're going to fall, aren't you mister!" He was right!

Later, my final performance as lineman did happen. My feet kicked out from a pole as they sometime did and I slid, hitting the ground, with one spur cutting my boot and penetrating my big toe. The "V" scar remains as a reminder. Thus ended my career as Apprentice Lineman, and my performance as "Big Bird." I had enough of that. Falling for girls, I didn't mind. Falling off poles was just too much!

Now where? That's the same question I asked years before when I quit a succession of after school and week end jobs, including flag man for an air crop sprayer.

Out of work for a few weeks I did a lot of day dreaming. I thought back to when I was foot loose and fancy free. I thought things were sure easier once. When I was a little kid, I had found a few jobs myself. In my teens, I inherited most of my jobs from friends who went on to better things. Before I became a teenager I also had delivered Liberty magazines and saved the bonus coupons that I had earned for prizes; I collected bottles and gritted my teeth when the bottle depot guy showed no respect for my precious gems, pitching them in the bin with others bruised and chipped. His carelessness didn't match my care, damn it! I eventually learned that I couldn't control what others did. So I'd merely mumble my curses instead when people slammed doors in my face as I tried to sell wall plaques for a friend of my mom's. After a bout of feeling sorry for myself, and wallowing around in the fear of rejection, I decided that wasn't going to get me anywhere.

Warehouse Man

So one morning, two weeks after I quit climbing poles for Sask.Tel., I dropped the, "if only it could have been different" stuff and instead, decided that I'd better get cracking and get a job. I answered a want ad in the Regina Leader Post and landed a job as a shipper at Groff Agencies that handled the top of the line luggage. A salesmen there had known my sister Pat from high school days. So I felt right at home. Someone knew me!

I felt good, that is till one day when I made a stupid mistake. I wrote up a numbered invoice wrong, and instead of voiding it with a line through it, and including it with other invoice copies, I scrunched it up and hid it. I couldn't understand what the fuss was about when the boss insisted that we look high and low for that numbered missing invoice. It never dawned on me that a missing one would suggest an item was taken out of the building without any record of what happened to it, borrowed, stolen, or lost. Did the boss think that I had snatched a bag? I hope not! Did he think that I "aided and abetted" someone who did? Well I didn't! That incident, plus boredom caused me to decide to leave. The boss never even saw me when I left. His secretary clerk said goodbye and that was that.

I wondered how many young people there were who weren't told, never knew, or didn't ask more about how things worked. What do you do when questions go unasked or unanswered at work, leaving some unnecessarily feeling they've failed? I wondered how many others felt themselves to be losers, as I did back then.

When I was at loose ends just out of work, I rode along with my old friend Bob to the Weyburn, Saskatchewan Mental Asylum. He was working as a draftsman, and had an inspection to do. I felt sad for the people there, but even more for myself. Bob had a good job. I had nothing. I felt useless, "a nothing!" My thoughts were those of the character who moaned

You don't understand. I could have been a contender. I could have been a somebody-instead of a bum, which is what I am, let's face it. 3

Escape seemed the only way out. I still remembered writing a letter to the La Ronge Conservation Office asking about the possibility of me trapping up north. The answer was "None!" I still thought there would be something for me to do up there. So I decided to see for myself. Having associated home with my failure and mom's nagging, I felt, since I was lingering in a mental wilderness, I might as well live in a physical one. So I said goodbye to mom and dad, and left for La Ronge with dad's parting words

"Son, there will always be a bed here for you, remember that."

I felt, in leaving, I was expanding my play pen. But I also wondered if I were slamming doors on opportunities, opening new ones, or choosing to be pushed or pulled along in life by reacting to experiences. Then again, maybe I was just being too damn weak to stick it out in a job. I began to wonder what all this living was about anyway? This answer came to me much later in my journey when I read

As far as we can discern, the sole purpose of human existence is to kindle a light in the darkness of mere being.
4

Years passed after leaving home. In that time I had a good wife and family, had taught school, worked for the federal government, gained a few university degrees and contemplated the future while living at Fort Simpson in the NWT.

Book 2

12 Saskatoon Seminary

Don't be an agnostic. Be something.   1

    While at Fort Simpson, I was asking myself what should I do? Then it struck me. I had heard that Harvey Hurren, whom I had known through teaching in Northern Manitoba, had just gone into theology at St. Andrew's College in Saskatoon. So I phoned him and asked "How are things?" We got talking, and I began thinking aloud about the possibility of also attending St. Andrew's. Then this poem came to mind,

> I fled Him, down the nights and down the days;
> I fled Him, down the arches of the years;
> I fled Him, down the labyrinthine ways
> Of my own mind, and in the midst of tears
> I hid from Him, and under running laughter.   2

    Those words like spikes tore into the fibre of my being. Wow, was I a blockhead! It appeared that God, so persistent, had finally caught up to me in his pursuit! It seemed like my Creator grabbed me by the scruff of my neck and said, "That's it Ken, no more running away, remember your past commitment!
    Indeed, I remembered a moment way back when I was about twenty years old, I and some other students knelt in down town Winnipeg's Young

United Church, and participated in "the laying on of hands." That declared us candidates for the ministry. Unfortunately, I didn't follow through with my intentions for many years. I gravitated into teaching instead. Then later, when I was teaching at God's Lake, the Revs. George, and Glen, who were attending a presbytery meeting confronted me with,

"Ken, just what do you want to do with the rest of your life?"

I think that they were telling me to stop fooling around and get down to business and finish what I set out to do a few years before. Yet, I still didn't feel any urge to study for the ministry. I recalled Poplar River, and that depressing picture of the deserted manse, and for a time, thought it all seemed so futile. Then I remembered ministers like the Revs. Ken and Ibbs who served at the James Evans' Memorial Church in Norway House and who sacrificed some of the best years of their lives to ministry.

Something special filtered through their personalities, something that I thought I'd like to have. What was that something? As I continued to think things through, I again experienced a pull toward the ministry. By that time, evening at Fort Simpson was long gone.

I remembered my resolve when I left the Hudson's Bay Company. I had decided that a person must give one's life to the most worthy cause that one could find. I concluded that would be to the greatest of them all, namely God. Who else?

So there it was. Lesley and I and our kids would go South. How would we manage that? We really didn't have any money. Nevertheless, somehow the wheels began to turn more rapidly as the days passed. I talked to the Rev. Dr. Charles at St. Andrew's College. Soon after, St.A's accepted me as a student and the Rev. Don in Saskatoon found me a position at Herschel, not too far from Saskatoon. I would take Sunday services as a student minister. As a family we would live in the United Church manse, and I would commute to Saskatoon for classes. That took care of our financial needs.

Only one thing was left to do. I would get to Winnipeg where Rev. Dr. John, minister at Regents Park Church would introduce me to his Church Board who, hopefully, would approve me, almost sight unseen, as a candidate for the ministry. That same day I would meet with the Winnipeg Presbytery Students Committee to seek its endorsement. It all happened. The Regents Park Board asked me how I found my faith. I told them about falling on my knees in that canoe at LaRonge, praying the Lord's prayer and reciting the twenty-third psalm my mother taught me as a child. At the Presbytery Committee, one person asked me what my view of "Atonement" was. At the time I didn't have a clue what he was asking. So I asked him what was his. The rest of the interview seemed to go all right. I was on my way as a full-fledged candidate for the ministry in the United Church of Canada, and in three years, if all went well, I would graduate from St. Andrew's and seek ordination.

The first year, I found the commute to Herschel from Saskatoon very tiring. So I asked the dean if I could stay in residence through the week. There was no room at the inn. So I approached the principal of the Anglican seminary. He said that he had a room serving as a clothes closet. He could have the students move their stuff out. I could stay in it. It had a radiator that bumped in the night. Some said it was the ghosts of Emmanuel and St. Chads. The room had a bed, and a table, with knee space between each. I was happy with that.

The second year we moved into Saskatoon where I did my ten-month internship with the Rev. Wes. He was an excellent listener, gave me opportunities to preach and conduct services. The congregation was very supportive.

The evaluation of my internship came about. I felt that one prof may have had problems with the outcome. He gave me the impression that he had some reservations about some of us mature students entering the ministry. Tom, an older fellow student who had been with the RCAF in the desert during the war, was a farmer, and seemed to get the same message. Anyway, whether the prof actually said it or not, I felt uneasy thinking that he thought that I was manipulative. Unfortunately, I wasn't sure what he meant. The only thing that I can think of was that another dedicated student had implied that I was a sponge. She didn't mean that I was good at absorbing knowledge. I wondered if she meant that I was milking the college dry by getting so much financial support as a married intern. She was single.

124

Every man, wherever he goes, is encompassed by a cloud of comforting convictions, which move with him like flies on a summer day.   3

There were times when, no doubt, people's views of me were clearly based on what I said. There was the time when I made it quite clear that I did not support the graduating class one year ahead of me. That class had made a decision to install, in St. Andrew's College chapel as a gift, a print of one of Salvador Dali's pictures, "Christ on the Cross." I felt that I had some idea of where Salvador Dali's head was when he did that picture. His life and motifs, I thought at the time, were not particularly Christian in the best sense of the word.

My views didn't go over well with some students, nor, for that matter, with some of the first year class. I had not associated with them much. I had little time for anything other than my family, my studies, and the congregations that I served. I was also feeling exhausted from conducting Sunday services, and working to prepare my MA thesis for printing. I don't blame them for concluding that I wasn't with them. Perhaps that business of labeling me manipulative may have surfaced partly from that, and the Christ on the Cross incident.

That incident did turn a light bulb on for me. I looked back on my life to that point and felt that in some ways I had been broken on the rack of experience. That caused me to believe that persons need to be broken by life's raw experiences before they can truly grow.

Man's mind stretches to a new idea, never goes back to
its original dimensions.   4

The St. Andrew's experience pushed, pulled and
stretched me in many directions. I revisited many of
my preconceived notions and changed some of my
thinking. I wasn't merely refurbishing my house of
thoughts, but gutting the insides and moving walls
around to make space for new views within. I
continued renovating through my seminary days and
well into my ministry.

When I thought about what needed to be done, I
remembered Lesley having to go to the doctor. She
sought to get movement back to her arm. He freed it
up after saying to her,

"Sorry, but this crunching has to be done if you
want to have free movement again. Otherwise, you'll
lose it."

I suppose that is true, also, when we as individuals
need to face how we are coming across as persons in
the eyes of others. What's that old expression?

"I am not one person, but three, the person I think
I am, the person others think I am, and the person I
really am."

The "Johari Window " theory, much talked about in
clinical pastoral care embellishes that simple idea.

How do others really see us? How often do we
really see ourselves? I think of the very faithful St.
A's Librarian and retired church history teacher. I
remember how he took my retired farmer friend, Tom
to task for dropping an "ancient " book on the floor
where it literally disintegrated. I remember as
students we once caught "Charlie" off guard. He
taught church history. At the beginning of one class,
he rolled down the projector screen with his back to

it. He couldn't figure what made us laugh. When he pulled down that screen, he revealed a girl pin-up picture. That didn't make him lose his composure. He just carried on with the lecture. I remember him also demonstrating how to baptize a baby by using a rolled up blanket. Nothing seemed to stop him from demonstrating his dedication to grooming us for ministry.

He really cared! Lesley and I remember him coming to our home when our oldest son was in trouble. We were hurting and he ministered to us. We remember also how for years Charlie sent us Christmas cards. He was the only professor who kept in touch.

I remember our pastoral care teacher talking about "walking around" something before he got to the kernel of the truth that he wished to convey. Our systematics instructor would have a conversation with himself in class, saying something like,

"Now so and so believed this, but then again this other person believed that."

Yet, when one or two of us pressed him on what he believed, finding it out seemed impossible. Eventually, after he wrote a book discussing the "Spirit," his beliefs did begin to unfold and his writing did express some of what was on his mind.

I experienced the same frustration with another instructor who seldom declared his own position on anything as chaplain at the University Hospital. He gave an introductory course on clinical pastoral care. I felt that he expected me, for one, to "spill my guts" but wouldn't risk himself. That was a bit too much! For handling the pressure I was under at the time was more than enough. I didn't need the stress of baring my soul in that setting and letting myself be that vulnerable, while someone else of my vintage hid in the bushes. I wondered why he did that? Was it because instructors feared that they would freeze students in their tracks on the path of learning, or what?

From my point of view that "hiding in the bushes," in so far as not sharing one's owns beliefs as an instructor, was wrong. Yet, my view didn't seem relevant when it came to an old revered patriarch of the college. Our grand Old Testament professor, Dr. Snell, walked through those 39 books with us. He pointed out the dramatic, the humorous, and so much more. He whetted my appetite to delve deeper into the life and times of the Hebrew people. Those who often attended and kept copious notes had an invaluable treasury of material for sermons. It made some of us even think that we could take a crack at preaching from the Old Testament. His points as they related to Bible characters also hit home personally. For instance in Genesis, where God called out "Where are you Adam?" God knew where Adam was geographically. But if that is so, what was God asking? Could it have been, "Adam, where are you in your thinking? Or in the vernacular of street people, "Hey man, what's happening?" that is, "How is it with you?"

It became very evident to me that Doc Snell was implying that anytime in a person's life, one can see himself or herself in the Bible. That was news to me. For I wasn't very conversant with the Old Testament, although I had taught Sunday School at Old St. Andrew's in Winnipeg when I attended United College. It never occurred to me that those ancient writings had anything to do with me living out my life; nor did it occur to me that I can, if I so choose, see myself mirrored in Bible characters as my life unfolded.

We soon had opportunities to take turn about preaching in the college's chapel, supposedly sharing what we had learned. Those were, for me, stretching exercises. Still the profs were very gracious in not tearing apart my meager offerings. It also seemed that as students we went easy on each other, knowing that our turn would come around. Besides, were we not to practice Christian charity?

Throughout two of the three years at St. A's, I preached each Sunday. After Herschel, the Wakaw-Rosthern charge offered interesting insights on how we as Canadians of mixed ethnic origins worshiped, played, and worked together. The Wakaw community revealed a people with a zest for living and working together. When not farming some men, shouting and hollering, often charged hell bent for leather around a race track in chariots driven by farm horses kicking up dust, not unlike the ancient Roman charioteers.

To my pleasant surprise, the Wakaw United Church congregation was a gathering of Hungarians and Ukrainians. Both fed me full on Sundays with cabbage rolls, perogies, poppy seed pastry and more. When I asked one man, who showed a pride in his Hungarian heritage, "How come, the United Church?" he answered, "In the old country we were like Presbyterians (one of the United Church roots) long before you people in Canada even thought of the idea!"

I guess he was referring to the reform tradition from which we, as a denomination came.

The two congregations were as different as chalk and cheese since the ethnic complexion of each differed greatly. Rosthern was more Anglo Saxon. Yet each, like many little country charges, bravely carried on, despite the sermons dished out by that inexperienced student and the lack of on the spot daily pastoral care. In fact, many congregations that I served as a student and ordinand, taught me far more than I ever offered them. What they had been doing all along, in an ad hoc way, was offering training grounds for would-be clergy and accepting the role as long-suffering, faithful, patient souls.

Years later, as many ministers long-in-the tooth have done, I dug out my old sermons, took one look through them, and wondered how I could have subjected anyone to them. Thank God for people who come to church, not because they like or don't like the minister, but because they want to respond to God's sustaining love. I found the formal internship at Mount Royal United in Saskatoon informative. However a supervising minister to Wakaw charge gave me only one bit of advice, "Avoiding using so many 'ands' in your preaching."

The moments of self revelation arrived. I began to get a glimpse of who I was. It didn't come from people telling me that I was a klutz at times. It came instead when I began to see that I would have to work out for myself who I really was as a person, and how I came across to others. Coming to terms with myself was one thing; with God, that was something else. I was also beginning to grasp the fact, as one put it that

Life is doubt, And faith without doubt is
nothing but death. 5

The message was becoming clearer; doubt, even self doubt and frustration, went along with this whole business of ministry.

That was something the Rev. Dr. John confirmed for me when he said ministry, and the training for it, is a marathon, not a hundred-yard dash, something I eventually accepted as a fact. From down in the depths of doubt, I found myself, when exercising patience, getting somewhere at last. Even these thoughts began to make some sense

Man, unlike any other thing organic, or inorganic in the universe, grows beyond his work, walks up the stairs of his concepts, emerges ahead of his accomplishments.   6

Remembering my reading of C.S. Lewis's "Mere Christianity" long ago helped to convince me at my head level that there is a Creator God. For if there is a garden there must be a gardener; if a watch there must be a watchmaker. I can't remember if Lewis said that. But back then it made sense to believe in a God that would create such a unique and intricate entity as a human being, me, of all things! People like Rev. Dr. John also helped me to see how God's presence was known and operational in people's lives.

At St. Andrew's College I began to collect and clarify my thoughts about what I believed. But, as when looking into a kaleidoscope, what I saw, and the beauty of it all, was ever changing as I responded to it, turning it about to see it in different ways.

I didn't feel as though my beliefs were like concrete and already set. To the contrary, I didn't have a flash conversion like St. Paul did. I couldn't say, as one person in an evangelical church said,

"That in a certain year, a certain month, day, and hour I was saved by the Lord and born again."

My finding a faith grew over time and brought me to these personal conclusions. We humans, though rascals, are spiritual beings. That is what makes us different from the rest of God's creatures. As St. Augustine said, our souls are restless until they rest in God. That makes me think that God has programmed us to be drawn to "Him." It is as if God's magnetic power pulls at the metal of our subconscious minds.

We humans are made in the image of God and not the other way around. I found when people take it the other way, they assume that their thoughts are God's thoughts, God's ways their ways. So if there was a tragic accident, and innocent people were killed, they would say something like,

"Well, God wanted our loved ones and so He called them away."

Thinking that God is a selfish, capricious God goes totally against the idea of God being a loving compassionate Creator, which I believe!

Evil in the world is not God's doing. We human beings produce it much of the time when we distance ourselves from God, keeping our Creator at arms' length, and blaming Our Source of Life for accidents and other disasters. The truth is that there is no way that we can, as humans, blame God for disasters. People create accidents, not God! People choose to build on flood plains, or in earthquake zones. People contribute to the carnage on the road. So we need not be surprised at the terrible outcomes, the product of human failure, not God's!

I believe we are our brothers and sisters's keepers, and can curse the deed but love the doer. Yet, we still are ultimately responsible for ourselves. We have the choice of being doormats, dependent persons, or not. I believe Jesus was saying to the paralytic,

"Your choice. You can lie there and wallow around in self pity, or you can go on with the business of living. "

I believe that some people victimize others, causing them to lose their self confidence. It's like this: Picture a big hungry fish, two little fish, and a fish tank: you have a fish tank full of water with a big fish swimming about. You relegate him to half of the tank, and slide a glass partition down the middle so he is limited to how much of the tank in which he can swim. Now, with the glass partition in place, you put two juicy, tantalizing tiny minnows for him to see but cannot touch on the other side of the glass partition. He, inevitably, charges through the water at a terrific speed expecting to satisfy his hunger, only to bump his nose hard against the glass partition. Each time he tries, his force is less. His enthusiasm begins to wain. Then when he swims about on his side of the glass fence totally bewildered, discouraged, and demoralized, you remove that glass fence. What does he do? Does he go and get his food? No! If that fish could speak, he might just say, "What is the use? It's all futile!" The result? He would starve. Many people, like that poor fish, having experienced many failures or rebuffs, lose their confidence, and just give up.

Going to college can present obstacles like that glass partition. Although I didn't have many meaningful conversations outside the classroom with the profs, as some did, I felt they were there for me if I needed them. I did appreciate the fact that those available to teach represented many different denominations. I, along with others, worshiped in the Lutheran and Anglican chapels. I attended classes taught by Lutherans and Anglicans. There I heard about Anglican students stamping out rug fires from incense burners, while Lutherans squabbled over moot points in theology. Having heard that, I felt better about the United Church and our scraps. Although I did then, and still feel, that we, on the cutting edge of the sacred and secular, do shoot ourselves in the foot sometimes, to the amusement of other denominations.

Where is the Life we have lost in living?
Where is the Wisdom we have lost in knowledge?
Where is the knowledge we have lost in information?   7

The issue over language and sexuality, though very important, often overshadows other important issues like getting in the trenches and getting our hands dirty instead of merely talking about it. Isn't one of our burdens as a middle class church that we are so busy with meetings, we forget that we need to help others? Do we forget that all people need to be able to say,
    "We are free, we are heard, we are safe, we count for something, we really do?"
    Isn't that what Christ had in mind? I felt in sync. with the person who said

 I love and venerate the religion of Christ because Christ came into the world to deliver it from slavery for which God has not created it.   8

You can see what I was up to already, preaching before I even graduated and got my testamur from St. Andrew's. Yet the day finally came when it did happen. The church ordained me in a hockey rink at Eriksdale in Manitoba. That time, when in the worship service I experienced the laying on of hands, I knew that was the real thing! It wasn't like the first time when I aborted over 20 years before in Winnipeg.

I was greatly moved at my ordination, also, because my family witnessed it. Lesley, Andrew, Mark and Marnie had gone through so much for that moment to happen.

The Right Rev. Stan officiated and signed my ordination papers. He was the same Stan whom I had met at Robertson camp when he was in his teens; the same Stan whom I had taught with at Norway House; Stan who eventually became Moderator of the United Church of Canada!

Norway House; what was there about that residential school where six people, three of Cree ancestry, became ordained clergy and, as contemporaries, had all worked in that school? What was there about the place that caused us to pray words expressing this appeal to God

Here I am Lord, Is it I, Lord?
I have heard You calling in the night,
I will go, Lord, If you lead me.
I will hold Your people in my heart.   9

At the Conference meeting where the ordination took place, we, who were newly ordained, had our placements confirmed. Back then, you usually got a phone call saying where the church wanted you to go. We accepted that the church would send us as ordinands to serve where needed. We also committed ourselves to stay at least two years. The family and I heard it was to be Glenboro, Manitoba. Our journey began into the unknown. What would the future bring? We were soon to find out with a few more surprises ahead!

13   First Backward Collar Church

We loaded our worldly belongings into a U Haul truck. Lesley, our daughter Marnie, I and a dog set out down Highway 1 to Glenboro, Manitoba. We had agreed to go to Glenboro, sight unseen. All we knew about it was that the Rev. Fred, whom Lesley and I worked with at Old St. Andrew's in Winnipeg, grew up there. That was enough endorsement for us. I drove the truck, while Lesley drove the car. We planned to overnight in Brandon. To our surprise one motel owner refused to give us a room because we had a dog. Tired and irritable, I mistook her attitude, thinking, "Here again, discrimination!" We did find a motel, though. The next day Lesley and I did our usual, what we called "a Cressy." The highway we should have taken ran by the home of the Wawanesa Insurance Company. Instead of taking that, we mistakenly headed across country and arrived in Glenboro by the back door.

The prairie stopped abruptly, blocked by sheds and houses. That was, without a doubt, a farming community. It had an "earlier era " look about it with its red brick houses. People had not built lately. The main street offered what a 900-population town could expect, a bank, co-op store, credit union, hardware, and the Camel Inn and other basics. At the W. L. Cafe, the owner's sons, Danny and Charlie, grew up hob-knobbing with the customers, excelling in "Reach For the Top" talent contests, and eventually leaving home to make good. Glenboro, like many towns with an unassuming wealth of intelligent people, exported its share during both world wars. The cenotaph attested sadly to that. Between those times were several devastating crop failures. Yet, despite hard times, many sons and daughters survived, rising to positions of prominence in city commerce and law.

The town, with its pragmatic Lutherans, staid Anglicans, and very intense U.C.'s got along well. The Lutherans and United had manses. We were to move in on arrival. However, my predecessor and his family were still getting the last of their belongings out as we pulled up in the truck and car. It was as if they moved out the back door as we moved in the front, or vice versa. Though a little unsettling, our comfort level rose rapidly when Bernice, a stalwart in the church, with a heart of gold and delightful gravelly laugh, came huffing and puffing her way across the road with cookies and juice. What a welcome! She was of good Icelandic stock, and could offer up some Icelandic phrases which, if translated, would make a warrior blush. The mischievous sparkle in her eyes, and her demonstrated determination caused Lesley and me to love and respect her to this very day.

Soon after we dropped our bags in the hallway, Bernice took charge. In just a few days, willing young farmers completely painted the kitchen, and made repairs throughout the manse. Another kindly, gentle soul of a man, wallpapered the front rooms. Soon the two storey brick 1920's vintage home, complete with parlour, felt warm and comforting. Of course, like all church manses, it had its own personality. The hot water rads hissed and bumped in the night, threatening to attack the new intruders. One did, more than once, almost scalding our son Mark when it developed pin prick ruptures and squirted at him, chasing him from his bed. The washer and dryer stood on the basement mud floor next to a cement cistern. When Lesley did her laundry, right from the beginning she felt eyes were watching her. Eventually a creature emerged to become her laundry companion, a friendly salamander.

Then there was Charlie, our pug dog. He replaced Rusty who went senile. Poor Rusty snapped, bit, and often stared into space, standing rigidly on all four legs as if hypnotized. Charlie, on the other hand, was a real gentleman. One day, driving into a farm yard, and stepping out of the car, I heard a tea kettle whistling sound. Looking around, I finally saw the source. There, lying snoring, was what I first thought to be a teenage pot bellied pig. Yet when it opened its eyes, I could clearly see that it was a bulging eyed "Pug." The farmer told me that was Charlie. I said,

"Looks like a great pet."

He asked, " Do you want umm?"

I asked, "You're giving him away?"

He said, "Sure, if you want umm, you can have umm. No use around here!"

Charlie joined our family, wagging his curly pig tail, snuffling and snorting. He would skitter about the house with his toe nails scratching away at the floor to get a good grip. So bashful, he would only drop his guard when the kids were at school. Then he'd nuzzle up a bit of fluff from the floor, and proudly prance about, balancing it on the ridge of his nose. Lesley was greatly amused. She was the only audience he would perform for. Sadly Charlie died. Dr. John, a veterinarian friend of ours, did an autopsy and found he had liver cancer.

Lesley and I had a great respect for John. Unfortunately, he eventually left Glenboro. We caught up with him a few years later in B.C. There he practices animal pathology, working with birds, reptiles, and other exotic creatures, no relatives of the cows and horses hanging about Glenboro, many of whom didn't take a liking to him as a vet.

Dr. John often dropped by the manse where I had my office for a time. I didn't like having the office in my home. So I gained an okay from the church board to have it down in the church basement. People would possibly feel more comfortable meeting me there. I would be less distracted, I thought, from household chores, and I'd get a sense that people would see that I went to work as they did, keeping regular office hours.

There was one draw back, though. At the manse I felt okay about surprising drop-ins. There two young troubled women, of whom I was unsure, came around frequently. I felt comfortable knowing that Lesley was within calling distance. Yet at the church, well, I wasn't sure! It's unfortunate that in this day and age, ministers have to be cautious, as do teachers, and other care givers. Now we must leave office doors open, and have secretaries or other colleagues close by to avoid possible accusations that could ruin a minister. Though when I approached retirement, feeling that all perceived me as perfectly harmless, I felt more at ease. It is sad that many ministers with a great amount of experience and training in counseling avoid offering it because of the danger of false accusations, just as doctors now "err on the side of caution."

A fine office soon took shape in the church basement. My carpenter neighbor, Darryl, saw me dabbling in oil paint. He had a picture of a beautiful African woman that he asked me to use as a reference for an oil painting. So Darryl and I made a deal. He would build the office if I would do the painting and draw cartoon figures on the wall of his little boy's bedroom. Done!

In my new office I found that I wasn't interrupted while writing my sermons, such as they were back then. On Sundays I would deliver them, which meant reading them, hoping that somehow I would connect with where the church attenders were in their thinking. People who attend church are very patient, sometimes to the point of being long suffering. Some of the wives of the fellows who nodded off to sleep during my sermons assured me their husbands were not doing so because they suffered from boredom. Their heads were dropping on their chins because they had exhausted themselves from early rising to milk the cows and nurse their crops along. Yet, in my own mind, I felt the ladies were kindly trying to encourage that young fellow who, green as grass, served up, "cold gruel" that even the cows might turn their noses up at.

Sermon making wasn't the only thing about which I had to learn. I had other stuff with which to contend. I had tried to make sense of why, for instance, grown men and women chose to switch partners while still married. Why would they blatantly think it okay when their teenage children saw what was going on? I just couldn't figure that out! Then again, I tried with my limited know-how to convince persons full of self doubt, saying that they didn't have to be doormats in their marriages or at work.

Yet not all was sad and depressing. The people in the inner circle of the congregation, as in any congregation, were the "salt of the earth." They witnessed through their dedication to their church, and by setting a high moral tone for their town. Some could be very judgmental. Yet, so many others were like Bernice. They rolled up their sleeves and gave their all, focusing on the task nearby rather than on others' faults. There were the sisters, Ruby and Sylvia, who for years along with Willa, provided organ, piano, and choir music. Willa wasn't possessive though. For a bit, when Lesley and I were in Glenboro, Willa, seeing talent in a young woman teacher, encouraged her to conduct the choir. Yet many years later, who is seen conducting? Why faithful and loyal Willa. Who else? She wasn't about to let the choir die.

I never sang in the choir. I knew that wasn't my thing since I couldn't sight read. Nevertheless I was flattered that one dear old lady in the congregation insisted that I sing some hymns on tape for her. I did, and for years after I had left Glenboro, a birthday card would arrive. In each card she assured me that she still played the tape. A person, especially a "minister" has a real time of it to keep from getting a swollen head. Still, just really getting my feet wet in the work, and tending to seek strokes, I grasped for affirmation, asking myself "Am I okay? How am I doing?

The need to be liked can be really detrimental in one's ministry. I found that sometimes a person needs to call it as it is, stating, "The king has no clothes." We need to face facts. Hesitation may cause a missed opportunity to be a prophet plus priest and pastor. It has not got any easier to perform those three roles of ministry in the United Church of Canada. Yet even back then, I felt, try I must! For then, as now, I knew that all are called to be faithful, and not necessarily successful. I hunch those great members of Glenboro United Church believed that!

Consider, Lena and husband Jim, who in my eyes, resembled the farm couple in the painting "American Gothic" by Grant Wood as prime examples of persons who, for better or worse, stood up for what they believed. They quietly, knowing right from wrong, seeing only blacks and whites and no greys, helped maintain the church's good name in Glenboro. The fact that they poured the walls of their farm home from concrete, symbolized well Jim and Lena's moral strength!

Lloyd was another down to earth man, who by trade was a sheep herder. He exemplified pioneer toughness. His weathered lined, brown face, and sad eyes told it all, of his wife dying and him marrying his mentally disadvantaged housekeeper, staying with her through thick and thin. He, holding his head high, looked up into the old manse trees which, too had weathered the storms, often climbed their gnarled and scarred branches to relieve their agony of dead, torn and twisted limbs. Those trees shared Lloyd's suffering and sorrow. The only difference was they groaned out loud in the wind, he within.

Then there was "J.C. of Chickadee land," as he called himself. The locals viewed him with tolerant affection, and his weird inventions with tongue in cheek. Though not taken seriously, many did admire him for sticking to his guns and having faith in his own beliefs. Once he lived out of town in a place surrounded by trees, sharing it with the birds and God's other creatures. Moving into town, he kept intact his unique frame of mind. That allowed him to debate with me to no end God's ability to find things for J.C. when he had absentmindedly lost them. J. C. would say with conviction,

"You know, I lost such and such, and you know I said, God will you find it for me? And God did! How's that for a good God?"

J.C. was good to me. When I needed people for Bible study, and the pickings were slim, he'd be there with his unique theology. I then had the chance to test my flimsy knowledge of the scriptures against the Bible according to Jay C. Give the community credit. Despite J.C's interesting peculiarities, they took him in, welcomed him, and when he was in need, provided for him to the very end.

Active community and church members can also be, not only charitable, but patient and very understanding. In United Church congregations there are persons who become presbytery reps. Some presbyters don't seem to find the fellowship that they need in their home congregations. It may be just because they don't move in the same social circles as those leaders of the church who serve faithfully on committees. People like presbytery reps. serve the courts of the church well. Yet one rep. found regular church attendance and contact with the local congregation more difficult. No doubt she, like other fine persons, had found this question challenging; should members of congregations, attending the different church courts, vote the way the local people want them to vote, or should they vote guided by their own convictions as individuals? Some say they listen to the debates on the floor of these various courts, and, moved by the Spirit, vote accordingly. Others say in a democracy such as the church, the representatives voted into the positions as delegates should vote according to the wishes of those who elected them. The debate raged on when it came to the "Issue" of whether declared homosexual or lesbians should be ordained. I have found that many ministers who differed with the views of their congregations lost the confidence of the congregations where the prairie conservative view held sway. Yet I felt that, for the church to be relevant, it must do as one speaker once said long ago

The Church should go forward along the path of progress and be no longer satisfied only to represent the Conservative Party at prayer.   1

Where some had labeled the Anglican Church as the Tory party at prayer, and the United Church in Canada as the NDP at prayer, Robert, one of my colleagues back then in the Carman Presbytery, was labeled by some, possibly unfairly, as an ultraconservative at prayer. For Robert was kidded unmercifully that he wore his clerical collar to bed at night. However, no one ever verify that. Maybe some kidded him so often to cover up our feelings of inadequacy. For he showed, both in the pulpit and at church meetings at all levels, that he had a fine analytical mind. If only he had been a card-carrying member of the NDP or Liberal party, instead of an enthusiastic member of the Conservatives!

The church, as I understand it, through history has struggled with the issue of church and state, politics and religion. In all my time in ministry, I have heard often that the minister should keep his nose out of politics. Many rural people have told me that ministers should definitely not air their views from the pulpit if they have any particular political leanings. I am inclined to agree, but with one exception. That is, if a minister really knows what he or she is talking about, and has done the homework, well, that's a different kettle of fish! When it comes to political issues, usually a minister would do well to share the basic tenants of the gospel free of uninformed opinion. That holds true, especially when it comes to farming issue debates, which seem to go on forever.

Of course, I found times when no one needed to muzzle a minister. Some people will keep their religion in one piece on Sundays, while sometimes scattering it to the wind the rest of the week. I had the distinct impression that some folks in the Rev. Glaeske's congregation, fine people though they were, didn't quite understand what the fuss was all about. Why were some United Church folk frowning on such worldly pleasures offered by the local drugstore which sold liquor and "smokes?" After all it was owned and operated by a sincere honest and active member of the United Church.

Just like human beings everywhere, we all live with contradictions, as did the Glenboro people. I guess that is what makes us human and helps God keep in shape chasing after us, as I once heard a farmer say, "I have wondered, have you, why there are so many different church denominations."

My answer was, God has made all sorts of different personalities; God also made it possible for different types of churches to exist to satisfy each of those. Thus those who tend to be very emotionally inclined fit nicely into the Pentecostal churches. Those who gain insights and meaning through the five senses fit comfortably in the very Liturgical churches. There they celebrate the Eucharist or Mass as Anglicans or Roman Catholics. Those who see everything in black and white, with no shades of grey, and are literalists, fit nicely into the evangelical tradition. Then there are the Lutherans and we United Church types who are a bit of each. Does that mean we corporately suffer from split personalities, or suffer from a schizophrenic religion? I think not! For neither Rev Glaeske nor I belong to a sick church. To the contrary, I feel proud of being United Church as I'm sure Rev. Glaeske felt the same being Lutheran.

He spoke with a good American drawl, proudly drove a Suburu car which he coaxed along by calling upon his mechanical know how. His annual stipend didn't allow for many luxuries, consistent with most ministers' or pastors' pocket books. So with that in common, I jumped at his invitation to go out in the potato fields and follow behind one of the potato harvesting machines. Those left many spuds, free for anyone willing to pick them up. Both of us, in a benevolent mood, felt we could pick enough to share with needy others.

Sharing was the key note of our clergy relationship. It was also that of our two congregations. We worshiped together in the Lutheran candle light service where every person there got to hold a lit candle. With the lights dimmed one also remembered the great feeling of awe and closeness that the CGIT vesper service evoked.

Our two churches also had in common the fact that we both had church bells. The Lutheran bell in its church tower was subject to the abuse of pigeons dropping unwelcomed gifts. Our bell, that I first discovered on arriving, suffered as a shut-in, sitting mute in the church hall.

Learning that a member of the congregation was a brick layer by trade, I asked him if he'd construct a brick cairn on which the bell could sit outside the church. He told us that he had not laid bricks for many years since he became a union boss, but he'd give it his best shot. He made a fine cairn with some very intricate brick work. The bell, proudly mounted upon it, offered a further challenge. I got the bright idea that we could get it to again peel with great gusto. It just needed a jolt from an electric gizmo activated by a switch inside the church building. A member of the congregation who was an electrical engineer might have made it happen. However, it stayed silent except, unofficially, on very special occasions. Lesley and son Mark made it cough up a ding and a dong on New Year's eve by sneaking down the street and giving it a few good taps. They, of course, were not the only people who did. Sometimes kids in passing would make it speak with a stone or two.

I cannot remember whether the old yellow brick Anglican church had a bell. I do remember Percy though. His last name was Shepherd, a fine name for a priest or deacon. Still, since we don't have priests or deacons in the United Church, I never did figure out whether he was one, or the other. Anyway, Percy had so well earned the confidence and trust of his flock that, when he planned to be away once, he had me lead a prayer book service. I couldn't believe he'd ask me to do that. I was astonished at the confidence he had in me, since we had known each other for such a short time. I, in turn, amazed myself that I could even entertain such an idea. Well, one seminary prof. often said,

"Work on the growth edges." Convinced, I

thought I'd give it a try despite my fear of the unknown. Happily, my fears were unfounded. I read, flipping from one part of the book to the other, feeling more confident as the service progressed. Where we in the United Church preached a sermon, the Anglicans heard a homily. Where we prayed a prayer, the Anglicans recited a prayer, at least I think that is what they did, so I followed suit.

After it was over, I left the Anglican folk without them celebrating the Eucharist, while wondering why I never knelt for prayers. I thought, " You know, we almost joined as one denomination." The Red hymn book, put together in anticipation of that happening, was chock full, I thought, of Anglican chants and hymns. I wondered why that marriage never took place. Was it because the bishops wanted to re-ordain us to legitimatize us in the line of apostolic succession? That may have become the indigestible fly in the soup. Maybe it was something else. Perhaps it was because we, in the United Church, remember our good old Presbyterian roots that forbid such a union. True, we sometimes get all caught up in joining others in denominational debates over how many angels can stand on the point of a pin. Regardless, as individuals we can find ways of respecting each other as friends. Percy and I were comfortable with each other. Most people in Glenboro were friends despite their denominational differences. After all, they had gone through a lot together as a community. So when they met and visited they had common memories that glued them together as "Glenboro-ites" proud of their little town and their achievements.

So many people stuck it out together. My neighbor, a retired druggist with a caring supportive wife, suffered a crippling stroke. He could really only watch rather than participate in the rhythm of the town. Yet he didn't roll up in a ball and shrivel away. There was also the couple who put out the local Glenboro Times newspaper. They were agents of Simpson's Sears and had their fingers firmly on the pulse of the community, even on its residents' buying habits. I remember also the young doctor. He replaced an older fellow who retired to his massive home library. That young practitioner had a quick mind and eye. When I asked him whether at times in diagnosing he slipped into his back room to refer to his text books, he replied,
"Like, I wish!" That affirmed what one wise person claimed

Education is what survives when what has been learned has been forgotten. 2

Those and others were Glenboro-ites in a town that never died, as Lesley and I discovered when we returned for a visit many years later. For the spirit inherent in the people still survived. In fact it was incredible that, when we drove by Mr.Rawling's house, there he was, as we saw him when we left, mowing his lawn. He stopped and engaged in a friendly conversation as if we had never left. Astonishing, since we had only lived in Glenboro for two years and been gone for decades!

In that time Lesley and I got acquainted with

others outside the church, some who moved away. Bob, who joined the Masons at the same time as I did, found that his legs couldn't hack the cement floors of his car body shop any more. So he left to become a Funeral Director in a bigger town. He had worked for the local undertaker who also was the ambulance driver. That conjured up some interesting scenarios. I can imagine the demands placed on that servant of the community. Someone may have called him to rescue the inebriated gentleman who decided to mount the town's huge sharp fibreglass camel, the town's tourist attraction.

Glenboro's camel, called Sarah, once stood by itself, visible to all from the highway. Now, she sadly is buried among farm machinery where she tries to poke her graceful head above those metal monsters. Her photogenic nature years ago invited kids to offer to take pictures of tourists standing in front of her. Once she had been the centre of attention. The Carberry people down the road, past Spruce Wood Park nearer the Number 1 highway, believed that she should be their mascot. They felt they had first dibs on the park to promote their town's attributes. Some Glenboro-ites suggested a donkey or burro might be better in their desert-like backyard.

The friendly rivalry between Carberry and Glenboro and other neighboring towns, Holland for one, was overshadowed in my memory by the tragic deaths that occurred on that highway passing through Holland. Many farmers lost their sons and daughters whom, they had hoped, would follow them into farming. Many parents never had the chance to see what their kids could do in carrying out the Glenboro tradition of making worthy contributions to society in and beyond the municipality. For many died needlessly, as road kill.

Tragedies are never easy, obviously, for clergy to deal with. Sometimes it becomes even tougher when a minister has to break the news of a loved one's sudden death. I had to tell an elderly lady that her son, who had just left her home, had died of a massive heart attack. When I broke the news to her, trying to be as gentle as possible, she was furious with me for saying such a terrible thing to an old woman. She stared me down saying,

"No, it's not so! "

The shock must have struck her far worse than it ever did me in my stay in Glenboro. The worst that I could think of then was when, driving home in a blizzard with Lesley and the kids, a truck suddenly pulled in front of us. Blinded by the truck's spray, I hit the ditch. Our Buick plowed deep into the snow and came to an abrupt halt leaving me clinging to the wheel in shock, thankful that we were still alive. We never did like driving that road, fearing for our lives.

Then we heard that, as a family, we wouldn't have to drive it any more. We were glad! For I had accepted a call to Moose Jaw. Yet, we left with mixed feelings, knowing that we'd miss many in the community. They had been good to us.

14 Moose Jaw Wilderness

I met a traveler from an antique land Who said: Two vast and trunkless legs of stone stand in the desert. Near them on the sand, half sunk, a shatter'd visage lies...Nothing beside remains, Round the decay Of that colossal wreck, boundless and bare...   1

I arrived one evening for an interview with the Moose Jaw U.C. Pastoral Relations Committee, having been invited by the Rev.B. At the time I should have figured that something was out of the ordinary. For normally it would have been the chairperson or secretary of the committee who would have arranged the interview. That evening we met and I had a brief tour of the church. To my surprise Rev.B introduced me to Rev.A in the sanctuary. It took me a few minutes to realize what I had not understood, that Rev.A would be the third minister, doing pastoral care and conducting most of the funerals. Rev.A, on retiring from a large church in another city had returned to Moose Jaw having with him, I found out later, his "family records." I believed that when he spoke to parishioners on the phone he could readily jog his memory about family details, names, birthdays, baptism and wedding dates, anniversaries, joys and sorrows etcetera. What a great idea having that information at one's fingertips before making calls at homes or on the phone! Once I caught onto how it worked, I used "family record cards," jotting down details about each family during significant pastoral encounters.
During my first contacts with the Pastoral Care

committee, and with Rev.B and Rev.A I realized that I had made every mistake in the book in seeking a call to Moose Jaw.

I felt like an outsider, one whose relationship to the two wasn't clearly spelled out in the interview process. Looking back, I kick myself that, having been enthralled with the idea of working in a prestigious, beautiful big building, I had neglected to seek a clear understanding of the job I was to do. I was pleased, though, to have been assigned a spacious office.

The position that I had put myself in was my fault, if anyone's. Where I fitted into the scheme of things was made clearer to me when Rev.B decided that he would covenant with the Official Board at a retreat which I was not to attend. For me that meant at the time that the Board was like the farm owner, Rev.B, the foreman, and I, the hired hand!

It was hard for me to pay heed to the Biblical text

Why do you look at the speck of sawdust in your brother's eye and pay no attention to the plank in your own eye?..2.

I also found it difficult to accept Rev.B's vision of the church. Yet, I assumed that I would have to play a part in making it come about, whether I agreed with the process used to develop it or not. I wasn't even sure whether the Board or congregation had taken ownership of it.

Here I was, in the beginning years of ministry feeling like a wounded bear, and regretting moving to Moose Jaw. I felt I should have taken up what I thought was an offer to move down east, where my gifts would have been used in an exciting inner city ministry.

Instead, I was performing up to five weddings on some Saturdays, baptizing children, many of whose parents had little or nothing to do with the church, and trying to offer a Christian Education program. It felt good, though, to be accepted and appreciated by the C.E. committee members. Yet the funding reserved solely for C.E., for materials, and equipment overawed me without any hope of my finding participants to benefit from all of that financial support. In fact, I began to feel the need to "produce or perish." I felt, unlike the "senior minister's" performance, the associate minister's was measured in statistical terms which was, by the number of participants active in Sunday School and midweek groups. I was in my forties. Perhaps a newly ordained youngster, grateful for the chance to work under ministers long in the tooth for a couple of years before striking out on his or her own, might have fitted in better in that church.

The problem in essence, now looking back at that bad dream, was that I found myself in a role expectation conflict. After becoming conversant with what's involved in marriage counseling theory, I believe that the players in the drama, I included, each had a hidden agenda that was never aired in the open. Thus, mistrust also developed, as in a bad marriage.

Now, I do have to say that both Rev.B and Rev. A were good to me in some ways. They welcomed me warmly when I first arrived. Rev.B showed me around the radio station where he did some broadcasting. Rev.A had Lesley and me over for dinner. Rev.B helped my son get a job at the cable TV station. As my colleague, he said to me one day, that he would never make me look bad in the eyes of the congregation.

It's strange though, how one's mind starts to think negative thoughts when one feels shut out. Though, I was given more than an ample amount of material resources to work with, I felt left out of the church family's important decisions. I guess back then I gravitated into that mode feeling even more uncomfortable about what often happened at worship. When it was my turn to preach, either Rev.A or Rev.B would conduct the service. I often felt one or the other referred to my sermon content in prayers after I preached. In that way I believed that they were making editorial comments about my sermon, editing it after the fact. Perhaps they thought that was necessary to put the people straight if I had strayed from their views. Reading some of my old sermons from those days, I could see where they would have found some pretty thin, and lacking coherence.

Yet, I was beginning to wonder if my two colleagues were dealing with me as persons would who wanted to distance themselves from another because of what he was doing. Was it because I projected the feeling that I wasn't approachable that caused the two not to level with me openly? Was that why Rev.B didn't have staff meetings where I was more involved in what was happening? There certainly was a lack of clarity and understanding, on my part, at least. No doubt back then, I could have benefitted from the knowledge about conflict management that I have now. I'm sure we could have relieved the tension and got on a better footing. Perhaps then Rev.B's and my relationship might have been better. Still, when I thought I heard him say,

"I'm not my brother's keeper," I assumed he meant that he had washed his hands of me. Then, when I believe I heard him say later in the year, words to the effect,

"Fish or cut bait. You have been turning me inside out and upside down, what do you want?" I believed that he thought that he had made all the effort in the world to help me settle in. I can now understand some of the frustration that he felt. I perceived that his view of the role of a minister in a congregation differed greatly from mine. Reflecting back on those moments, I can't help but think that some viewed ministers as tribal leaders rather than as enablers or coaches. But whatever view was adopted by ministers and congregation, I believed that it was the church's Official Board, representing the congregation, that ultimately made the decisions and worked in tandem with the ministers who implement policy. I did not see any minister as the "prime minister " in a congregation!

I understand Andy, chair of the Board, and Gerhard, two very capable people among others on the Official Board, also believed that. In my opinion, they fought hard to keep the decision making power over policy and programs in the hands of the congregation, via the Official Board. In the literature today on church growth, there is much said about the need for ministers to have a vision, and how to sell that to the congregation, pursuing it with unrelenting vigor. Maybe even back then I was asking myself which vision is the legitimate one, the minister's private one, or the church family's, namely the congregation's? Who is to set the agenda for the congregation? While struggling with that issue for several weeks, it came as a surprise to me when one member of my Support committee, said,

"You have trouble with authority, Ken, don't you."

It was then, really for the first time, that I realized some active members of the congregation saw Rev.B as the "Boss." I realized then that there was no way I could fit myself into what I perceived would be a master-servant relationship, especially in a church. I kick myself that I had not, from the outset, asked that in the induction, (now called "covenanting service," that Rev.B, Rev.A, and I covenant together in the presence of the congregation. Then we could have made promises that clarified what our roles, and working relationship would be. I would have sought to have equal status on the Official Board with other staff. Then I wouldn't have felt that members of the congregation saw me merely as Rev.B's helper. Thus I clung to the idea, as one put it, that,

All your strength is in your union, all your danger is in discord   3

I now find that the whole affair may have been one where I was perceived as engaging in a power struggle that was, in the eyes of many, not the thing

158

for an "associate" to do. In my effort to find my way
into the life and work of the congregation, I might
have been more effective in having that happen if I
had explored with Rev.B who those people might
have been when I believed he said to me once,

"I'll have to consult with my advisors," or
something like that. In the mood that I was in, I may
have passed it through my mental filters and heard
him say instead,

"I'll have to consult with my people."

What I heard made me feel even more closed out
of some inner circle of unknown power brokers within
the congregation. It left me believing that more
transparency and openness would have been helpful.
Rev.B had access to my support committee. Yet I had
no idea who was in his. Even today, I find repugnant
the thought of such a dynamic existing in a Christian
church.

Everyone is more or less mad on one point.   4

There was no doubt, back then, that, I felt very
much alone, wallowing around in self pity at times.
When I walked through the peaceful park across
from the church, I would see a family of mallard
ducks waddling their way up a mound toward the
library. No one allowed them in, but people fed them
the crumbs. I would ask back then, Is it fair to say my
family and I were relegated to much the same
position? Just as those ducks were not let into the
library, accepted for who they were, neither my
family nor I felt that we were affirmed for who we

were. The swans who seemed to crane their necks to feed and admire their reflections in the park's pond water, reminded me then of Rev.B and Rev.A. That was the state of my mind. I felt the two pros were patronizing me. Yet I should have remembered what one funeral director said to me when I complimented him on his ability to keep his cool when under great stress. He said,

"I'm somewhat like a swan, On the surface I look that way, but underneath my feet are frantically churning away to move forward."

Such insights into reality helped me to think, perhaps Rev.B and Rev.A have feelings, too! No doubt they were also hurting over the pain inherent in our unresolved role conflict.

Despite the festering that was going on, Rev.B and I did what we felt we wanted to do. Rev.B was, I believe, talking about creating a pathway of pictures depicting Christian motifs and stories on the walls throughout the church building. I had some vague memory of him allegedly wanting also to do something to buy up adjacent houses to provide more space for parking; also to salvage and find a place for a grain elevator from a Canadian expo exhibition. He had already installed an aircraft-like search light in the sanctuary balcony to provide lighting for airing the services on the local cable TV for shut-ins. He agreed that I work on coming up with a song book, "St. Andrew's Sings." That was a challenge because I had to write to copyright holders for permission to include their songs. His secretary operated the offset press to make copies.

I also put together a catalogue of opportunities for people in the community and congregations to participate in mid week and study groups. What I found out, though, was one could offer all the programs in the world, but to get people to participate in them was another story. Rev.B's idea of offering different speaker series such as the Dobson productions, giving tips on parenting, generated public interest. Also, his having Bible College choirs come and sing, gained good size audiences. Thinking, though, of growth in the spiritual depth of the congregation, I had my doubts that anything that we were doing had much impact to generate that growth.

St. Andrew's seemed to be in a survival mode. I felt it was hanging in there to celebrate its great visual brick, mortar, and stained glassed presence in the community, while barely managing to meet its operating costs, despite having endowments for Christian Education. There seemed little energy left to provide an outreach ministry to the immediate or global community have-nots. It was, in my view, just looking after itself out of necessity.

Struggling in my own mind with this dismal outlook, I began to think about pursuing a Doctor of Ministry at St. Stephen's College.

The Robert Schuller course that Rev.B brought in, which I attended, did not satisfy my need for growth, either. In a sense, it merely rubbed my nose in this whole personality cult stuff that I began to hate with a passion. Was it because, I knew I'd never rise to become such a figure, but secretly wanted the public to notice me in that way; or was it because I felt such ego trips by some ministers such as those on TV do injustice to Jesus Christ's cause? What an inward struggle!

I reached the point where I was desperately groping for a way out of Moose Jaw. I found that the St. Stephen's College people were not the least bit enthused about me working on a doctorate of Ministry program. Looking back, I can understand why. So I looked at another option. I spoke to two profs. from the University of Regina social work department. We talked about the possibility of me studying for a master's in social work. They gave me the impression that was a real possibility. However, I let that drop. I wonder where my family and I would be had I gone through with it. Life certainly has its twists and turns and I believe we are the choices that we make in life, and the results, well

> Yesterday, all my troubles seemed so far away, Now it looks as though they're here to stay. Oh, I believe in yesterday. 5

I gained a real sense that Lesley had a difficult time trying to play the role of the "minister's wife." In particular, to do what some expected of her in what she and I perceived, whether rightly or wrongly, as that of functioning in a social stratum not unlike what one would find on a military base. "Knowing one's place" certainly wasn't Lesley's normal function. I did not feel that there was any room in the church for a conscious effort by anyone to perpetuate social classes.

The building itself, in some ways, unfortunately invited illusions of grandeur. The building's court yard had high vaulted ceilings with hanging banners reminiscent of a medieval castle. It sported elegant white wrought iron tables and chairs, harkening back to a more prosperous era when one could imagine that high tea would be served from delicate China cups.

Yet the church photo directory, that I helped with, didn't make that kind of statement. To the contrary, the collection of photos of members suggested the church family consisted of people from many different social and economic strata.

I recall the dilemma that Old St. Andrew's faced in Winnipeg years before. It had become an inner city church, one that in its hey-day was considered very prestigious. However, when Lesley and I worked there, only a small remnant of the well-to-do worshiped there. Those few came from across the city for what seemed nostalgic reasons. The largest number, who were often very poor, came from the surrounding neighborhoods. While at St. Andrew's, Moose Jaw, I often had the feeling, that those who were served well, were not the "great unwashed," but "the haves." Even within that group, I thought the leadership base consisted of those better "blessed," both financially and socially, outside the congregation.

I always felt uneasy with the temptation to give more attention to those who had the potential to support the church with bigger offerings, even though I knew better. Yet, ultimately, it is often the story of the widow's mite repeated in the church, namely it's the poorer folks who can least afford it, who collectively give the most. I tried not to know what individuals gave, either in the fall canvas declared on commitment cards, or on the Sunday offering plates.

I did appreciate, though, knowing what it's like sitting in the pew, and getting a glimpse of what the whole business looked like from the point of view of the congregation. While on holidays, before I began work at St. Andrew's I attended a Sunday service in which Rev.A baptized a child. Just as he finished and handed the child back to the parents, he collapsed. There was great consternation in the congregation. I felt I could do nothing else but jump to my feet and, call for medical help, and continue with the service. I stumbled along trying to keep my composure, and feeling the spirit move, delivered a brief message. Rev. A seemed to recover from this first warning of a heart attack and business went on as usual. The only thing I heard was via the grapevine that, "He even preached a sermon!" I never knew to this day whether that was an affirmation or a criticism on how I handled that situation. I thought what a strange introduction to the beginning of a ministry in a new place. I'll not forget that incident, for it illustrated for me, that it's not wise for a minister to return to the place where he had such a long successful ministry, any more than it is wise for an athlete to force himself to keep going long after his prime.

That question "Have I still got it?" no doubt haunts many clergy as they approach retirement. It did me even when I was in the beginning stage in paid accountable ministry. Then in my forties, I had many bouts of self doubt. Such as the time when an RCAF instructor from the base kindly, and I mean kindly, informed me after a service when I had baptized his son that, during the baptism I referred to "him" as a "her." Fortunately, I got his child's name straight at the end. That experience for a time caused me to doubt my ability to keep my wits about me in the presence of such capable people as those flyers.

St. Andrew's had many families who had close connections to the military. There was the very attractive, intelligent single mom whose husband, a "Snowbird" pilot, was killed, leaving her with a bright young son. What could the church, or I for that matter, offer those gifted people who were constantly exposed to influences outside of the church, seeking their time and their talent?

St. Andrew's competed with the secular world. If that wasn't enough, it also competed with another United Church nearby for the people's attention. Winning could, in time, decide which of the two lived on or died a slow painful death. St. Andrew's had been Presbyterian and the other, Methodist, before union in 1925. Both stubbornly held on. A myth also existed that when a fire gutted St. Andrew's, the other large church invited St. Andrew's congregation to join with them. No way! A province-wide canvas was done to rebuild St. Andrew's. Like Phoenix it rose from the ashes even grander than ever under Rev.A's very capable leadership. Then when the other church's dome was threatening to crash down into its sanctuary, It's alleged St. Andrew's leaders had the audacity to invite the other church to crown St. Andrew's Christian education building with its dome. So the legend goes.

The folks at St. Andrew's did do their best to respond to the leadership of their ministers. Evidence of that existed in the craft store to which a former Anglican Church Army-turned United church minister helped give birth. The generosity of the congregation lived on. The people's long standing habit of being good to their ministers also lived on. For example Fred, an optometrist, gave me an extra pair of glasses when I had my prescription changed. When I asked, "How come?" he said his office had made a mistake and ordered an extra pair, so I might as well have them. I believe he was just being generous, a habit he seemed to have, as did others.

A kindly, elderly retired doctor found time for me. I was pleased when he invited me to join him on one of his daily walks. We walked through the cemetery. I commented on the dates on many stones indicating that people died young. He pointed out that many in their forties way back then were in very influential positions in the town including one mayor, and more than one alderman. I then asked why many live longer today. He replied,

"They were too damn stubborn to die!"

That made me wonder if I should ask someone, quoting the words of one writer,

Do you think my mind is maturing late,
Or simply rotting early?   6

Another kind person, for whom Lesley and I had a great respect, did not hold any position in society. Yet she could hold her head up high, and she did, proud of her accomplishments as a professional sales clerk in an old established department store. Pearl, who dressed smartly in immaculate apparel, including white gloves, in dress reminiscent of by-gone days, attended church punctually and regularly and spoke with quiet pride of her daughter, an accomplished medical doctor living in the United States.

There were, of course, other members of the congregation whose reputation, unlike Pearl's, suffered under a dark cloud of suspicion at the time. Having heard that a man with a connection to the United Church was accused of murder, I felt he and his family needed ministering to. I was told that wouldn't be such a good idea. I accepted that view, assuming that others were reaching out to the hurting families involved to offer support. It seemed to me that, if not the accused man, at least his children could use immediate pastoral care.

I believed then and now that ministers struggle with the question, who should take the initiative, the clergy or the people when they seem in need? Should we wait for persons to reach out for help or take the initiative and accept rejection gracefully if it comes? The obvious answer is, take a chance and reach out. Yet then again, maybe the person just isn't ready. The question then follows,

"Well, when is a person ready to receive help?"

There is a danger in being paternalistic, causing people to even start using the minister as a crutch.

There is also the danger of a person to whom you reach out turning on you, taking their frustrations and anger out on you. That happened to me. I was asked to visit a person, who was, I believed, on stress leave from work. I thought the visit went well. Yet that person claimed later, in a letter, that I had breached confidentiality in talking to her supervisor about the visit. When I got the letter threatening to have me defrocked or something like that, I shook my head in bewilderment. I had no idea that I had been indiscreet or unethical. I certainly didn't think, that by talking to her supervisor in general terms, and not divulging our conversation, that I had been unethical. I believe that I had merely suggested to the supervisor, who attended St. Andrew's, that she might affirm her since she also was a member of the church family. That significant pastoral encounter also shows the sensitive relationships that some professionals may have with their colleagues when they are members of the same congregation.

I was getting to realize the importance of active listening skills, playing back or paraphrasing in my own words what I think a person said. Then I would assure the other person that I've heard accurately what he or she actually said. I was also becoming more convinced of the necessity of leveling with people, being open and honest with one's feelings. Though I soon realized such openness comes with great risk.

One day I said to a friend that I was dropping the boys' group that I started with his encouragement, because I did not feel there were enough

participants. He said, very emphatically,
   "Ken, you blew it."
   I felt that he was implying that I was incompetent
in not succeeding to build a strong group that his
grandson could enjoy being a member of. I asked
myself, would he have been so upset if his grandson
had not been a member? Who knows to what degree
emotions and personal involvement colour one's
thinking and estimation of the competence of the
leader or coach? I have heard often from teachers
and coaches that it is not the kids who are the
problem, but it's the parents! Sadly such

   A prejudice is a vagrant opinion without visible
   means of support. 7

   Lesley and I truly appreciated all that this man, in
his role as school psychologist did for our son Mark,
measuring his skill levels, interests and abilities. He
went beyond the call of duty. So I can understand
where he might expect the same from me if I were to
call myself a professional. That raises another
question; is a clergy person a professional or what? I
found the answer when Lesley and I tried to organize,
recruit and conduct a camp when Presbytery asked
each congregation to manage one of many camps
through the summer. I barely survived that camp.
Our cabin leaders, for the most part, were older
teens. We used to say we had more trouble with
them than we did with the young campers. But for
the experienced kitchen and water front staff, we
would have felt very alone in the job. Somehow we
got through the ordeal with a resolve never again to

make that mistake of putting on a camp where the young volunteers did not understand their roles, nor commit to the common good of all the campers.

Something amazed me! No matter how much planning and preparation one does, sometimes things just blow up in your face. The criticism sometimes comes from the least expected sources. It happened when one of the two church secretaries read and possibly typed the material that I compiled for a wedding preparation course. One section, which I got from a very credible and reliable source, include some questions related to sex in marriage. I fielded some criticism for that particular content. Rather than have it become a tempest in a teacup in my view, I dropped it from the course material. I realized my mistake in not taking the material to the C.E. (Christian Education) committee to seek their approval before coming up with a typed draft. If they had approved it, I would have been on firmer ground.

The process that I used in doing pre marriage counseling included the use of the Taylor Johnson Temperament Analysis material. The couples had the opportunity, after answering questions to have the answers graphed. In that way they declared features of their personality which might enhance their marriage or clash and thus raise havoc in the marriage. Sometimes I would, using that cliche, boldly go where angels fear to tread, suggesting that the marriage looked like it would be a disaster, based on those and other questions asked of the couple. More than once, I heard later that my prediction had come true and the couple had split up.

I believe it's tragic that some women and some men will make elaborate wedding preparations, send out the invitations, and then, right up to the time when the bride walks down the aisle, be extremely unsure about his or her decision. Some just don't want to "let the side down " by pulling out before it is too late, because mom or dad have gone to all the trouble and expense to have it happen. A bride or groom, who knows it's just not right, may also go ahead with it anyway, for fear of losing face in the eyes of their friends. I felt then and now that we as ministers really don't want to be the agents of misery. Some of us feel that all weddings, as in some European countries, should be civil weddings. Later, those who really take Christianity seriously could have their marriages sanctified in the church. Whether that would become a norm in this country, I'm not sure. Still, I am convinced that it would be great if some church or agency offered pre-engagement courses, wherever possible, to head off at the pass those couples who are not sure, and are going ahead anyway, knowing full well that to marry would be wrong!

Sometimes I've found that people will fly off the deep end and fall in love, and in the process, leave a lot of wreckage behind, as well as set out on a path to self destruction. They leap before they look. One day someone drove this truth home to me in spades. A distraught middle-age man appeared at the church office wanting to see a minister. Somehow St. Andrew's tall bell tower acted as a beacon drawing people from what seemed far and wide. With the downtown city park at its front door, an inviting spot for some lost souls to bed down, the church was put on the spot to help them. I listened to the story of the lost soul who had been a successful, married Baptist minister down east until he ran off with his organist. He had "the world by the tail." He broadcast on radio, had a big, prestigious congregation. Then he "fell head over heels" for the church organist and fell flat on his face, losing it all. What to do? He wrung his hands in despair. For, after leaving the city, his wife and children, giving up his church and his reputation and moving to another town, the organist left him high and dry. I felt like saying to him, "You damn fool! " However, I didn't. I had nothing else to tell him that I felt would help, other than to say here is a couple of dollars that will get you down to the Salvation Army that has more resources than I can offer. What is that expression?

When you feel down in the mouth look around, you will see someone worse off than you!   8

Well, I was directed to that thought when I compared that poor guy's problems with my own. Sure, as an associate minister I felt, as I said before, that I had to publish or perish. I believed I had to produce programs that would entice droves of people to get involved in the church when I knew that the demographics were not there to make it happen.
Yet, I still had opportunities and choices that poor fellow did not have, having burned his bridges behind him. Still I saw myself as a fish out of water. I

shared that with an understanding judge whom I had asked to be on my support committee. His reaction was to refer me to the Bible passage,

"And if any one will not receive you or listen to your words, shake off the dust from your feet as you leave that house or town."   Matthew 10:14

That made sense, though the advice hurt. Still, rather than create a fuss in the congregation, I decided to do just that. For I had adopted a code of ethics, part of which stated that a minister must keep peace in the congregation and avoid being a lightning rod. So, I decided to leave thinking,

I must lose myself in action lest I wither in despair.   9

I understood that the word got out that I was "flaky." I did not feel that I had earned that reputation, and had no idea where it could have come from.

I did regret that Lesley had to remain in Moose Jaw until our house was sold. St.Andrew's congregation had lent us ten thousand for a down payment on the house. I really felt bad that Lesley had to be subjected to remarks about me that were untrue and unfair. We were not separating. I wasn't giving up the ministry for good because "I wasn't good at it," and there had been no "hanky panky" going on that I had perpetrated.

I would in time learn that I cannot be responsible for other people's responses to my actions, a truth that stood me in good stead in the future. I phoned

Ernie with whom I had taught school at Fort Chimo many years ago. He pleasantly surprised me by remembering we were once colleagues. I had found his name and number in the Prince Albert, Saskatchewan phone book, having heard that he was up that way consulting for an Indian Band Education System. I asked him if he had anything going on up there that I might be able to do.

"Yes, at Stanley Mission, as school principal. Interested?" "I am! "

So it came about that I became the principal of an Indian Band-run school near La Ronge, Saskatchewan.

Such is what is to be? The pulp is bitter, how shall taste the rind? 10

I told Rev.B that I was going to find a job where there was more money. However, that of course wasn't true. Having been turned off temporarily on ministry, I felt I could do no other than leave.

As I reflect back on the Moose Jaw wilderness experience, where I served as a reluctant associate minister in a multi-staff church, I now realize deficiencies existed. For there was a need for greater active listening skills, a working knowledge of conflict management, job descriptions, and for the staff and congregation to covenant together within the context of a clear mission statement. Without such, Caveat Emptor!

15 Northern Indian Band School

I felt on edge driving the icy gravel road between Lac LaRonge and Stanley Mission. I heard later that it was wise to travel equipped for emergencies. One fellow who slid into the ditch kept himself from freezing to death by gaining warmth from candles till he was found. As I drove, white knuckling all the way, I remembered a government worker in Yellowknife disappearing en route to Fort Rae. People suspected that he went off the road into the muskeg and sank out of sight. Fortunately, neither Lesley nor I hit the ditch on loose gravel heading north, hemmed in by miles of monotonous uniform evergreens leading from Lac LaRonge to Stanley Mission.

Ernie had arranged for me to meet with the school council on my first trip into Stanley. He obviously had vouched for my credibility and credentials, for other than an in depth discussion of the possibility of resuscitating the outdoor hockey rink, the meeting seemed one of "let's get acquainted." Though, I did hear one response to the interview, " That guy sure talks a lot! "

When I think back, I recall a quiet exchange between two of the committee members barely within my hearing. Later, I asked about that because each had a twinkle in his eyes. It turned out that they noted the similarity between me and an Indian senator whom I resembled from the neck up. We both had monk-like bald heads. I never knew whether their first impressions of me were a plus or minus.

Still, some things did click in the interview. I had felt very comfortable with the people I met. The job was mine beginning in February, with an indication that, if I so chose, I might have the option of continuing into the next fall term. The school principal whom I replaced left under some kind of a cloud which I never asked about.

One of my first encounters with one of the school's idiosyncrasies turned out to be the bell system. It, like many other systems inherent in that building, architecturally created to evoke "Indianess," challenged me to try to understand how it all worked.

The library addition, with its teepee-like beams from B.C., and other sophisticated features, seemed very romantic, though somewhat limiting in useable space. When bells went off at most interesting times, when the open area concept of moveable partitions between classes contributed to distractions, then the building really got in the way of what it was really meant to be: that is a school where teaching and learning was foremost, and the grandeur of a building, secondary.

The locally born engineer no doubt did his best with his limited resources to keep the water, electrical, and all other systems operating to their optimum. Still, the frequent fly-in of technicians to do this and that suggested a simpler, less trouble free system might have sufficed. Hunting down the engineer frequently was a chore that I didn't enjoy. That grappling with the idiosyncracies of the building's operational system caused me more and more to concur with one ecologist's view that

Small is beautiful. A study of economics
as if people mattered.   1

Right from the outset of my stay in Stanley, I was
determined to follow that old saying "KISS," that is,
keep it simple, stupid. I kept telling myself that often.
Consequently I took the liberty of changing the high
school schedule so that the teachers taught the core
subjects almost every day. We didn't announce "this
is day three, or this is day five" of a several day
schedule. Monday was Monday, and so forth. No one
seemed to complain, so I kept the new arrangement
in place.

I had this strange idea that tidiness was next to
Godliness, rather than cleanliness being next to
Godliness, especially since my son Mark and I were
batching temporarily. With that fixation I poked my
nose into the primary grade classrooms. What I saw
in one was utter chaos. So when I was complimenting
the team of teachers, I didn't include the one whose
classroom that I felt was "the pits." Well, that stirred
up a hornet's nest. For a brief time I felt my
honeymoon period with the teachers had ended. It
was quite amazing to me how the gang rallied
around that one teacher from the South. What I did
want to avoid was a "we, they " dynamic developing
between the teachers and me. I felt there must be
ways to help bolster morale. So I got a coffee
supplier to install one of his machines free! The catch
of course was that we'd buy his coffee.

As a principal, I had perks. Once a month, the
various school principals met with the chiefs to

report. The trip to Lac LaRonge turned out to be a break from Stanley Mission and an opportunity to share in Chinese food at the local cafe with administrators from Lac LaRonge and elsewhere, including the Indian Band's Education boss. He impressed me with his obvious astute political sense, tempered by casual dress and mannerisms.

Unlike the local people, such as that education boss, some "outsider" teaching staff seemed so up tight. Back at the school, I wasn't impressed with the fierce determination of one teacher to have two windows in his teaching space, divided off by padded movable partitions, while his teacher neighbor had none. I tried to appeal to the "two window" teacher's sense of fairness, without success. So I lost patience and got one partition moved over so both teachers had one window each. I made a bad mistake, though, in underestimating the dogged determination of the "two-window teacher." He was out on holidays when I had that happen. On returning he found that he had lost a window. He was not pleased! I couldn't believe the primitive need to assert territorial rights displayed in that event. Then I recalled a National Film Board cartoon that depicted a fence being moved back and forth with the end result, the demolishing of a dejected flower, the victim of others' selfish pride. I felt wistful at what that cartoon depicted about human nature and the need to mark out boundaries despite, the consequences.

There was on staff another teacher whom, I sensed, also had a need to guard his space. He was a Sikh.

He dressed accordingly and kept his distance from the rest of the staff, giving his attention to teaching high school math in a very meticulous and professional way. One couldn't fault him for his professional ethic, nor for the way he formally revealed refined hospitality when inviting me to his residence for tea. In contrast with the rest of the teaching staff, including me, he had polish. Despite his professionalism, the writing was on the wall. The Indian Band would not renew his contract. The reasons? He allegedly suffered the inability to blend in with the rest of the teaching staff, and instead aligned himself with the former principal, with whom the staff had problems. It appears no one can escape politics even in a school setting. It wasn't that he was of a different ethnic background than the Caucasians or those of North American Indian ancestry that caused him problems.

For also on staff was a young Canadian who was second generation Japanese. He, unlike the Sikh gentleman, quietly went about his business, socializing with the rest of the teachers, yet without comprising his own personhood. The students and other teachers respected him, perhaps because they knew that he had a background in the martial arts, but also because he projected a respect for others, and accepted them as they were.

Another young teacher with less refinement, swaggered about and revealed his limited vocabulary when speaking, especially to the boys on his basketball or volley ball teams. He often called the boys "Bozos" which I took as a pejorative term. I watched the expressions on the players' faces, but couldn't tell what they were feeling. They did not convince me that their happy faces, and laugher revealed their true feelings. The young teacher had control of the gym time and the new school bus that he drove, and they no doubt knew that he called the shots.

I chose to teach the high school English in a small room off the library office. To my amusement, I became conscious of some of the teaching staff and students listening in on the other side of the partition to hear how the new kid on the block handled teaching chores. After all, I had only arrived in February. I never did hear what their verdict was. Ernie, the school consultant, having got me the job, showed an appreciation of my choosing to both teach and administer. That was enough affirmation, since I had a great respect for him!

The task of trying to bridge the glaring gap between two cultures, and in particular, to make Shakespeare and other Saskatchewan departmental English exam material relevant, was a formidable one. It left me feeling that those who wrote curriculum for northern students had a huge task to adapt the contents so that it wasn't totally beyond their reach. Back then most knew more about hunting, trapping, fishing, dances, bingo, cards, and what they picked up from characters who frequented the bar scene in Lac LaRonge, than they did about Western classical literature and the Arts. Such seemed far from the thoughts of the native adolescents. Yet they were expected to write

Departmental exams geared to kids in the south.

Even their own native culture, taught throughout the grades by two young native men, took a back seat to their sports. I even wondered how acclimatized the two native teachers were to their own culture. When the community put on a concert, those two played the part of two characters, Bob and Dave, "Hosers " featured in a Canadian TV production called the "Great White North," complete with toques and beer bottles.

I spent a lot of time when I wasn't teaching roaming the halls, whistling to let people know that I was coming. I quite frankly didn't know what else to do. I wasn't about to "rock the boat " at that stage of the game when half the school year was over, and I hadn't a clue yet in which direction the school was going. What I did know for sure was what I came with, the knowledge that when you make a change in one area it affects all the others. I had nudged and tested the whole ball of wax by rescuing a window for a teacher, ensuring a supply of good coffee, tinkering with the high school time table, and daring to question one teacher's classroom management skills. Now it was a wait and see game to see how the teaching body would react to my invasions on their social space that had taken shape long before I arrived. The staff had already established the pecking order. Who was on the in, and who wasn't, had clearly been spelled out. The native and white staff had worked out a way to understand each other's views while jockeying for elbow room. All that had happened.

The young woman teacher soon to marry an RCMP member when she went south, had been acting as principal. Now there I was, trying to earn her respect and gain and maintain credibility with the rest of the gang. An interesting challenge! It was also a challenge to bite my tongue and watch the local school and settlement engineer juggle his time and energy, while at times feeling frustrated with the complicated systems for delivering the necessary utilities.

I wasn't clear whether the people's living conditions and circumstances drove some to drink excessively. Was it the fact that here they were with a modern school with all the conveniences, yet exposed to the fact that there was a great disparity between the houses of the teachers and those of the local people? Or was it because they were not only trying to escape their reality, but were trying to muster up enough drive to break through their natural native politeness barrier to confront "the haves?"

There might be something in that view. Once, a native member of the School Board arrived drunk at my door late at night, pounding to get in, shouting and cursing a blue streak. I had never met him and had no idea what his problem was, nor was I then about to find out. I dialed William, the native school counsellor and community worker. I heard his skidoo pull up. Shortly after, all became quiet outside and I went back to sleep. I learned long ago the merits of leaving the people to deal with their own. Thus, it surely made sense to me to see local native RCMP at work on reserves. Yet it made even more sense to follow the Hudson Bay Company's policy of promoting local native persons to management, but never having them stay on their own reserves. Having them serve elsewhere where they were less inclined, out of necessity, to favor their families or friends, allowed them to act impartially.

One would think that living in the north without tremendous traffic would offer perfect peace. That was not so! The stillness of the night was often shattered, even though the house that the Band assigned me, distant from the reserve folk and teacherages, suggested that as a good possibility.

My first night and thereafter offered surprises. I was wakened by the outdoor tap running. "What the heck? " Peering out from behind the closed drapes, I saw someone filling his pails, loading them on the back of his skidoo and roaring away. I wondered why the build up of ice just outside the basement window. Now I knew. I was tempted to turn off the tap from inside the basement. On second thought, no, I'd wait and ask around. To my dismay I heard that it was an accepted custom that the persons, whom I assumed were "non treaty Indians" living just across the road from the house, got their water from the principal's tap. I thought there had to be a Canadian compromise to that tap-filling night and day routine.

It seemed that others perceived "my house"as a convenience rather than a private residence. I was secretly glad that Lesley, having driven up alone all the way from Moose Jaw to visit, chose not to stay. I wondered how she would have responded to that, and to the Lac LaRonge native school superintendent, right out of the blue, informing me that an anthropologist from Saskatoon would be staying with my son Mark and me for a while. Both the superintendent and the anthropologist were likeable guys. I enjoyed their conversations. Yet the element of unpredictability prevalent in the air, shook me a little, since I was just starting to adjust to other changes.

I gave myself an assignment. Rather than just do my job and keep my mind and body centered merely in the life of the school, I'd get out and see what was going on in the community, especially in the church for, in one person's words

A man who puts aside his religion because he is about to go into society is like one taking off his shoes because he is about to walk upon thorns. 2

Worshiping in a building dwarfed by the school, I listened to an Anglican native leader. The old man sat on a chair in front of a handful of women cradling babies, and a few elderly men. Where are the teenagers? My question was answered when I couldn't help over hearing some of the boys telling a teacher that Sunday the bishop would confirm them. I got myself over to the very old, but newly painted church around the bend of the lake. What a transformation! The bishop, with miter and staff, proudly processed, followed by several young people, boys no longer dressed in sweats, but in black pants and white shirts, girls in skirts and blouses. The boys' raven black hair was slicked down, the girls' hair permed. I was surprised to see those boisterous young people very subdued and respectful, kneeling in front of the bishop to be confirmed.

Within a week of that celebration the community experienced two more exciting incidents which seemed very much a part of its unique life. A plane crashed near the public dock by the HBC store. Half submerged, with one of its wings askew like that of a wounded bird, it presented a pitiful picture with boats buzzing about full of curious people. No sign of passengers being removed, dead or alive, caused me to seek information, but to no avail.

Such excitement often represented tragic losses in many forms. Very early one morning I saw through my window a shack engulfed in flames. Later that morning I tried to find out if anyone had suffered injury or died. The answer was, "Yes," and "No." Someone said that he heard screams from a couple of young guys, but that was all I could find out. Not that there was a conspiracy of silence in the settlement among the people; rather I concluded it was just that I wasn't yet in the loop nor privy to what came through the gossip grapevine.

At the school I heard that there had been some squabbling about which direction the community TV antenna dish should be pointed. Some wanted sports, others wanted soaps or whatever. Controversy didn't raise its ugly head, though, over the selling and distributing of pull tab gambling tickets. In fact the losing tickets were scattered about throughout the school, on the playground, and all about the neighborhoods. It seemed it would be a futile exercise to try to prevent the students buying tickets from one of the School Board members and others.

It would also be a futile exercise for me to try to speed up the sequence of events happening at the community-sponsored Winter Games and festival. The casual approach of the organizers to keeping things moving was perfectly maddening to someone like me from the outside. I should have either pitched in or relaxed. I did neither. That day I got involved in a half-hearted way as a spectator before I eventually went home to engross myself in my painting, with little success.

Though my painting was a flop, fishing for pickerel was a great success. It didn't matter whether we cast from the dock, or in the company of the HBC manager in his boat; my son Mark and I always had a feed of pickerel.

June's end came quickly with me still pondering over the interesting Stanley Mission phenomena and its residents. They seemed somehow to muddle through while knee deep in the outsider's materialism, yet still whisper in their actions, "Indianness."

Bags and boxes of discarded completed class assignments were left to put in the burning barrel after the teachers left. I tried keeping it from scattering to the wind. So much paper! It seemed symbolic of the futile effort to contain the invasion of white's culture into every nook and cranny of the peoples' traditional way of life. Ironically it was the native primary teachers on staff who had already bought into the south's materialistic way of life, that gave the children most of that seat work. Since I came to Stanley Mission I had tried to look around to see evidence of the native culture as I remember remnants of it years ago when I was with the Hudson's Bay company. However, all I experienced, while walking the shore line in front of the native houses, was a question from a fellow who approached me and asked,

"Are you looking for something?"

That question stayed with me for sometime. I asked over and over,

"What exactly was I looking for?"

Long gone from my thinking was that romantic search for the "Noble Savage" written about by Rousseau, and remembered by Edgar Rice Burroughs in his Tarzan series. Gone also from my thinking was the idea that I would leave the ministry and go back into education, a thought I had when I left my last congregation. Where, then, would I look to find my calling? I hunch my mind was made up when I had gone South during the Easter break. I stopped to check out a church at Maple Creek, written a few church congregations, and to my pleasant surprise got a good indication that members of Rosedale United Church in Winnipeg would be interested in me as their minister. I accepted the call.

Still it was with mixed feelings I resigned the principalship at Stanley Mission and, having got that out of my system, set off South. Before leaving, I was deeply touched by the staff, in particular, the native teachers who gave me a bead work gift, a "keepsake." I felt good in having my self confidence back, feeling that I had done a decent job, and having Ernie affirm it in writing. Now what would the future bring, given that

Much I have learned from my teachers, more from my colleagues, but most from my students.   3

16   A Fort Rouge Church

Moving back to Winnipeg was incredible. It seemed I had gone a full circle roaming Canada. I had boarded with a dear old lady on Morley Avenue for a short time when I was out of work, just before I answered a telegram from the Rev. Ken McLeod to go to Norway House. At Norway House I met a fellow with whom I had taught. His dad and mother lived just down the street from Rosedale United Church, located just a couple of blocks from Morley Avenue. It was if I had been programmed to be in synchronization with some ultimate plan.

That neighborhood, not far from some prominent buildings, was split in two by Osborne Street. Those people who lived around Rosedale differed from those who lived on the other side of Osborne. They were of the blue collar or "hard hat" class that included many railway workers. Those on the other side in Riverview were mostly professionals or white collar workers like those who lived on Churchill Drive which ran along the river. That was the way it was until some larger homes in Riverview became boarding houses and a building, once an elementary school, became a school to upgrade young adults.

The communities on both sides of Osborne did see themselves as distinct and different. The rivalry was there. Thus the two United Churches, one which had been Methodist, (that was Rosedale), the other Presbyterian (which was Riverview) had members whose families went back a long way in their respective churches.

They were well steeped in the neighborhood's history. Cam, for one, a retired school principal and proud active member of Rosedale, gave a tour to remember the old fair grounds that once proudly had a presence near the river. As we followed him around, we tried to imagine in our minds' eyes what it must have looked like, a real "Coney Island" with a giant toboggan slide. In the summer there were rides, and a race track, all meeting places for kids, couples, and other grownups of all shapes and sizes. Now it was all gone, invaded by houses, where in some back yards, the soil sketched out where once ran the race track.

Not only houses invaded the glorious past of the area where Rosedale Church stood. Others also invaded. The Dutch Elm disease worms hung by thin threads, making walkers feel grubby when they brushed hair or clothing. The trees wore sticky belts around their middles to keep the beggars from crawling up to hang from the branches, but nothing seemed to keep them down. Trees began to die, their limbs, like members of church congregations, turned grey and lifeless and dropped off. Would that be the fate of either Rosedale or Riverview churches?

After I had been a minister at Rosedale for a while,

I saw a glimmer of hope despite surface appearances. For I didn't think that calling the members apathetic was fair. True, I did find that many folk felt that, since they retired, and they had "done their bit," they were quite prepared to leave it to the young folks to keep things going. I thought Rosedale United could flip into that irrevocable survival mode, which would ring its eventually death knell. God forbid! However, hope still lingered throughout the congregation. There was a kaleidoscope of loyal and persistent characters that could save the day!

Henry, the choir director, for many years put out a newsletter with the help of others. At first, he used the old fashion Gestetner, requiring the typing of each page onto a stencil. Once inked, it was rolled on the Gestetner's drum. What a messy business! Cam, then got a reconditioned huge rumbling old photocopier. It cranked out copies at a tremendous speed, and jammed just as fast. Still, it got the word out about what was happening at Rosedale. It told of Sunday School. It told of Henry's wife's Junior choir, of the adolescent son of a railway engineer who sang solos. It told of the CGIT Vesper Service, and the small Boys Brigade, a precursor to the Boy Scouts.

It didn't state the fact that old Baden Powell used a lot of the Boy's Brigade stuff to launch his own boys' program. I had attended a Boy's Brigade training session outside of Toronto, heard about that, and how the Canadian outfit was engaging a young Methodist minister from the States to work his way across Canada, promoting the parent movement of

Scouts.

Despite the coming and going, the fading in and out of boys and girls midweek groups, there continued to exist within Rosedale a core of committed people who came up through young people's groups. Young people had been active in Winnipeg, as one old timer said, "from the beginning of time." It was hard to believe their activities went back that far. Still, I had no trouble believing that many married couples in the church, then in their fifties and older, had met in the choir or in "young peoples."

There were also some singles of that vintage, mainly women. I asked one dear lady why she never married. I found her answer sad.

"In those days," she said, "Women who got married had to quit their jobs. If you liked your job, you chose it above a husband."

Nurses and teachers, in particular, were forced to decide, where today women may choose a career over marriage, or both, without feeling coerced.

Many women, both married and single, through the UCW, (United Church Women) were the backbone of the church, as they are today. Marg Edye, a very intelligent and committed church member, realized the fact that young women do need a care and support group. Though not "young," she got a group of young women together. She mothered them along, and we saw the group grow. She knew, as I did, that younger women would have a hard time breaking into one of the established UCW units. The members there had been together for years, and there was no question that the generation gap was clearly evident. People in those groups remembered vividly the "Great Depression," and thus had a definite, different, outlook on life.

Some folks, like Gordon Edye and Marg, appeared to stay current. Gordon, with one foot in the past, modestly shared his experience as an RCAF pilot, and railway conductor who, in later years before retirement, taught railway rules. Both Marg and Gordon, like many leaders in congregations, showed unselfish, gentle generosity with no sense of self importance, while suffering more than their share of physical pain.

Many of the church leaders represented the Canadian ethnic mosaic. I was proud to belong to a country which didn't boast of its melting pot mentality. Instead it encouraged the different ethnic groups to continue to maintain as much of their old country distinctive cultures as possible. One Dane, named Carl, did that well. He showed leadership both in Winnipeg and in the Scandinavian Club, and at Christmas decked his tree with Danish flags. Pride in country of origin prevailed at Rosedale. Henry's family was German Mennonite. He married Marie, from Scottish roots. They had met in high school musicals when both played lead parts. To celebrate their differences, yet union, they once staged musicals. One depicted what it was like when two different ethnic extended families saw two young kids get together for life. Not only did it appear that the Enns marriage succeeded, despite extremely different family backgrounds, but also another couple proved

192

that a successful marriage arrangement can happen. Phil, a university professor, was an ardent member of the United Church, his wife an active R.C. He sang in the choir while his wife attended elsewhere with the kids. When the kids had something going on in the RC church, Phil attended there. When he had something special going on with the choir, his wife and children were there to applaud his performance as a soloist. Who says mixed marriages can't work?

Who says, also, that active church members can't have a life outside the church, or that if you go to church you can't have any fun? Henry dispelled that myth. He sang and performed for years at a posh restaurant called the "Hollow Mug," while serving his church. He was also a Junior High principal in a job that called for steady nerves. Colourful figures, full of life, did indeed inject enthusiasm into Rosedale. What Marie and Henry did outside of school and church, would boggle the minds of many who had less energy and imagination. They owned an acreage near Henry's politician brother's farm. On it they had a railway box car for their horses, a caboose, and, a complete railway station. Whether the atmosphere of their Fort Rouge neighborhood, where a railway round table had existed over the years, rubbed off on Henry and Marie, one will never know. Whether Henry, of good German Mennonite stock, felt up-rooted from it, and so sought roots in Canadian nostalgia, I will never know.

Yet, some psychologists believe that it is the subconscious part of our minds that really calls the shots. That, deep in the complexity of our mental computers are the programs that cause us to do what we do. We think our conscious presence is consuming information and making decisions, but I hunch that we are just kidding ourselves. Perhaps Henry was motivated by a voice deep within that is the same voice that motivates us as Christians.

Despite having "toys," Henry and Marie appeared to be the least concerned about material things. In fact, their demonstrated generosity went beyond merely letting Lesley and me stay in their home while they were away, and we awaited a place to rent on first arriving in Winnipeg. They astonished us by leaving their doors unlocked, protected only by a friendly Elk Hound. That dog was very hospitable, allowing anyone to enter to pick up farm eggs that they sold to help friends. You could call them gullible and very trusting or darn right naive. On the other hand, Henry obviously knew of the criminal element that lurked about. For, one day, he went to the rescue of a person being attacked, and took off in pursuit of the thief at his own peril.

Others less spry than Henry, who had wives displaying an inordinate amount of patience with their men, held powerful positions where they were highly respected for their knowledge and skills. One was a retired doctor, who claimed to have been a good diagnostician, and no doubt it was true! The other was a retired fire chief. Both had their hearts in the right places. Over the years they supported and worked hard for Rosedale United Church. Still, like many, they did have trouble, I think, letting go of power. In fact, I hunch, they were grieving that loss terribly. That made it an interesting challenge not to bruise their egos any more than had already been done, when they stepped down from their respected positions in their chosen professions. A question remains wherever congregations function. It's this: is there enough opportunity in churches for very capable men, like those two, to exercise power and expend the energy that they still have? For, no doubt they, like other professionals, look for outlets to siphon off that energy in a productive way, without running roughshod over others.

Still, there also needed to be room in Rosedale for other willing workers to do their part. Despite those high profile figures, there were persons who somehow found a niche that others didn't want. Perhaps the others didn't want those jobs requiring on-going weekly commitments. One such niche finder named Claude, a Baptist, faithfully ushered with others without fanfare or fuss. Though I never saw his wife at church, I sensed that his faith and loyalty to his task determined his coming. What is it they say about the old time mail carrier? "Neither sleet, nor hail, nor snow will stop mail delivery." Well that was true of Claude; neither controversy in the church, nor difficult people, would stop him.

I presumed that I knew what I was doing. Having read something about the way to generate church loyalty, I sold the idea to the church Board of having a lapel pin designed with a rose motif. Claude was one of the first to get a copy.

I found in Rosedale, as I had in some other congregations, that little Trojan horses will invade the inner sanctums of the church to gain a foothold. One new couple were all hot to trot with Amway products. They showed their intent by moving in and about through the congregation as people would at a cocktail party. Yes, it was true that some active members of the congregation were into rival products such as Shackleys, ordering them more for themselves and using a room in their home for storage and display. However, they weren't using the congregation as a pool of possible new customers. I had heard of "Amway churches" that promised a new way of life, where persons would prosper and grow rich while somehow thinking that God ordained and blessed them to do so.

I never felt comfortable with fast talkers who invaded people's private spaces. So I could understand why some people hived themselves away. Still, I found it a frustrating task trying to make contact with people who lived in apartment buildings. To gain entrance one had to give ID by talking to a wall, listening for a voice, then entering by pushing at a door to coincide with an irritating buzz. I must confess that more than once I was tempted to wait till a resident unlocked the door, then scurry in at a person's heels, disappear out of sight down a hall, and run about leaving pamphlets at every door to advertise Rosedale Church.

It was a real job to get to see people in their homes, and in hospitals. In a place the size of Winnipeg, parishioners were scattered about; not only in the neighborhood, but in apartments throughout the city, and in many hospitals. Some were as far apart in the city as many towns are distant from each other in the country. Often I'd get to a hospital to visit a patient, only to find that person had gone home or transferred to another hospital. Fortunately back then, unlike now, I could ask for the pastor's box containing cards filed by denomination. Quite often I would find someone "in" whom I knew lived near the church. My visits were mostly welcomed. Wearing my "dog collar" helped, giving me access to everywhere I wanted to go in the hospital. Now I and many of my clergy colleagues are frustrated that, because of "confidentiality rules," we are given no more access to the patients than the general public has been given. Thus many clergy feel that their stringent professional ethics count for nothing. The prevailing mistrust of institutions as we move into the millennium causes me to wonder whether institutions such as hospitals don't even trust other institutions. It surely is a suspicious world we live in where the well-being of others suffers in the process. That is very sad! It is also sad that we are more and more relegated to computers that become gate keepers of information! Unless one gives the correct pass word, no information surfaces. It seems ridiculous that hackers and those who often don't need to know, do know, and many of us who are not as well versed in key punching, but need the information, are shut out. That brings up the age old question,

" Do you fit people to the administration, or do you fit the administration to the people?"

Despite the cumbersome environment people are

forced to live and work in, there are still examples of where the human spirit and courage prevails. At the municipal hospital on the fringe of the Riverview neighborhood a few patients bravely faced each day encased in iron lungs, victims of the long past polio epidemic. One person, then in her thirties, having endured the insults of the iron lung since a young woman, had unselfishly released her husband-to-be, despite the fact that he still loved her and wanted to marry her. "Greater love hath no one..."

Other unselfish acts of devotion abounded within that hospital. Delia, a robust, bright, outgoing person suffered a stroke. She lay flat on her back, her blue eyes open, blinking, but with no recognition of even her faithful husband, Ray. He sat holding her limp hand day after day, week after week, only leaving her side to go home to shave and shower. Often I would stop at Delia's door, knock, step in, and know that I'd find Ray behind the door looking into Delia's blue eyes. She never spoke a word, yet I believe somehow that couple, who had lived many decades together, continued to touch each others lives. Ray's intense devotion moved me to tears. I saw, then, what the words
"...for better for worse till death do us part," in the marriage vows, really meant.

Without suffering myself, I also listened and heard about many in different circumstances who struggled as victims of sexual abuse, persons who had loved ones suffering from anorexia, men and woman who, despite how much they tried, just couldn't share their secrets and hear the fact that God had already

198

forgiven them, or it was okay for them to think or be the way that they were.

I remember visiting one young woman in a hospital, who, though not identifying with the United Church, did desperately want to share with another her dark mental anguish and lack of self worth. As she wrung her hands in despair, she told of how, when baby-sitting her sister, she had driven the family car. The car went out of control and crashed. She lived, her little sister died. Her father blamed her and said,

"If anyone should have died, it should have been you, not your baby sister!" One wonders whether her feelings of guilt, magnified by her father's outbursts, would eventually "send her around the bend," as it had others whom I visited in the hospital, many who languished in silence.

Then there were the survivors, the street wise whose survival skills were honed to axe head sharpness. I teased one frequent drop in. I asked him if he thought that he ran a trap line. What did I mean? Well, he told me that he had a regular route that he traveled throughout the Fort Rouge area, rummaging in many bakery, supermarket, and cafe dumpsters.

"It was surprising how you could feed well on what you found. What waste! Good stuff still, thrown away, Lucky me!"

I asked why he didn't just stay at the "Sally Ann" (the Salvation Army Hostel). He yawned and softly said,

"Oh, I wouldn't stay there! I like to sleep under the

bridge. It's safer there. At the Sally Ann guys may steal your shoes when you're sleeping!"

Some characters passing through and dropping in at Rosedale Church, labeled "gypsies," rather than sleeping under bridges, slept in their cars. Their arrival at the church door was just as predictable as geese arriving in the spring. The line that they used to solicit money for gas and groceries was also predictable. Their "trap line" wasn't just a part of Winnipeg, it was, (from hearing from clergy in other provinces), a big chunk of Canada.

Having heard just about every imaginable story about hardships, and having seen or heard of money given for booze, I no longer questioned persons needing help. I just gave out meal vouchers honored by a local cafe and denied cash for bus fare, (a common appeal). In doing so, I sometimes got an ear full of abuse. What frustrated me the most about that, was the return, time after time, of an elderly obnoxious fellow who had in tow "his old lady," who was blind. He appeared to have forgotten that he had frequented Rosedale so often with the same line. When I took him up on that, he blew, shouting,

"That's what you are here for aren't you, to help! What kind of a Christian are you anyway?"

Feeling he had worn out his welcome, I asked him to leave, only to experience his presence again. His memory often failed him.

It was very hard to give parents with small children "the bum's rush" as many would have me do. One day, two women appeared at the church door with a couple of little kids shyly peeking out from behind their mothers' skirts. The spokeswoman of the two told how they had no where else to turn to but to the church.

"No home, no food, just arrived in town, and the kids are hungry," and on she went. I suggested social services. She lost me with her convoluted reasons why she expected no help there. Yet almost in the same breath, said that she and her friend wanted to join the church. Another story accompanied that surprise.

I found it futile to check with social services. Bound by confidentiality, they would never give me information to verify or discount a story. So it really came down to how good I was at judging character. Then, I blew it, even though I had sworn I'd never be taken in again. Still, those two played on my sympathies, especially for their kids, and on my ego. I would rescue them from their predicament as the "great white knight in shining armor." I phoned the local thrift store, an apartment was found, trucks arrived with beds, the whole lot. Then the two descended on me "to learn more about the church." I gave them a membership workbook to do something with. They did. The silent one looked up and copied out every scripture text noted, reams of it which I certainly didn't ask for! Whenever they brought in an instalment of copy work, a new request would follow,

"Perhaps some of this or some of that, for the children you understand!"

I was beginning to feel very uncomfortable, thinking they viewed me as gullible enough to think I expected copy work payment for goods. One day I noticed that they hadn't been around for a while. I asked about them, only to find that they had disappeared from the district. A few years later when I had left Winnipeg, I heard that the spokes-lady had discovered that her little girl had healing powers, and was gathering quite a following of people across the border who were desperately seeking help. Wonder of wonders. One thing I knew for sure, those characters never caught that contagious condition from me!

Still, despite my feelings, I felt I had to pray, using words such as ,

O God help us not despise what we do not understand. 1

In contrast to those pathetic charlatans who, damn it all used people, were so many mothers, genuine, authentic people who cared for their children and for others. Lesley worked as a teacher's aide down the street from Rosedale at Lord Roberts School that integrated special needs children into the regular classroom setting. One very healthy youngster, with whom Lesley struck up a good working relationship, told his mother that there was this lady who had been at Norway House. It turned out that Lesley knew Lily, the boy's mother, as a child, at the Residential School. Now she was a successful mother and wife in a good interracial marriage.

Many people from the north were living in the district in homes, some which they rented from an Indian housing association. I felt honoured when I was asked to conduct a funeral with Indian participation in our church. Dullas Robertson's mother had died. I remember, when I was a young man working in the Norway House Residential school, hearing from the United Church minister there that there was a young man from "down river" who wanted to become a minister. With no native ministry program in place, as there is now, he went to the States for his studies. Then years later, I was to meet him. Matilda and many more fine folk from Norway House also gathered for the service. The smell of sweet grass, and the soft sound of the Cree tongue brought back fond memories. We had a celebration of a life well lived, and for a very brief time, a sense of oneness as Canadians.

Rosedale not only was blessed with the presence of many original Canadians, but also of persons who settled in Canada after the second world war. Fritz, for one, who lived across from the church, seldom attended services, but his wife did. He had worked for the railway as a technician having, he said, gained experience in radio work flying rescue missions with the German Lufwaffe. Sadly, as he began to approach retirement years he got cancer. Like many who had exhausted all that the medical profession could offer, he reached out in desperation to seek help from claimed cures, using electric magnets and the like, but to no avail. I still picture in my mind, Fritz in his hospital bed, knowing that his immune system was shot from radiation, vulnerable to any microbe in the air, still wanting to have his wife and two teenage boys near him.

Ministers get a real lift from weddings and baptisms, but regardless of how often we have confronted death over the years, we never escape the feeling of loss. Just as seniors constantly experience the loss of friends and family of their vintage, to remain in a constant state of grieving, so also, I believe, clergy grieve almost weekly. It hits even harder when a fellow clergy dies young. Rob, a well loved young minister, full of energy and enthusiasm for life and his work, who had just settled in his new congregation, having come from Steinbach, developed a rare disease and tragically died. What a huge loss! We who knew of his great musical ability as a song writer, worship leader, and so much more, found it so hard to accept! His new congregation, young and old, celebrated his life. They drew pictures, wrote poetry, and stories, throwing themselves into supporting and caring for Rob's wife, children, and each other in the face of death. What a healthy way to deal with grief! Time would never fill the empty space in the lives of those who touched Rob's life as he touched theirs. Still, a hymn he wrote, now in the new Voices United hymn book, continues to help celebrate his life whenever it is sung.

Funerals are never easy. They can drain a person conducting a service, especially if the funeral directors and staff are either not known, or just see themselves as doing a job. Many funeral homes have, in my view, become very impersonal, having been taken over by big corporations. Where once funeral homes had a small town, "We know your family well, we care," feeling about them, now as big business, that touch is lost. There was a time, even in the big city, when I worked with those who really had a keen interest in the families of the deceased whom they had known from way back.

However, the coming and going of new people at the funeral homes made that a thing of the past. True, there were exceptions. I found it interesting when a new face would appear, such as the woman ex airline pilot of Slavic background, who knew the language and could, as a funeral director, minister to north end families. Then there was Neil, who had sold his business to a conglomerate, but still was able to maintain his long-standing respected family reputation. What he had going for him, I thought, and which I respected, was the fact that he still did house calls. Working out of a store front office, and as a good Lutheran, he apparently recognized the importance of having funeral services in churches as opposed to in funeral chapels. Maybe he just wanted to maintain a low overhead, but I hunch it was more than that.

I have found many sad people, who haven't necessarily had anything to do with the church before seeking help. One day I had a call from a young wife and mother whose husband had allegedly committed suicide. He lived by the river. I heard he jumped off a bridge. Behind his home was a big garage housing his street rod, a customized car that he had babied along, giving his all to make it just perfect in his eyes. The day of the funeral was a real happening. The street rod club members came out in full force to give him a grand send off. They embellished the streets surrounding Rosedale with vehicles, cherry reds, bright yellows, and chrome, almost blinding one in glare. The roar of the engines following the service shouted a goodbye that I've never heard since. What a tribute that was!

What we anticipate seldom occurs; what we least expect generally happens. 2

Many funerals definitely share a note of sadness. Yet at others, people provide pathos, not only as part of the eulogies delivered, but also in other unexpected ways. While riding in the lead car or coach to and from cemeteries, funeral directors and I have often swapped stories about bizarre things that happen at funerals. There is the story of the minister conducting the grave side service, losing his footing and falling "ass over tea kettle" into the hole. Then there are the times funeral directors would personally just like to forget. The son of a funeral home owner, as a fledgling funeral director, had the task of driving the coach (a polite word for hearse) to the foot of the stairs leading up to a great prestigious downtown cathedral. The church dignitaries stood very regally awaiting the coffin. When the dignified young man stepped out, strutted to the back of the coach, and opened the door, his mouth fell open, aghast! He had forgotten to load the coffin. Without a word to the waiting dignitaries, he leaped back into the driver's seat, gunned the engine and drove off like a scared rabbit, leaving all gathered and waiting dumbfounded, and wondering, "What the ... !" Needless to say, his father wasn't amused when he arrived back at the funeral home to face the music and try to quickly return to the church with his forgotten cargo.

Stories of such disasters are numerous. Like the time a beginner funeral director meticulously attended to the thousands of details funeral directors must deal with, only to arrive at the grave side to find that he had forgotten to include the minister in the procession. He breathed a sigh of relief, and so did his boss, when the minister drove up to the cemetery a little later in his own car with a bemused look on his face.

This of course can't match the horror stories that are legendary in Ireland, which have happened even here in western Canada. A funeral director told this story. He once arrived at the funeral home, having stepped out for just a brief moment, to find the coffin open, which wasn't unusual. He was taken aback though seeing the family and friends of the deceased holding their own private wake and toasting their dead loved one in a very raucous manner.

When I think of toasts, it's usually about toasts at wedding receptions. Winnipeg receptions were often very enlightening and exciting. Sometimes, with more than one wedding in a day, I'd say grace at one held in posh surroundings, indulge in a main course, then be off to a Ukrainian marathon to eat dessert and enjoy seeing the groom king, and bride queen decked out in traditional garb and glittering tiara. Our United Church seems open to celebrating with people of different ethnic and denominational backgrounds.

Across the lane from our home lived an Italian family. The husband grew beans hanging from vines, made wine, and had roaring heated discussions with his good wife who gave back as much as she got in shouting words of affection. That couple's son, in love with his future R.C. wife, needed an annulment from his previous marriage by the church to be married Roman Catholic. Meanwhile, the couple wanted to live together as husband and wife.

"Would I wed them?"

"Sure, why not! However, let's get a priest participating if possible." Done! A young priest came and did most of the service, apart from the pronouncement, and in leaving said,

"I'm not supposed to be here, you know!"

I knew! Still, there was no evidence of children from the groom's first marriage, and somehow that made it all right.

Children sometimes were in for surprises. A couple in their nineties asked me to perform their marriage, but their middle age and older children were not to know till after the wedding. They wanted to elope. They were married in the church lounge behind closed doors. Before the wedding I had asked them,

"Why, at your age?"

"Well," they said, "We live in the same senior high rise. We eat together. We play cards together. We play shuffle board together. We do almost everything together. We might as well live together."

In a way, they did not surprise me, having heard the same kind of reasoning before.

That elderly couple reminded me of "some people's kids." I recall members of a family in Glenboro, Manitoba who frequently gathered around their mother's bedside. She was 104 years old and then some. They would often say, "Sing us a song mom." Their mom was a tiny, childlike soul. With her knees to her chest in a fetal position almost buried in quilts, she would slowly open her eyes. Out would flow one old gospel hymn after another sung in a faint squeaky voice, bringing tears to the eyes of her 70 plus year old children. Though their old mom could not carry on a conversation, her mind could recall those gems as if taped on a recorder, a gift she could still share.

Young children, an essential ingredient of a church, also shared by frequenting the church building. Many parents brought their kids to church and stayed to worship. Some parents, having other things to do, dropped them off for Sunday School. Throughout the week a day care operated out of the church basement. Evidence of energetic children at work and play caught grown-ups attention. Still, not all favoured that flavour. It seemed that when some people grew older, especially some who had taught, their nerves became frayed more easily, and their tolerance level for children became lower. They forgot that children were not little adults. Thus I had often fielded complaints, even about Rosedale's polished gym floor being abused. "No black scuff marks please. Those damn kids are ruining the floor!"

Even the well-meaning janitor, having an aversion to unnecessary messes would, immediately following a wedding service, practically shove the last wedding guest out the door, closing the double doors quickly to keep the confetti out of his church. Someone once suggested rice, but then the pigeons would leave their messy splat offerings at the door.

Rosedale's brick exterior, for some reason, evoked a turning inward rather than friendly welcoming outward appearance. It projected a very private space, and, like many churches, must have been intimidating for new comers to enter sensing the unintentional message,

"Don't mess this place up!"

I felt it would take as much courage for anyone new to walk into a church for the first time as it would to enter someone's home uninvited. People quickly get to know whether they are welcomed. I felt the fewer of those kind of messages sent, the better.

There were of course some persons who thought we could do without "undesirables" who entered unseen in the dark of night. The numbers 666 appearing on a church window let it be known that not everyone loved Rosedale United Church. The office file cabinets were broken into more than once, suggesting our popularity was based a little on any money we left around. To save the cabinets becoming battered cadavers, we left seed money on the top for the customary intruders for their usual quick get away. We weren't sure what remedy to apply though when one morning Mary, our church secretary, and I found the church safe dragged near the exit door in the sanctuary, obviously left behind in a bungled getaway. The worst was yet to come. Mary, a trusting soul, had left her purse unguarded in her office. As a consequence, someone stole her car. It didn't surface again till months later when, of all places, it was found intact in a hospital parking lot. Apparently it had been parked there for some time.

It is strange how people don't notice things. Cam, a man with an interesting sense of humor, planted a tomato seed among the flowers by the church's well-trafficked front door. The tomato plant grew, raised its head above the flowers, bore a few bright screaming red tomatoes, practically shouting out " Hey, we're here!" Yet, would you believe it, no one noticed the flower bed intruder till Cam mentioned his creative experiment at a church Board meeting. "Oh yeah," was the most response his confession gained.

The need to make people aware of what's happening around them and also of others' needs has always been a perennial problem in the church. Usually ministers don't feel comfortable asking for "extras." Yet, convinced that confidentiality was critical, I believed that finding another place for the minister's study was very necessary. So it happened. Before the move, my study was in the adjacent secretary's office near the front entrance. A glass partition had served as the only wall between the secretary's office and the minister's study. With all respect to people who came off the street into the church, I had wondered how much private conversation was heard before a study was created from a room near the pulpit, out of ear shot of traffic, at a distance from people who didn't really want to eaves-drop. Upon moving the study, a counter was installed on the secretary's office door to provide some sense of safety for her while alone in the building. A church door buzzer also helped to ease some of the secretary's anxiety by allowing her to visually screen those who entered. The only problem was the glass by the front door wasn't clear so she couldn't check to see exactly who wanted in during office hours.

A series of stained glass windows enhanced Rosedale's sanctuary, depicting the life of Jesus Christ and his parables. Those were installed over a period of many years. Each was a memorial to a person or family long gone. I found them fascinating, so much so that I encouraged a young woman who was taking a photography course to photograph them. Copies were made in black and white and included in a booklet giving the names of donors and the deceased, along with a brief description of the Biblical references.

That action resulted in me getting a deeper appreciation and understanding of the lives of those gone before, many of whose adult children continued to identify with Rosedale. It also satisfied my need to get a handle on, not only the present, but the past. For each congregation, like a family, had so much unsaid when members met. It was not only they in body, but all the cultural baggage, and memories that they carried which cropped up in conversations. Like most ministers with so few years in a church family, I was at a disadvantage, coming cold into their decision making exchanges.

Sometimes, knowing church members backgrounds and the church family's history gave a better understanding of any resistance to change.

Change of course, no matter whether positive or negative, is stressful, but I felt in a dowager church like Rosedale, change was needed if, for no other reason, than to get people out of their comfortable ruts. That seemed very necessary since one definition of a rut is "a coffin open at both ends."

Resistance haunted Rosedale. I had an idea that dimmer switches could be installed in the sanctuary to better set the atmosphere for worship. A few were skeptical."It couldn't be done!" But it could!
For, new to the congregation was a young man who had been an engineer on sea-going vessels. He was very conversant with such things. Yet, like many newcomers, and even some long time members, he hesitated to "step on toes." It was true, as in any church, people carve out their little niches or spaces, things they want to do, and God help anyone who invades those spaces. Thus the young innovative man got the subtle message and felt very uneasy about installing the dimmers. But I encouraged him to go ahead. Somehow he thought that I was the ultimate boss. I assured him that it was God working in and through the congregation.

I sometimes wondered what there was in me that had that need to encourage congregations to install dimmer switches in sanctuaries. Was it just because I wanted their attention when I preached, and had the fear that they would find something more interesting to do, such as read or count the fly specks on the ceiling? Sometimes I questioned my motives. You'd think, especially at Rosedale that I'd want to have as much light as possible to be in eye contact with the congregation. The sanctuary was very long and narrow, and, as in most churches, people chose to sit way back, leaving the minister thinking two things; either install a conveyor belt so that he could push a button and they would all move forward en masse, or install a pair of binoculars. I must confess those silly images came to mind when I tried to establish contact with the folks when I preached.

Pierre Burton had written a book called "The Comfortable Pew." The last thing I wanted was to see the Rosedale people feel too comfortable and complacent! Yet it was easy for them to be just that.

Fund raising was no problem, nor meeting the church budget. The congregation was blessed with some shrewd business men such as the distinguished old gentleman who, with the church Board's permission, sold RRSP's and gave his commission back to the church. There were also other known figures in the congregation like Jack, the retired fire chief, who conducted the annual fall canvas for years. He would let the finance committee know how much they could expect in pledges, then suggest about 80% of them would be honored, giving a figure that the finance committee could then use in budgeting. On top of the benefits gained through the skilled persons in the congregation, there was a huge bequest from which the congregation, keeping the principal intact, withdrew only the interest for operational expenses. That was a mixed blessing, obviously, for it encouraged the people to "rest easy on their oars." Indeed Rosedale was a very comfortable church, in more ways than one.

So when people like me tried to encourage Rosedale to consider amalgamating with Riverview United Church, the Rosedale and Riverview congregations, at the time, didn't seem to really find that too necessary. They already did one thing together as neighboring congregations almost across the street from each other. They competed in curling for the "Golden Broom" that Jack devised. Great fun, but to amalgamate? Eventually though, someone said,

"Well, let's form a committee or two made up of people from each church and see where that takes us."

Years later, long after I had left Rosedale, it took the "Issue," that is the possibility of homosexuals and lesbians being ordained, to help bring the two congregations to marry. Ironical wasn't it!

The Spirit did move, though, in another direction, causing me to be less down in the mouth. Jack and I, walking along the river bank one day, shared a dream in response to the question, what needs to happen to help people who are aging and are active in the immediate community to stay where their friends are? The answer, a housing development in Rosedale-Riverview District. More dreaming. It could be built beside the Senior Leisure Centre on the soccer field. Sorry, no space. Where else? Pull down some houses! No way, that would defeat the purpose! Where then? Let's ask the local town Councillor, Don Gerry. He has a stake in the community. That man went to work with the city manager types. God bless him.

215

Property was found in the neighborhood with the front door opening onto Osborne St, the back looking out on the river. CMHC money, consultants, the architect who built Winnipeg's first Lion's Manor for seniors, seniors center reps., reps. from the Legion, and both Rosedale and Riverview churches all got their heads together and it happened! What a great outfit! Not only that, but a hope that I had, to see every apartment balcony on the high rise look out on the river, happened too! What did one wise person say

> If you have built castles in the air,
> your works need not be lost;
> that is where they should be.
> Now put the foundations under them.   3

Oh so true! I had never received any great award in my life time until then, so I did appreciate the one that I hunch Jack and the Counselor got me from the City. But I feel it belonged to all who made something come true, perhaps something that they had always had in the back of their minds. I got something else from that experience, namely the realization that it takes political will, public funding, local initiative and hard work to make anything like that happen.

Back in Rosedale, as elsewhere, I always felt myself to be a down home boy. For my personal preference, in so far as church was concerned, was to give attention first to the local congregation, then to Presbytery, and if any time and energy were left, to Conference. In Presbytery I found myself on a students' education committee volunteering to put together a handbook or guide for congregations who wanted theological student interns to work and learn in their congregations. I solicited ideas from the other provincial church offices, and Church House people. It was only after completing the job that I found out that the Toronto office had a person on staff doing that very thing.

Presbytery seemed so big, since it was made up of reps. from all the different congregations, and a resource staff. I felt a little sad about where it placed its priorities. I guess I recalled the "good old days " when Dr. Fred, whom Lesley and I worked for in Central Winnipeg Missions, really did an outreach job in trying to meet the needs of marginal people living in and around the city's core. I wasn't really sure that it was still being done by anyone with the same gusto, and meeting the same success that Fred and company generated.

I knew, though, that I couldn't continue to flop over in my seat and go on nostalgic trips into the past. I had to continue to sharpen my skills to minister. The University of Winnipeg, once United College, offered courses in Marriage Counseling, one of which I took, thinking that it might be a route for me to follow, with the end game being a registered marriage counselor. In the class sessions where I interacted with other students, I painfully learned something about myself. The wife of a minister in Winnipeg really got to me with what I thought was her judgmental, sanctimonious attitude. We clashed often. I felt others went to her rescue because I would come on too strong. It took me a few years to get off my high horse and realize that I clashed because I saw in her much of myself that I didn't like.

That same dynamic may have surfaced when a fine man, a long time-devoted member of Rosedale, and I clashed. In a heated discussion which seldom occurred, since I usually played the "yes man," with him, he surprised me! For I believe I heard him shout out in anger,

"Whose church is this anyway, your's or mine?"

Well, that really hurt! The last thing I would ever have wanted was to be perceived as some character who thought it was his prerogative to run the church. I felt that he had questioned my integrity. So my response triggered, If that's how he and others see it, that's it, I'm out of here!

It's amazing how one's intent in speaking doesn't match the impact. I believe today that he never meant it the way I took it. Yet, back then, having heard very little affirmation for my work from Rosedale's Ministry and Personnel committee, and despite the care and support I received from Gordon and Marg and a few others, I felt that after five years it was time to go. Lesley and I sold our house to a prof and poet from the University. We paid back the ten thousand dollars the congregation loaned us for a down payment on a house, sadly took Fred, our basset dog to SPCA, got rid of some furniture that I got at the hospital nurses' residents auction, and moved into an apartment which to our dismay looked out over a noisy Pub.

Looking back on our stay in Winnipeg, there was

218

the work in and through the church which gave us satisfaction. We both had contact with Mark and Marnie and enjoyed traveling the city to garage sales, and buying ice cream treats at the "BDI." Lesley had some of her side of the family, friends, work at Lord Robert's School, and CGIT. I did some pottery, browsed and bought at the annual Hospital Auxiliary book sale.

Lesley and I found by living in the city we could enjoy a private life apart from the church family. We got to know and admire many people both active in the congregation and beyond. Many were remarkable, showing great courage and imagination, especially in how they solved many of their personal problems. A lady who waited tables for years chose to be a single mom to raise her boys which she did successfully. Her husband was a drunk. But rather than divorce him, she bought the little house next to hers, "for him," so the boys could have a dad despite his nonsense."

In keeping with the spirit displayed by that caring woman, Lesley and I were heartened to hear later, after we left, of the generous understanding of the Rosedale Church family. The members were true to their reputation, a bit crusty on the outside, but when the chips were down, they were there when suffering souls needed them. A fine young man with a wife and two sons who "came out of the closet" to declare himself a homosexual, much to everyone's surprise, was welcomed back to teach Sunday School. A fellow whom everyone trusted implicitly, went off with a bunch of the church's money. He was forgiven, and accepted back into the fold without being broken. No doubt the stranger who left a lot of money to the church years before must have felt welcomed, helped, and loved unconditionally, without the Rosedale people doing anything other than what came naturally to them. It is very clear, Rosedale took to heart the Matthew 25:35-40 Bible passage.

I remember, looking back, that I had given my request for a change of Pastoral Relations in January and while continuing at Rosedale till June engaged in that age old game of courting for a call. The rule was that a minister could only negotiate with one congregation at a time. Yet, either congregation or the minister could write for information and check out other candidates or congregations by phone, Fax, or whatever. Often someone on a congregation's Pastoral Relations Committee would know someone in the congregation where the minister worked, and on the quiet check him or her out that way.

I heard from two rural Ontario pastoral charges, one in the tobacco country, another near Ottawa. The latter spokesman invited me up for a ride in his ultra light aircraft which scared the flipping daylights out of me just thinking about it, The tobacco country congregation I felt, wouldn't do since I was against smoking, period! Williams Lake congregation sounded appealing since I knew a friend there from the Arctic. In talking to a tough old gal on the phone, I made the mistake of asking if there were any roads up there. The people and I might have got along okay since cattle country appealed to me a bit. Then there was another northern B.C. congregation that kindly hosted me, but after a meeting with the committee I felt that wasn't for me. Flin Flon, Manitoba was a possibility, and so the courting went on. A phone interview with the folks from Mission B.C. resulted in a trip out for an interview. There I should have been tipped off on the interesting weather. A kind member sported an umbrella, but I was slow on the uptake, and the match was made. Lesley and I would move to Mission.

17 Mission City On the Fraser

Though the mountains shake in the heart of the sea; though the waters roar and foam, though the mountains tremble with its tumult, There is a river whose streams make glad ...Ps 46

My first night in Mission City was spent alone in the church manse. I undressed, climbed into bed, and began to read myself to sleep. Suddenly something flew close by my face, casting a fluttering shadow on the wall. I jumped up stark naked, and flailed away in a frenzy with my shirt to knock it senseless. Having finally nailed it, I threw it outside, thinking I'd get rid of it in the morning, only to find next day the bat had disappeared. An interesting introduction to Mission City! I learned later that all that I really had to do was open a door and the bat would find its way out of the house on its own. Still, I felt the stress of settling in would be enough for Lesley. She didn't need to meet a restless bat after a tiring trip from a Manitoba CGIT camp.

I got to Mission first to greet the U Haul, kindly driven by a young man and his friend from Winnipeg. Later I picked Lesley up across the bridge from Mission. I felt uneasy driving into town, knowing that the mountains or the coast had never enthralled her. Before coming, I had given her a rosy picture of a modern thriving town. Yet to my dismay, what she saw first as we drove Main Street were bales of hay, and people in frontier dress evoking a real gold rush scene. It was "Pioneers Day."As we drove up the hill to the manse to pull into the back driveway, I glanced over at our neighbours' Anglican rectory. I thought, "Oh no, She will see that bathtub in their front yard! " Lesley must have felt as dismayed as she did when we flew into Grise Fiord many years before!

We did eventually settle in after the visit of another bat which we suspected came down the fire place chimney. Other surprises followed. On the top of the U Haul truck I found a big white sign reading "Low Clearance" I wasn't sure whether that was some kind of omen. Since I had no clue where it came from, I leaned it on the rotten, moss-covered garden fence. I suppose a philosopher could have a field day reading some symbolic meaning into my discovery.

Mission itself was uniquely fascinating. It was made up of five smaller communities, Silverdale, Mission City, Hatsic, Dewdney and Deroche, all on the north side of the Fraser River. A bridge crossed the river near a road bottleneck where the Royal Canadian Legion building stood. The town hall, built out in the country, accessible only by vehicle, gave the civil servants less drop-in traffic to deal with. Two

Federal Correction Institutions, a minimum and maximum, stood nearby.

Memories of Mission were marred by the confiscation of orchards and fruit farms, fish boats, and other private possessions from the hard working, long established Japanese Canadian community. I and others in the congregation felt terrible about hearing that even the land the church now held once belonged to the dispossessed people. Tomiko, a grand lady in the church family, told of how her parents buried family treasures, only to return to find them all gone without a trace, stolen! She and others often spoke quietly of their smoldering anger. Yet Tomiko never let that get in the way of her friendships in the church. Besides, she said, "Others had it done to them too! "

Now, I couldn't picture neighbours back in those war years, taking advantage of the Japanese Canadian folk when they were down. Yet I shudder to think that I might have gone along with the mob that drove the folks inland and stole their possessions.

Having come from a mixed ethnic background, Slavik and English, and called names because of my looks, I felt for other visible minorities. So when I was put on the spot to consider an invitation for a native Indian dancing group to perform in the church sanctuary, and I declined, I hoped that they wouldn't label me a racist. I had seen imported Indian dances accompanied by drum chants. So I felt a more suitable place would be in the church gym rather than in the church sanctuary. Also, since I compared those performances to those used in competitions at Pow Wows, I felt that any worship or spiritual value would be scant in nature. I doubted that the Anglican and RCs represented on the Christmas Bureau planning committee, seeking a venue for such a performance, would consider having it in their churches. I also believed that, not only would the congregation feel uncomfortable having the dancers in our worship centre, but had I recommended it to the Board, I would merely be patronizing a sincere group of people who celebrated their Indian identity.

Clearly people outside the United Church had many different ideas on what we were all about. I bumped into one young man from a different denomination who took me to task for an article published in the local newspaper. I titled it "Different Gloves on the Hands of God." The intent was to say God travels incognito and can appear when and where God chooses. It is presumptuous to say,

"God, you will only show yourself in Jesus Christ, and not in other ways."

That young man, so sure of himself, was most insistent that "one door and only one" would lead to salvation. He stated that a person must confess Jesus Christ as Saviour and Lord or be damned. I had a problem with that fellow's idea that, once "born again," a person had a guaranteed ticket to heaven, no matter what kind of life that he lived on earth. We parted agreeing to differ, but still needed to talk some more. I never met him again.

I sat on the RCMP Citizen's Advisory Committee, believing that the church needed to continue to reach

224

out in the community. Two active members of our
church were Stan, the staff sergeant, and his wife
Marge. For a while I hadn't realized Marge and I had
been in the same class at Brandon teachers college
years ago. It wasn't only because of that, or their
commitment to the United Church, that I began to
feel a common bond with the couple, but because I
appreciated what Stan was doing in his community.

He opened an RCMP store front office down town,
addressed seniors' safety concerns, and even was
willing to field trivial complaints. He even listened to
me tell of someone stealing the heads off our front
yard poppies. Stan did all of that while dealing with
heavy duty stuff such as hydroponic drug growing,
and murder. Yet, he still had the human touch and a
sense of humour. I heard that more than once he
played a trick on his dad, a farmer back in Manitoba.
While golfing he substituted his dad's ball when he
was looking the other way. When his dad took a
swing at it, the ball went absolutely crazy, going
every which way. That was Stan, one who impressed
me with his consistent prairie boy at heart approach
to life. He took what happened in stride without
getting too overwrought, flavouring it with humour.

He told me once that in his late teens he kicked
around two ideas. One to make the RCMP his career,
the other to take up the offer from a family member
to accept some free land to farm. He opted to apply
to the police. One day while out working the land, he
saw an RCMP vehicle kicking up dust as it rapidly cut
across the field. He was to report to the training
depot within days. So, as Stan said, "Well, that's the

whole story and here I am, way over thirty years later. "

Stan never did talk much about how he saw his efforts being received by the community. In my case I felt that in Mission City I got more feedback from the community at large than I did from the congregation. There was the odd negative return for my efforts. Once it came right out of the blue. On Remembrance day, as Legion Chaplain, I often gave the message to a patriotic gathering. Proudly marching with the comrades, my clumsy footwork often caused the one in front of me to limp when I stepped on his heels. Embarrassing! Still, since he didn't turn about to ream me out, I felt invincible and accepted as "one of the good old boys." That is till, after one Remembrance day, I got a letter from someone coming down on me hard for what I had believed was a well thought-out message. I strongly sided with peace, having learned the painful truth that one must take a stand, recalling the Bible prophet's challenge

"How long are you going to keep hobbling between two opinions?" What is it they say? "We are the decisions that we make."

Rapid change began to transform Mission City before and after we arrived, leaving the bitter memories of greed brought on by war in the dust of the past. Newcomers took advantage of rocketing housing prices in the Big City caused by offshore money. People there sold property for over $200,000 or more, moved to Mission, and bought houses for a little over half that, banking the rest. Others escaped the prairie's bitter cold to retire in a warmer climate.

Lesley and I never found that to be true. Sweaters helped keep the damp out. Still, the damp bed sheets, mould, slugs, a backyard garden of moss instead of grass, left me thinking the next thing would be for moss to grow on the back of my neck. The rain, which never deterred parents watching drenched kids play soccer, didn't frighten off the influx of prairie "puddle jumpers." In fact, the joke was someone should issue certificates to genuine home-grown BC types since they were so few. Almost everyone came from somewhere else, it seemed.

Mission City became the haven for "the haves," but also for the "have nots." Often a couple of ladies from one of the many group homes aroused my curiosity. With their heads down they scurried about, reaching with great concentration deep into the streets' refuse bins with one hand, the other holding cups of coffee. It appeared that the powers-to-be in government were emptying out a mental institute, placing former residents in Mission City group homes and elsewhere in the Fraser Valley and main land.

Not only were there clusters of people from many places to form a larger and different Mission City, but church congregations proudly sported different denominational signs. When a fight flared up in a congregation, a sign would come down, be changed, and a new sign would appear somewhere else declaring not a split, but another denomination. The process reminded me of cells dividing. Two new churches for example surfaced. Ministers sometimes became like Lone Rangers. One pastor formed a hybrid Baptist church. A Lutheran minister bought the old RC church to form his own congregation.

Fortunately, St. Andrew's, despite the "homosexual issue" stayed together as a congregation, losing only a few members. The congregation proclaimed business as usual. Some denominations denied the presence of homosexuals or lesbians in their pulpits. Yet my understanding was that they could be, so long as they didn't practice; a novel idea! I felt that it would almost be impossible for most persons to jump through all the hoops in the United Church leading up to ordination if they were seeking same-sex partners. Even if they did, they would find it difficult to be accepted or function in many rural charges. So for me it wasn't a "big deal" as an issue.

Many "salt of the earth" Mission City 's members were very family oriented. The "Hatsic girls," then in their seventies, had married "boys " long ago whom they had met on farms. Many women while picking berries, or cooking for harvesting gangs, met fellows who had ridden the rails through the provinces to BC, during the depression.

The wealth of Mission City centred, not only in the depth of character of people, like the Hatsic girls, but also with latecomers who actually were moneyed. Vic Hollister, a generous gold mine owner from the States, did much for Mission. He got a high school breakfast club going to encourage would-be drop outs to stay in school. They were to "bird dog " trades people, working in jobs that they might like to do, to see what was involved and find out what training and education they needed. It was that man who connected me with the high school co-op learning

program. Through it, St. Andrew's United Church got
some badly needed data entered into the computer,
and a young man, dwarfed at birth, got some on-
the-job experience. Much good evolved from this
man, Vic. He was a vet who flew in B 29 bombers
during the war and shared his loyalties with both the
USA and Canada. He had connections across the
border. Yet, he shared his resources and leadership
skills locally through the International Rotary club,
the Presbyterian church, and other causes.

I found, as I did with Quebecers, that people in BC
were more north-south oriented than east-west with
the mountains forming a natural barrier. They did not
convince Lesley. though. She would have no part in
buying cheaper cheese, milk, and other dairy
products in Sumas, USA, only twenty minutes from
Mission. Lesley, for one, and myself to a lesser
degree, believed in shopping locally. Her reasoning?
If people didn't shop locally, stores would close and
the town would die. Opportunities to shop were there
in down town Mission City. Unfortunately, the town,
cramped as it was for space and parking, really had
only two streets in its core, each running parallel to
the river, which you could call its business section. On
the "main drag " were, among other businesses,
Klas and his wife's coffee shop specializing in
German pastries. In the heart of the business section
was the Green Village Restaurant operated by a
Chinese and Vietnamese couple who served food of
both nationalities. On Railway St. the "old lady," who
impressed Lesley and me with her courage, ran a
second hand store offering affordable furniture and

stuff that she picked up from garage sales in her "clunker," an orange van. Despite being bowed over with a bad back, and mothering a teenage son suffering a kidney disease, she struggled on, usually with a smile.

The "old lady " and her son, and others, old and young, did enjoy a break in the grinding routines of making ends meet, though. For, under winter skies spilling rain that often seemed to soak right into one's bones, the annual Christmas Candle Light parade enticed swarms of people to descend to the main drag from streets and roads above. The parade, like a tinsel festooned, dancing creature wended its way down the narrow main street lined with eager people. Music, laughter, ooh...s and ah...s, rumbling engines, and sirens increased the usual street cries. Now that was loud for the parade's voice added to the sounds that Lesley and I heard, day and night, even within the walls of the manse. Windows open or shut, no matter! The roars of drag racers, trains, planes, boats, the clicking grinding shake and shingle mills, shouts from the local corner hotel, and even the cymbal sound of hub caps swiped off cars in the dead of night, invaded our premises. Just think how much noisier it would have been, had the once busy fibre glass plant still been in operation. Yet, if there was a choice between noise and the reopening of that plant that employed many, it would be no contest. It was sad that in some remote board room a few made a decision that affected the lives of so many deserving people who lost their jobs.

Many people labelled "transients " passed through

Mission. As in Winnipeg, I gave out meal vouchers honoured at a local cafe. Once or twice I reluctantly arranged for a room at the local hotel but often felt duped. I thought, If only the Salvation Army had a hostel in Mission City, rather than just an alcohol dry-out centre way out in the country. Then we'd be getting somewhere in helping the poor souls. As it was, they had to come with cap in hand to a stranger like me to make demands for themselves. Once in a blue moon a needy family would really tug at my heart strings. Such a family did surface. A woe-begotten twelve year boy showed up at the church door. "Would I help?" His mother and younger brothers were stuck at the corner. His mom's car was out of gas. More help resulted after an appeal to the congregation for bedding, furniture and more. Lesley and Mary-Ann loaded up at the Mennonite (MCC) second hand store in Abbotsford and made a special trip to Deroche with some "really good deals." An artist couple donated a hundred dollars from their meagre income. The twelve-year-old spokesperson for the family was very polite, and his family looked very deserving. The mother said that she knew a United Church minister in Calgary. Something had happened there, as it did in Mission City. For within weeks, the family disappeared with no forwarding address, leaving all who helped hurt, deflated, and hesitant about responding again to appeals from needy families.

Once in awhile, though, a character would come along whose story, if it didn't quite have a ring of truth about it, nevertheless aroused one's interest. A slim, wiry old merchant marine dropped by asking for help saying,

"I'm off to visit my daughter out east."

And some weeks later,

"I'm now on my way back home, could I work around the place for some cash to buy a little food and tobacco?"

"Sure," I'd say, "you can dig a bit around the fir trees that the boy scouts planted beside the church."

He'd get right at it, his feeble frame and tattooed arms really put to the test. He'd shove his broken glasses on his nose, and persist for a bit. Then I'd give him a few dollars and he'd disappear, only to reappear the next year with both of us understanding each other. I took a liking to the old fellow, partly because I thought, "What you see, is what you get." I also enjoyed him telling me that he didn't hop freights. He travelled in style in the second engine on most trains.

"It was warm in there and no one hardly ever bothered me," he'd say with bold-faced sincerity, and often with a sigh, scratch and say, "I'm really getting too old for this kind of business."

I felt the old boy never did anybody any harm. He wasn't like the inmates who had no respect for others' rights that I met when serving on the Citizens Advisory Committee at the minimum security penitentiary. Learning about the program for victims to confront criminals, and a program for sex offenders, dispelled in my mind the ideas that the inmates lived in a country club atmosphere. Having seen the cells and learned about the restrictions placed on the offenders, I was reassured of the merits of the system.

I did feel though, that kids who did "doughnuts " with their cars ("beaters"), and those who shot out car windows with pellet guns on drive-by shootings, could use a tour or two through the institution's facilities. They needed to hear the iron doors slam shut behind them, and have "lifers" share their stories with them. Then they might just tone down their ridiculous behaviour!

Yet, I'm not sure about the thieves who preyed on the elderly, such as dear Margaret, our neighbour. Once a purse snatcher mugged her. Another time, while she was away, her house was broken into. Thieves took jewellery that her late husband had given her. She lost her lodge life membership pins and other irreplaceable treasures of very little monetary value. Margaret was a sweet old lady, and at age eighty five didn't deserve such treatment. She had worked and slaved on the farm before her husband's premature death. She had carried heavy wet laundry around for years at the hospital to survive and raise her children as a single parent. Margaret not only kept her spirits up, buoyed by her solid Christian faith, but she offered passers-by the beauty of her flower garden that she nurtured and brought to life every spring. More than once she climbed the Manse back steps and secretly left little parcels of baking, vegetables and such. That was Margaret. If those who harmed her would only have sat and visited with her, I'm sure they would never do it again. For they would appreciate that caring, special person as Lesley and I did.

I kicked myself that I didn't hear the break in, and felt bad about it afterwards. We lived right next door. Ironically neither did a jail guard who lived right across the road hear or respond to the break-in. His German shepherd dog unfortunately seemed to bark all the time and not just as needed. I left a couple of notes asking politely, if he'd try to keep his dog from lunging at people walking on the public side walk, and if he'd try to stop his dog's incessant barking. The Jail Guard wrote back, "You stop harassing me, or I'll take you to court!"

Despite the fact that people needed jobs, a citizens' planning committee, appointed by the mayor, which I chaired, did turn up its nose at having an industrial waste disposal transfer station locate near Mission. Working with representatives concerned with environmental interests from the BC Law Society, along with a highly respected doctor, we warded off what might have been future disastrous chemical spills, especially from trucks crossing the bridge over the Fraser River.

Clergy, I found, are not always seen as having any thing to offer outside the church precincts. Mission City's mayor at the time, a woman with NDP credentials, thought otherwise. Through her initiative I had the opportunity to get a glimpse of the procedures leading up to the unionizing of the local credit union.

Though a rural town, many in Mission City's population were very cosmopolitan. The doctors at the hospital could tap the best expertise through their home computers. People like the wealthy Sikh family "on the hill " above the shopping centre, did business all over the world. I believe I can attribute my five-year ministry to the strong and diverse leadership base within St. Andrew's congregation. They were rugged individuals with lots of talents.

Lillian, the church secretary, a Cape Breton Islander, and proud of it, knew just about everything that was happening with people in the church. If you wanted to know anything, "Ask Lillian." Oh so true. Church secretaries really are a source of knowledge, and so have a lot of power in a congregation. When I first dug into the life and work of the local church, I tried to get the decision-making out of the office and back in the hands of the Official Board members elected by the congregation. I found that to be necessary in more than one church family that I had served.

The people outside the church office were more than capable and dedicated to boot! John and May, both strong personalities, were caring and committed to the church family and the neighbourhood. Both retired from hospital work. They often took the "bull by the horns," lifting, driving, baking to make life much better for many. I sometimes got John off track, enticing him to relate his war stories. As a veteran, having joined the army in his early teens, John could vividly relive his battles and prisoner of war experiences. His descriptions were bloody and very graphic.

Don, a dentist who also served in the war, and his wife Ethel, were like an older brother and sister to

Lesley and me. Don served the Mission City people for over thirty-five years "pulling teeth" he'd say. With the same dedication he wrestled with the church sound system and the political intrigue inherent in most congregations.

There were some other faithful church members, more long suffering than Don; Muriel, the organist for one. She matched her dedication to Windebank Plumbing, a business her uncle started many decades ago, with her dedication to her church, both playing and sharing her beautiful voice. Though the Windebank business was sold out of the family, Muriel stayed on, suffering somewhat in silence as a valued employee. For with Muriel came the goodwill and incredible knowledge of a business within which she was raised. It seemed that her church music was the melody, the business the harmony, though the business now and then sounded a discord or two.

The Mission City congregation could boast of others like Muriel. The membership included persons from many professions and callings, accountants, the town administrator, pharmacists, teachers, doctors, and foresters, But unfortunately there were very few trades people such as plumbers, and electricians. It seemed so typical of a middle class United Church. The consequence of having very few trades people in the congregation was that the repair bills often mounted up. When the church boiler threatened to give up the ghost, it sent the property committee into a tizzy. The A frame building with attached CE rooms and auditorium sat itself down on a concrete pad. The concrete once contained an architect's dream of having the heating pipes encased in that concrete. Heaving happened, pipes ruptured, and the mess caused a new heating system to live within the building. That no doubt disturbed the army ants (or whatever they were) causing them to rise up in arms, march through the building, and gradually ingest and digest the building's footings. The building, thrown up in haste years ago, resembled a summer cottage lacking sufficient insulation and security features. Doors and windows were "paper thin," thus offering costly challenges to keep repaired and free of break-ins.

Fortunately Mission City was blessed with the volunteer services of a man with a strong business sense, who knew accounting. Doug and his wife Lorna had returned from serving a stint through our national church in Papua, New Guinea There Doug worked in tandem with a local manager of a Coop. The intent was that some Canadian know-how would rub off on the local manager who would later take over and run the business. Lorna taught nursing. When she and her husband returned to worship at St. Andrew's, she got the congregation to sponsor a "woman at risk " from Iran. That woman, a widow with two young boys with Persian names, proved a challenge. She apparently missed the great wealth to which she had once been accustomed. Reality had set in. Though church members were making a sincere effort to meet the one year commitment to support the family with shelter and necessities, as the Federal government required, still she wasn't satisfied. Misunderstandings occurred. That made the life of the project a very rocky one, unlike a previous "boat family" sponsoring project. Yet, as it has been said

God tempers the wind to the shorn lamb.   1

The congregation did indeed find the strength to fulfill its obligation to help that "woman at risk." The church family also reached out in other ways. For years the congregation provided space for a unique day care, which in time, began to spill over into other rooms in the place. The church charged rent, but began to wonder whether it was worth competing with the day care for space. I, for one, also had to admit that the vocal outbursts and wailing were very disturbing. Unlike the day care staff, I wasn't trained to work in a special needs environment. Believing that the church activities need not have to work around those of the day care, which appeared increasingly to impinge on the life and work of the church, I approached the church's Official Board, asking if the members would revisit the day care's contract. The Church Board decided to ask the Day Care Board of Directors to seek another place to operate.

The congregation got bad press. I felt some people were accusing us of being insensitive, callous, selfish, and not sympathetic to special needs children and their parents. By confronting head on a smoldering situation, and being willing to take the knocks from the public spurred on by bad press, a "win, win" resulted. A man who heard of the day care's plight came up with financial resources to build its own independent facility in memory of his child. The centre was named after that donor, and proved to be a far better facility than anything it had before. That freed up space for more church-sponsored programs. The experience verified the need sometimes to confront a festering issue head on. For as Ben, my former ethics teacher in seminary often said, one can suffer from "paralysis of analysis."

Looking back on that experience reminded me not to fret for, in the words of one

> When you are getting kicked in the rear it means you are in front.   2

I learned that trying to accommodate others by providing space, often has its draw backs. "Look before you leap " still seems a good motto. Like the church, I leaped without considering Lesley. Bob, a piano teacher from Lake Erroch, had limited resources. It seemed he had inadvertently encroached on someone's space in the Anglican church, where he had given piano lessons. He was asked to leave. I heard about it and suggested he could rent the manse basement. He did. His students used our one washroom upstairs, and Lesley's laundry room became his waiting room. Lesley suffered in silence while more than one child, favouring one particular song, beat it to death. Bob accepted the fact the well-meaning arrangement wouldn't work and found a more suitable home for his fine monster of an antique piano.

Oh, the beauty of avoiding beating around the bush with people-a lesson I found reinforced by the actions of two new-found friends. Decisiveness seemed to be a word not found in everyone's vocabulary, but it was found in Co and Maniam's! They, as church members, were great supporters of Amnesty International, and had a deeply ingrained sense of responsibility that helped ensure St. Andrew's church kept its integrity. Their staying power was, as kids say, "Awesome! " Co's frugal ethnic, strict attention to detail as church treasurer for years, in the end, earned the respect of those confessing to be "spendthrifts." It's often said that church treasurers need nerves of steel to keep churches afloat. The UCW's financial bail out every summer wasn't always quite enough.

   Maniam and Co's hard work and sacrifice extended far beyond Mission City or, for that matter, Canada. The couple made it possible for a niece and nephew to have a country where otherwise, they would have been landless. The couple's efforts resulted in the two that they sponsored gaining good professions. Both Maniam and Co had, as youth, survived the dreadful occupation of their homelands, Co, by the Nazis, Maniam by the Japanese land forces. They knew hardship from an early age. That obviously affected their approach to life, displaying a mix of gentleness and toughness. I admired the likes of Co and Maniam, and Hank and his wife Lee. Hank and Maniam, commuted for years, logging thousands of miles, to get to hospitals where they worked. They were examples of people who, despite exhaustion, dug deep within themselves and found energy to give to their church and its causes. They did that despite the pain, suffering, and even the frustrations of the wider community that were often dumped on the church. Somehow the human spirit never fails to prevail over adversity.

The human spirit, I believe, may not necessarily always win. Nevertheless, hanging in there to see it through certainly helped even when the future seemed bleak. I marvelled at the courage that so many whom I knew demonstrated every day, that they could still struggle to draw yet another breath.

Bob, a St. Andrew's member and volunteer, one day, after hauling a truck load of free, frozen broccoli and fish from a plant shutting down, broke the news that doctors had diagnosed him as having the fatal A.L.S. disease. Prior to that, even though knowing something was wrong with his body, he hauled and labouriously spread gravel on the manse back driveway, all without fanfare or any expected reward. I watched him slowly die that year, his frail body shutting down a bit at a time. I remember his wife once standing on a chair and with Bob replacing a hall light fixture in the manse. Now she couldn't bring back the light into his eyes.

"Why do bad things happen to good people? "

I had too often turned to the book of Job with Bob and others, and painfully said,

"We do not understand all the intricacies of life. All that we know is that God is with us, not only in the joy, but in the suffering. We are never alone! "

Mart Kenney, the famous band leader, another member of St. Andrew's, also shed tears when he watched his loving wife Norma Locke slowly die of a brain tumour. Her courageous fight, comforted by family and friends, and even their giant Bouvier dog, gave meaning to the last days of her life. Her cremains were interred in the park where the Norma Locke House is located. Norma was instrumental in leading a fight to save the old RC. Indian residential school grounds from the developers, to preserve it for public use. Like Norma, Mart Kenney was amazing. He still did "gigs," in his eighties, having bands awaiting his arrival to lead them in major cities. He also served on the town council for years.

Others in the church did not live quite as exciting lives, but still found ways to contribute meaningfully to their church and community. Julie, who lived down the lane from the church, over the years conscientiously went far beyond the call of duty as chair of the property committee, to give the church building the attention it demanded and deserved. Her faithful dog accompanied her on her voluntary nightly inspections of the building. Whether it would or could protect her if she was attacked went unanswered, but as she said,

"It was some comfort to know that I wasn't alone."

Julie's matter of fact, shrug off compliments approach to her service to her church was matched by Bill. He was a kind tough "old bird" who lived in Matsqui. Encouraged by his good wife, despite her stroke, Bill not only grew an impressive vegetable garden, but produced a sea of pumpkins every year;

"For the school kids, to come and get for Halloween," he'd say. Once, Bill surprised me, and no doubt the kids, by pointing up to a tree saying,

"I bet you didn't know pumpkins grow in trees."

Sure enough, a pumpkin up above cast an orange light on my shiny bald head. Bill's family and others had made Mission City their church home way back when the church was located near Main Street where the library then stood.

Other persons who had been around a long time sang in the choir. The space in the choir loft was apparently limited by the number of chairs provided. When Lesley and I arrived, that was made very clear by the comment of one choir member that, "There isn't any more room up here," The "think small attitude" underlined the need to follow the rule of thumb: the more parking spaces you have in the church building or outside, the more people will come. For people to feel welcomed and comfortable they need "personal space." Given that is so, the size of church facilities determined the size of the congregation. It would grow no larger than it was. Some families, bless their hearts, didn't pay any attention to that theory or the unspoken message from a few that there was no space in the choir. They just laughed and joked their way into the good graces of the congregation sharing their open trusting nature, and most, including myself, really appreciated their God-given talents.

The Taves, Mary-Ann, and John were like Bill, full of fun! They were from good Mennonite stock, and met in Bible College which they called a "Matrimonial Bureau," The enthusiastic two, with their children, brought new life to St. Andrew's United Church. While they were there they sang, strummed guitars, and taught, linking up with another neat family where the husband played the drums, his wife, the piano, and the children pitched in with their music. One can only imagine the incredible blue grass sounds that filled the clear mountain air up at Steelhead, where lots of their flower generation-like types lived to dance and make music.

What delightful characters were the Taves, a real breath of fresh air! Picture in your mind, years back, a couple of kids in their late teens hitching rides, their faces encrusted with ice, their eyes peering through a Manitoba winter blizzard, oblivious to the stranger staring them in the face. They did that! Picture them again years later, driving a dilapidated T.V. Beverly HillBilly-like camper truck, across the same prairie, destination Ontario. Picture them again, returning with their camper trailer wearing a strange looking hat, a load of roped down furniture and other household stuff. Going home-that's right, through the mountains, but not before stopping at what they called "The Taber mall," (that was the town dump). Why stop? Of course, to pick up a big old "could be cleaned" bread pan to add to the truck's hat collection, and a cast iron frying pan for Lesley. Good-byes sent the Taves family rumbling off toward the west. Back in Mission hills expecting their return would be their sheep that answered Mary-Ann's "Baas," and their goat that thought it was a person who often loitered on their back stoop expecting lunch. Also awaiting their homecoming were rows of raspberry canes to attend to, a big garden, chickens to do up using their rubber plucking machine, home brew, sausage to prepare. and Mary-Ann's baseball coaching chores, something she had done for years.

Mission City had no shortage of other characters. Lesley answered the door one day. A gentleman reached out and handed her a loaf of sour dough bread. I had forgotten to tell her that a retired doctor in town, a sour dough enthusiast who even wrote a major paper on the stuff, had offered me a taste after I had heard that he had that hobby.

St. Andrew's church worship times also enabled a glimpse at the thinking of others. When I first arrived, the service wasn't to start till Min, a long time choir member, flew in through the door from Silverdale. A few Sundays later, services began to start promptly at eleven a.m. Min found I had this thing about punctuality, a hangover I guess from my teaching days. The year I was in charge of the Rotary Carol Festival Min again asserted her preference, arriving late for the choir performance, to her surprise.

Min, like so many other women whom Lesley and I admired, kept tight calendars. She gave much of herself to the church and to the hospital women's auxiliary, raising funds through the thrift shop, and pushing carts about the hospital. She helped the patients to get their minds off their pain and loneliness.

Some patients confronted their pain with silent resignation, only going into hospital when it was absolutely unbearable, thus revealing the power of the human spirit to overcome the worst of times. A young mother with M.S, who was confined to a wheelchair, still cared for her children in a rented home since her house had burnt down. Her circumstances were in glaring contrast to the young hospital administrator, who with illusions of grandeur, I think, refurnished his office suite to equal that of royalty.

It seemed to me that though people live in a place like Mission, many still live in different worlds. Depending on their life styles, they were labelled, "yuppies," the aging hippies and "draft dodgers" from the States, the "hard hats," commuters and seniors. Many seniors lived in nursing homes and senior complexes in town such as St. Andrew's Place. Years ago Mr. and Mrs. U.G. Mueller and a young United Church minister spearheaded its creation and shared with others in getting it off the ground. U.G. and his wife had been active leaders in the Co-op movement back in Saskatchewan and lived by high moral and ethical standards. I felt, though, in my many visits with the couple, that U.G. wasn't the man that he once had been. Age had eroded his intellect to the point where one day his wife phoned me,

"Ken, you must come over and do something with UG. He won't believe me that you didn't ride up in your horse and buggy to see us the other day. Please do come!"

I found that so often wives ended up nursing their aging husbands, in and out of nursing homes. Sometimes they walked long distances winter and summer to be at their husbands' side to feed them, wheel them about, and even change their diapers. Whenever I interviewed a couple in preparation for marriage, where the man was much older than the woman, I would ask the woman if she would be prepared to feed and toilet her husband when he became old and frail. So many sad pictures surfaced: a wife reaching out to moisten her husband's cracked lips, only to have him open his mouth like a little bird expecting food, bringing tears to her eyes.

I also visited a retired school superintendent who had suffered a severe stroke and lost his ability to speak. He only talked with his sad looking eyes. Yet despite, that, his wife continued to tend his needs with love and affection. From a nursing home, an elderly man wheeled his wife, suffering from dementia, down the street, through church and back to the home.

Then there was Winnie who had been a prairie railway station agent's wife. May and John, or I, would get a call that Winnie was "on the loose again." Once a friend rescued her while she was carrying a garbage bag down the middle of the bridge overpass, totally oblivious to the traffic rushing by her, brakes squealing and horns honking. Another time, Winnie walked into a parishioner's home. The lady called me,

"Winnie is here, I don't know what she wants."

I phoned the nursing home. I asked,

"Do you know where Winnie is?"

The staff replied, She's in her room! Why?"

I whispered to myself, "Guess again!" but said, "Because she just dropped in for tea a few blocks away from you."

No one had heard the warning door buzzer when she left. A more noble picture in the same nursing home was that of a dear elderly couple, arm in arm, shuffling down the hall with the most tranquil looks on their weather-worn faces.

Not every senior enjoyed such secure peace. Elderly parent abuse was not uncommon. One mentally ill mother suffered emotional abuse from her adult son who insisted that she identify with and support the religious cult in which he wallowed. She was so troubled because he wanted her to forsake her friends and religion. The torment that she went through was hard for me to watch in the months that I knew her. I grew very irate seeing cults such as the J.W's practising "shunning." When Lesley's and my good friend, a United Church minister died, his oldest son, who grew up in United Church congregations, but married a J.W. wouldn't go to his dad's funeral. It is sad when children choose to stay away from their parents because of religious beliefs.

A Postscript: I heard that many years later the oldest son did reconnect with his family after he and his wife left the JWs.

Often adult children, as many elderly parents say with some sad resignation, "have their own lives to live."

Sometimes an elderly widow will even out live her married son, as did Mrs Coffin. Then, because of constant phone calls, demands to come right over, indirect repetitious hints of being neglected by friends, the care givers "burn out." That leaves folks like Mrs. Coffin to adjust to paid "strangers " from Home Care. I felt really low when I had to say to Peggy,

"Look, I've a couple of hundred other people

whom I am called to minister to as well as you. I'll pray that you'll understand."

It is so frustrating that people like Peggy, who insist on living in their own homes, don't realize that, sometimes it is only possible by making unreasonable demands on so many care givers. In order for them to stay put in their own homes, they often become very shrewd and manipulative. I felt controlled that way when Peggy would even phone my predecessor, then living in Vancouver, causing me to feel very inadequate. I became even more uptight when I got it into my head that, more than once, he and his wife would "come to Peggy's rescue." Then I'd be the "heavy" on the scene, having refused to run across the street to answer her beck and call when she felt bored or lonely.

It was because of the Mrs. Coffin incident that I soon realized that, although my predecessor had left town in body, his soul kept marching on through the lives of the community. Like many other clergy in other towns, I felt that he showed that he found it hard to let go of "his" congregation, as did some in the congregation of him. I found out that some in the church family looked upon him as a father figure. Some people repeated his wife's name often saying proudly,

"She did this, and she did that" or "That's not the way she would have done it."

Lesley tried to get it across that she was not the minister's wife who had gone, while I tried to strongly convey the message that I wasn't "He" who had left. I became very annoyed by the frequent return of that man on the invitation of church families to do funerals. I often berated myself for not discouraging the practice. I felt put on the spot. If I objected, the family would think that I was less than understanding or caring, putting my own interests above theirs. If I put my foot down with him I would, perhaps, be showing that I felt very insecure, which was a "no, no," and a sign of weakness in character. I tried to give this conscientious servant of God the benefit of the doubt.

Had he merely stopped with funerals, I might, over time, had got used to the interference, or someday found the courage to confront the man. However, he never stopped there. He often wrote articles, published in the local newspaper, on social issues. People reading the items often would assume that his stands on issues represented those of the local church of which I was minister, or those of the United Church of Canada. A quiet-spoken gentleman and devoted church member whom I respected for his integrity, a former pharmacology prof., knew him as his minister for several years. I asked him to talk to that retired minister about his annoying habit.

Yet, I did accept that, just as it is hard for a parent to let go of a child, and a child of a parent, so also is it very hard for some ministers to let go of their congregations, and for some members to do the same. I recognized that it would be hard to match the role expectations engendered by my predecessor who, in the eyes of many, had been a seven-year success. No doubt many were going through a grieving process. Presbytery had told the congregation that they should consider an interim minister for a couple of years to get the man out of their system. However, St. Andrew's called me. It must have been a surprise to Presbytery that I stayed five years.

Despite the haunting presence of that well meaning, devoted United Church minister, my predecessor, lurking in the memory of the St. Andrew's people, I still felt that I was ministering. I had to also believe that I wasn't so hard hearted in comparison to the man's "fatherly and caring nature."

Serving on the board of the local Palliative Care Society gave me the opportunity to interview visitors to the bedside of the dying at home or in hospital, even if they were not closely connected to our congregation. Many dying persons witnessed to me with their courage. In one instance a young dying father sat surrounded by his worldly possessions that he was selling at a garage sale. The pain of seeing a man face death head-on was both profound and sometimes tear wrenching.

Yet it was never as painful as hearing how people deliberately caused death: a murder in a park, drug house violence at Deroche, drunken or drugged out kids wrapping their cars around poles or, stoned out of their minds, drowning in an overturned car in a few feet of water. No time to say "good bye's " or have second chances. What waste!

Then there were the suicides. Sometimes people were really left with a dilemma. One local legend claimed that a family wanted to have their loved one's body interned in the local RC. grave yard. At first that seemed impossible. He had committed suicide, an act frowned upon by the RC. Church. A solution was found. They dug the grave so that his body would be laid with his head outside the fence and the rest of his body within the church yard. Why that way? Because, they reasoned, it was his brain that made the decision to take his life, not his body.

Many tragedies happened, though, that were not the doing of the victims. I found it very hard to minister to a mom and dad whose tragedy hit the local paper.

"A helicopter log harvesters tragedy. Ben killed 150 metres from the spot where his 45 year old brother Todd died, struck by a tree during a helicopter shake -block operation 6 kms. North of the head of Power Lake."

That terrible tragedy was overshadowed by a horrible axe slaying of members of one family, a 9 year old girl, her 11 year old brother, and their mother and dad who had married in the nineteen-seventies. Their teenage son, and foster son axed them to death while they were asleep.

School friends and their parents were devastated. Their anguish was tormented even more when they heard that the slain girl was planning to overnight at a friend's house, but the friend had a cold.

The T.V. people wanted cameras in the church for the funeral. I said, Absolutely not! They were very understanding and I allowed the unobtrusive presence of mikes. But I told them they were to be well out of view of the door of the church with their cameras.

Everyone in Mission was tormented by the tragedy and asked over and over "Why?" My prayers were with all touched by the senseless, unexpected event. Like other moments, it will leave scars in the memories of the Mission City community no doubt forever, along with several unsolved murders.

It seemed that Mission City continued to have more than its share of tragedies. Some were hard learned experiences. An elderly couple at Deroche had waded into the river near their country home. The husband tried to save his wife who lost her footing. They both drowned! A family member asked me to commit their cremains on their property. After the appropriate words of committal, I released the cremains from the container, throwing them. They landed on a small bush in the couple's garden. To my dismay many particles appeared like minute bone fragments. I encouraged those present to make a hasty retreat before they started to ponder how the words, "Ashes to ashes, and dust to dust" could really be relevant in that instance. I chalked the experience up to bad planning on my part, cautioning myself to never again take anything for granted. The couple deserved a more dignified send off than that!

I conducted a more appropriate committal service for a couple whose lives were instantly snuffed out by a careless driver. He passed on a tight curve in the fog and rain on the nearby highway-a real killer strip at the best of times. The couple had owned a fantasy theme park depicting Disney-like characters, that they had laboured over for years. I committed their cremains to a grotto that their adult children created in their park garden.

While in Mission City, I experienced so many needless deaths including the death of our dear friend and mentor. He, his wife, Lesley and I went all the way back to old St. Andrew's United Church days in Winnipeg. His death seemed so unnecessary!

Much to his wife's disapproval, following retirement he had insisted on filling in at different churches in the Fraser Presbytery while they were searching for new ministers. His style of doing interim ministry work often demanded long days and hard driving. He had promised his wife that, on retiring, they would travel as a reward for their work in Canada and as Missionaries in India. They would visit their kids and grandchildren. One day he suddenly suffered terrible chest pains. Rather than get to a hospital quickly, he drove himself to Abbotsford miles away. His wife insisted that he go to hospital immediately! He reluctantly did. I visited him the next day. "No problem!" he intimated. I heard the next day that he had died of an aneurysm! I conducted the funeral. His long time friend and school mate gave the eulogy. He and his friend had agreed that when one died, the other would do the eulogy. My friend had the last word though, as he often did. Picture this: his last wish was that his remains be scattered from a galloping horse on the family farm back in Manitoba. I wonder if it happened?

Just as he had been one of my mentors I felt that I too, could help students by sharing my experiences.

With that in mind I signed up for a Supervisor's course at Vancouver School of Theology. The course became somewhat of an unexpected nightmare for me! One trainer often criticized me for interrupting, telling me to "bite my tongue." He made me feel like a little boy again. He told me to forego my bad habit of "butting in." He also implied that I had a hard time relating to women. That came as a surprise to me since I had been working with women for years, and married for many more. Surprised and down in the mouth, I felt beaten!

That criticism as to how I came across in a group, and the hassle of fighting traffic each day from Mission to Vancouver got me asking, do I really need that? My feeling of indignation was amplified by the fact that, if I were to become a supervisor of theological students, I'd have a long road ahead. I was told to take a Group Dynamic lab at Naramata Training Centre before I could do the job. After the course, I stewed awhile in my own juices, licked my wounds, vowing never to follow-through to become a supervisor. Yet, eventually this truth became incarnate

Our greatest glory is not in never failing but in rising every time that we fail 3.

A post script: I did become a supervisor, thus verifying what I heard the one trainer and critic say, that I showed remarkable resilience. Good for me! It also proves the fact that

When an emotional injury takes place, the body begins a

process as natural as the healing of a physical wound. Let the process happen. Trust that nature will do the healing. Know that the pain will pass and, when it passes. You will be stronger, happier, more sensitive and aware. 4

Despite the pain of confronting death so often, the ministry had its moments. I often cringed when a mother would phone and say,
"We're thinking of having the kid done,"
(meaning baptised) That conjured up in my mind all kinds of images. Nevertheless I did baptize, finding pleasure in celebrating a child being incorporated into the one church with Jesus Christ as the Head. Still, I believed that God accepted all children, whether baptized or not, for, to me, our Creator is a loving and caring being and does not reject anyone.

Weddings could also be a joyful time, not only for the wedding party, but for me. Just as I didn't turn anyone away who wanted a child baptized, I never turned away any man and woman who wanted to make their vows in the presence of God. If they perjured themselves that was between them and God. I wasn't about to take on the burden of feeling responsible for their decisions. The odd time a person said to me,
"Don't you feel responsible for that marriage break down?"
My answer, "Of course not!" Persons must ultimately be responsible for themselves. The church is not called to be a crutch for human beings; nor should it, in my opinion, make mental cripples of persons who darken the doors of the church. People should not leave their brains at the door of the church before

they enter.

I often wondered how three interesting wedding couples made out. Henry was, I believe, the head of a biker gang. I found him to be a real gentleman in my presence. When the wedding party left the church on their big Harleys, Henry, his wife, and guests, flipped up their tails, and gowns, revved their engines, and moved off in fine formation, followed, by elderly bikers and their wives in side cars, suitably helmeted, goggled, and off with a roar. An afternoon wedding followed accompanied by sedate harp and flute chamber music. The very refined sight was enhanced by the smell of leather still hovering in the air.

Another day, a couple did a free fall to eventually guide their parachutes to land in the church backyard in front of the guests and me. Stripping off their jump suits they paraded into the sanctuary and were married in great style.

Moments, unlike those, did arise however, when I shuddered, having heard what the wedding hostess confronted. I had no doubt that May, our wedding hostess, could handle herself in any situation, having once worked in a store front street clinic in the toughest part of Vancouver. She did most of the wedding rehearsals. At the weddings she also acted as "a trouble shooter." Sometimes, she had to call upon all her past experiences to deal with surprises. Once a groom and attendants took the liberty of setting up a bar in the back Sunday School room before the wedding. Another time, some characters broke open a six pack on the church front steps before the bride arrived. And yet, still another time a ring bearer, carrying a pillow with the real ring, swung the pillow around his head just for fun and lost the ring in the church narthex. It was five or so minutes before the service. Perspiration dripped into the groom's eyes, glistening with tears of frustration. Fortunately the ring was found just before May planned to offer to let the groom use her wedding ring to fill the temporary gap. May once even mended a tear in a groom's pants. The combinations of challenging, unexpected events were many. Yet she conquered them all! I, like May, often had to revisit this truth to be non judgmental while serving

When we see men of a contrary character, we should turn inwards and examine ourselves. 5

I had my share of surprises too, especially when couples came to me seeking to be married. A young lady once came accompanied by a young man who made no bones about it that he was a cross-dresser. He didn't fight with her over the fact that she had, without asking, given all his finery to the Salvation Army Thrift Store.

Another time a ragged and tired looking young fellow whose bony knees were showing through the tears in his jeans, asked if he could be married in the church. He would be willing to work off the cost of a wedding since all his cash went into his boat in dry dock. Fine, done!

Stranger things were yet to come! One day someone outside the church family, a very troubled lady in her fifties shared her problem. She found, to

258

her dismay, that the person whom she was married to for many years wasn't a man after all, but a woman. Apparently her "man" had been raised in the back woods of another province as a boy. As an adult she faked male behaviour for years, binding up her breasts and remaining well clothed in bed. The poor distraught "wife," to my amazement hadn't caught on for years. Now she wanted to know if the marriage could be annulled. I suggested that she contact the minister who performed the marriage, or better still, the person who issued the marriage licence, Wow, what a dilemma!

I wasn't surprised over the years at bizarre human behaviour. I did once find it troublesome, though, when a young woman, for whom I had performed a wedding, came crying, saying that she found out after the wedding that her young professional, up and coming husband,, had deceived her. She discovered he was a regular customer of a sex shop mail order house and had "very kinky views about sex."

I regretted that I had not spent more time and energy counselling the couple. I made the mistake of being mesmerized by the young man's professional air, and his logical delivery of information. I also thought the bride-to-be was very intelligent, cautious, and streetwise. Obviously I was mistaken!

It takes some doing sometimes, to maintain faith in human nature. Just before I arrived at Mission City some kids trashed the church, tearing pages from the pulpit Bible and leaving the congregation feeling uneasy. The culprits merely got a slap on the wrist and one boy was made to help our caretaker Billy for a while. I felt he would rather not have had the kid around since obviously the trust wasn't there.

Intruders with devious intent were not uncommon in churches, as I found out even before ministering at St. Andrew's, Mission City. Yet still I was taken by surprise one morning. When I unlocked the church outside door leading into the hall, a head poked out from my study, then quickly disappeared. I was tongue tied for a moment, then I shouted

"Stop, stay right there!"

I heard a thump, then the intruder escaped around the corner and was gone. When I stepped into my study I found a Jughead comic book and some junk food wrappers and containers on my desk. It appeared that when I opened the door into the church I must have roused him from his sleep on my desk, his bed for the night. I heard later from Billy, the caretaker, that he had chased that character quite a way till he lost him in the bushes. I had some sympathy for the intruder. Billy chased him into the blackberry bushes. He would have suffered what I did when I tried picking black berries. I felt that thorns had constantly clawed at me.

Yet, not all strangers were unwelcome like that night prowler. One day a fellow came off the street to make an offer that I couldn't really refuse. He offered to do a mural for free, provided the church supplied the materials. Immediately I thought of the wall between the church kitchen and the lounge. It had been declared impossible to do anything with, for many thought its varnished surface couldn't be painted over. I suggested the artist have a look at it. He did, and given the freedom to pick his own theme and motif, he went ahead, not the least concerned about the wall's varnished surface. The result? A mural made up of little simplified figures depicting the completing of a jig saw puzzle. In conversations with him, I found out that he had been in a serious vehicle accident and received a generous insurance settlement. Thereafter, feeling his life had been spared for a purpose, he committed himself to painting murals in schools, institutions and wherever anyone would let him. Before he started on our wall, he told me that I could find a sample of his mural work down the hill at the drop-in centre and social service's offices, which once was the Mission City hospital. I saw and was impressed. I was also pleased with our mural. It was a sequence of figures trailing across the wall culminating with a figure reaching out to ponder how to fit in the last piece of the puzzle, "of life." Looking back, I thought, what a rare unselfish figure in this day and age, a modern day Johnny Appleseed with a motto,

"Have paint brushes will travel."

That fellow caused me to look within myself, and also within the United Church of Canada, to find out whether that unexpected dedication to a good cause was evident there within me and in others.

In the United Church there are no bishops to act like political party whips to provide extrinsic motivation. One's motivation must come from within. Fraser Valley Presbytery to which I was required to belong and answer to, and in theory receive support and encouragement from, met in various churches throughout Fraser Valley. I often found driving to those places intimidating, looking down deep gorges, at hovering rock faces, and manoeuvring around hair pin curves on narrow roads.

I felt the same way when meeting retired military chaplains, serving in pastoral charges. At times I felt really out of my league. I felt like the new kid coming from the other side of the tracks (river), from a church family that was looked upon less favourably than others. Now I see that I was off base. At the time, though, I felt like I was tiring, like one of those hooked sturgeons dragging a boat up and down the Fraser River.

Another way to look at it allegorically: Fishing in the Fraser was far more complicated. One had to know about the different regulations for different fish runs. It wasn't as simple as I remembered fishing in prairie lakes with a simple Len Thompson spoon or two, and few regulations. In Presbytery I never really caught onto the game, and so didn't know how to fit into the system. In fact one day one of whom I considered a "power figure" in Presbytery, a clergyman-who eventually went east, whisked by me during one of the breaks. In passing he asked me if I'd serve on the Stewardship Committee. Later, he reminded me of my commitment. It had totally slipped my mind. I said,

"I have no idea what you're talking about. Are you sure you were talking to me?"

He was very loud and abrupt and said,

"Absolutely! There isn't anyone else here that looks

like you! "

I became totally confused and reached out for help
to a fellow minister I had known years ago at Norway
House. He had recently retired as a military chaplain
to serve a church.

"You didn't hear me volunteer did you?" I pleaded.
He just grinned, showing I'd get no help from him.
Later I realized that he hadn't been anywhere near
me when I was asked to volunteer. I came to the
conclusion after that experience that I'd take the
advice of James Glass, with whom I had once taken a
Church management course at VST in Vancouver. He
offered this advice,

"There are ought to's, want to's and have to's.
Don't do the ought to's, you will never make anyone
happy. Do the have to's to pay the rent, and the want
to's to be happy."

Remembering that, I decided I would do the bare
minimum for Presbytery. I also resigned from some
other community activities that I felt were "ought
to's" and did the "want to's" instead, which mainly
involved working with the St. Andrew's congregation.
So I got a Demit from the Masons, resigned my
position as president of the local Rotary club, and
started to give some thought to finding more time for
Lesley and me to do things together, and to revisit
some of my hobbies. For it was becoming obvious
that I was on the verge of burn out.

It was while reexamining my place in the scheme
of things that I experienced what I thought at first
were interesting flashing lights within my good left
eye. It began after I had lugged a lot of chairs back

to the church auditorium after the funeral of a prominent shake mill owner. I remember that day, just as some evangelicals remember the day and the hour when they were converted. In my case I found myself in trouble. I described for my doctor on paper what I was seeing. It was like looking through a screen made up of small dots like a newspaper photograph. My doctor in Mission City referred me quickly to an ophthalmologist in Abbotsford across the river whom I felt at the time was run off his feet with patients. He sent me home untreated. After a week or two my condition got worse. Back I went. He told me to get to hospital in Burnaby immediately. I drove myself in with Lesley at my side. It was a close call. I almost lost my sight in that eye due to a detached retina. I returned to Mission City with eyes looking like they had been dipped in red food dye. I thanked the Rev. Golightly for conducting one wedding I was to do. He was apparently worse off than me, suffering from macular degeneration. Fortunately he had the service memorized long ago and did well.

When the chips were down Lesley and I found that people were there to minister to us. John, an excellent driver, picked me up at the hospital. I sported a patch on one eye. John led me in a stupor from the hospital by the arm to his car and brought me home. I remember that much.

Driving about in Mission City for a prairie person was stressful at the best of times. I worried about Lesley driving about in what we called her "rust bucket," a Volkswagen Rabbit purchased from our next door neighbour, an RCMP officer who brought it down from the Yukon. When Lesley wasn't tearing back and forth between Silverdale, Mission City, Hatzic, and Deroche as a special needs assistant, she sometimes went with me on visits. Sometimes, we found ourselves on a slippery slope, fearful of not being able to coax the car further up the hill, nor to ease it back down.

Our good friends John and May, on the other hand, as home grown BC-ites , had no trouble navigating hills summer or winter, mud or snow. In fact one winter, like caring inn keepers, they kept watch for stranded people who couldn't slither up one slippery street made worse by heavy wet snow. What those travellers were experiencing, I was too.

I appreciated it when people let me know of others whom they thought their minister should visit. I had problems, though, when a person wanted to sic me onto someone who was "a bad one." I would have no part in playing the canine role let loose by its owner. No doubt a few viewed me as the congregation's hired gun. I often did a lot of praying to keep from becoming a cynic. I was finding, with all that had happened, that my patience reached an all time low. I wasn't getting much joy out of the work anymore. I felt after five years that I needed a change. Yet I was not in a mental space to put my name on the list of ministers seeking a call. Lesley, I believed felt the same. She never did take kindly to the presence of the mountains fencing in the valley. Even the Fuji-like mountain seen from our kitchen window that people ooed and awed over didn't enthral her.

I got to appreciate, in time, Lesley's need to feel flat land rolling under the wheels of our car. Yet drives about the valley basin, sniffing what we called the "Matsqui Miasma,"calling out to the cows, knee deep in lush green grass, "Hello ladies,"didn't take away Lesley's homesickness for prairie and wide-open spaces. I often said there are vertical and horizontal thinkers. Lesley was definitely a horizontal thinker, looking for lots of sun and sky.

Many months earlier I had played Frankie Lane's "Wild goose song " at a funeral for one of the prominent lumber mill owners. I wondered if that was merely to fulfill a need that I had, namely, to muse over my longing to be free, or was it because I legitimately believed it right for a man who loved the outdoors? How much of what a minister does, is interwoven into his own subliminal needs?

I longed to be like the forty-five-year old whom I saw at early morning swims. He, a man with staying power entered the iron-man contests every year. I, on the other hand, couldn't say

"I was weak in spirit, but strong in body."

I was pleased, though, one day when Lesley and I visited Westminster Abbey on the hill to hear one of the brothers giving us a tour. He stopped in front of a couple of angel figures and asked,

"Do you know what is the angel's favourite song?"

"No" we said, thinking he'd tell us something very profound. "I Ain't Got No Body " (a once popular song title), he said.

Well, I ain't no angel, but I could relate to that, for

I felt quite drained. Yet right there so near to me was a perfect place for me to recharge my batteries. Many did by attending retreats at the Abbey, coming away refreshed and energized like those batteries that just keep on ticking and ticking. Regrettably I didn't do that. Instead, I started to see the prison bars, and not stars. Blinded by the clear cut eroded hills awash with mud and debris making way for new subdivisions, I lost sight of the beauty of the intense green, flowering foliage and rolling hills, a setting for the jewel-like abbey.

I started to see young teens wrapping themselves around poles in car accidents, as suicides in disguise. I felt it depressing that a school principal friend felt anguish when it seemed to me that the government of the day devised a way to cause a devastating rift between school principals and the teachers union. He once had a wonderful working rapport with his teachers. But then he was ostracized for trying to avoid the teachers' strike pickets by conscientiously getting on with his work.

I found it deploring to hear of a clergy's behaviour who was at St. Andrew's before my predecessor. When I was on the scene, he solicited funds from parishioners to grub stake his trip to another country, having done so without really touching base with me or the church Official Board. Clergy ethics seemed beyond his understanding.

I began to whisper under my breath, "Oh, the heck with it. I'll direct my thoughts and actions toward something more positive." My motivation was imbedded in this definition of God

What I mean by God is not the manager of a small, fourth floor department of life called religion. What I mean by God is the owner and operator of the entire business. God is either God of all, or he is not God at all.   6

With the view that churches could cooperate more, I talked off the record to the Anglican and Presbyterian ministers. I had thought that it would have benefited the Anglican, Presbyterian, and United congregations if they shared a church campus with common office and Christian Education facilities, and possibly separate sanctuaries, or one adaptable to different worship styles. Since St. Andrew's United church had land to spare, and their churches did not, and since their church congregations were seriously thinking of pulling up stakes and building elsewhere in Mission, the timing couldn't have been better. It made a lot of sense to suggest to the governing bodies of the three churches to consider pooling more of their resources.

Well, it didn't happen, and that was depressing. So also was it a bit much when attempts to seed an alternative idea to utilize St. Andrew's church spare land to build a seniors' complex. It, too, didn't go beyond the talking stage. Despite all the efforts of my good friend Don to make some good things happen, nothing much worked to get the church in sync. with our vision of St. Andrew's becoming even more relevant in the community.

I felt there was no need for those outside the church to paint all church denominations with the same brush. Anyone who did that I felt needed to be at the fielding end of this advice of ancient times

I bid him look into the lives of men as though into a mirror and from others to take an example for himself.   7

The United Church of Canada, staying true to its statement of faith was and is on the cutting edge between the sacred and the secular. Yes, we shoot ourselves in the foot some times trying to point the gun of righteous indignation at wrong. True, we sometimes put ourselves in the line of our own cross fire while seeking to make things better for others. Still, we do position ourselves in the front lines where the church should be. Despite my despondency, I felt good about the United Church, and abhorred the methods of others who sought, with glib talk, to convert to their own particular brands of denominationism the weak who were driven to their knees by "bad things happening to good people."

I was at the point where I felt that I was also watching plays develop locally but never scoring. I heard well-intentioned people, including myself, pontificating, finding our voices in a way freezing in the air. It was like the way the Last Post sounded when a Legion member's tape recorder started freezing up at the cemetery and offered inarticulate irrelevant wooooo sounds.

Oh, if only I could have been as effective as my friend, the school principal had been. He translated his military zeal to defend his homeland into great enthusiasm for presenting dramatic children's performances for Remembrance Day. I also felt wistful that I didn't have his commanding presence about me. He had an ability to get people to volunteer for jobs, as did Roddy, a lawyer who had made a gift of a computer to the church in memory of his father-in-law. Recruiting was never my forte as it was Roddy's.

I thought, also, if only I showed the humility and willingness to sacrifice as much as did one church member, an airline pilot who, before retiring, skilfully flew the Andes Mountains. He had enjoyed his work, but willingly sacrificed his career to care for his wife, a traffic accident victim.

I caught myself thinking more about the "if only's." However, before they got me completely down in the dumps, I revisited in my mind the kaleidoscope of characters that I had met, remembering even more people making up that wonderful wealth of colour and light. There were those I called the minstrels, a bunch of part time musicians, old in years; but could they make music to strut and shuffle to! The long white bearded smiling fiddler I married off to a lady who could play just about any thing you passed her way. I remember their garden wedding and the joy I felt. I also almost forgot the fisherman who was taking his new boat up the coast, and asked me to christen it and say a prayer over it. I felt honoured. That was good stuff!

I remember Sue and her dedication to the Junior choir, and Ron who, for many years, led the Senior choir and taught in the Dewdney School. His professional commitment to those two, and to his school band, as his students said, "was awesome!"

I guessed when thinking of those fine folk, as examples, it all came down to what that one famous playwright said

> This above all: to thine own self be true,
> And it must follow, as the night the day,
> thou canst not then be false to any man.   8

I almost forgot the pleasure I gained from what I thought was an innovative way to teach the Scouts' Religion and Life Award by using a unique paper plane that Grandpa Forgie taught me back when I was a kid in Regina. I was relieved to see that, by using it as a way to capture and keep up the interest of the kids, who literally were on the fly, my need to gain a positive response was met. Little moments of satisfaction weren't enough, though, to energize me.

So, after the five years at St. Andrew's, I was wallowing around in the bitter and the sweet, and starting to think very seriously of a change, not only to survive, but to grow. I accepted that to grow, the mental and spiritual stretching causes some pain. Yet how much more, and where would it take place?

Then to my surprise, completely unsolicited, came a letter from the Pastoral Relations Committee of a prairie town church. The committee secretary wrote,

"Since we notice that you have been five years in your present charge would you consider coming to our church?"

I wrote for and received more information. Then, after talking it over with Lesley and the people by phone, I tentatively accepted. Lesley and I took a bus trip out to see the town in January. We had a good look, met some of the people, returned to Mission City, and submitted my request for a change in pastoral relations effective June 30th. I had learned about fishing, lumber. Now I was about to learn about cattle, and sugar beets, corn, and other field crops, and above all else, about those great people who grow them.

At a memorial graveside service that I performed for an owner of a Chinese Cafe in Mission City, candy and a needle and thread were given out. The candy to taste the sweetness of life's experiences, the needle and thread to sew up the wounds, and the hurt remembered. At least that is how I understood it, as I will think of the Mission City venture: Sweet and sour, yet good stuff for Lesley and me to remember as we moved on to meet up with just a few more surprises.

18 More Than Country Folk

First impressions of Taber

As we approached Taber, our conversation was broken off by the harsh roar of a passing truck. A sharp bit of rock hit the windshield, leaving a ding at the driver's eye level, an annoyance in a day full of anticipation as we looked forward to meeting new people. Turning left at the lights we saw Knox Church on the corner of 50th and 50th, across from the well-treed Confederation Park. It was a heart-warming impression that lasted as we began to settle into a small town, and learn about southern Alberta farm and ranch life.

Farm Life-Alberta Style

One couple, among many, who made us feel at home were Doug and Dora. They, like many farm folk, were a team who generously opened their home to all who came their way. Thoughtful Dora, in the spirit of a former 4H Club mother, let no opportunity go by to value others. Her gifts of recognition included home baking, ice cream cakes topped off with CGIT or other church group logos. Doug, Dora's husband of many years, could have just shaken his head in dismay at Dora's dipping deep into their hard come-by resources. Doug's view, like many self reliant farmers and ranchers, seemed to be, "do it yourself, nobody gave me anything, inheriting nothing but sweat and toil," Yet he, too, opened his home and heart to young and old to show he cared.

That is not to say that Doug and Dora could not in the heat of the moment lose their temper like any farm folk, while cajoling a few more years out of older farm machinery scarred by the welding torch. They were only human! Yet, unlike some of us city bred, they had goodness burned into their souls from grit and by golly living as very young newly weds. They endured hard years of everything, from breaking horses gently instead of causing snorts, and foaming mouths that kill horses' spirits, to bites, kicks, and falls, burns, and burrs. Thus from the first, as weary farm hands, Doug and Dora scrimped and scraped to buy their land.

In my Taber stay, driving down the middle of township gravel roads into farm yards, and meeting the likes of Dora and Doug, I learned how working and feeding land and cattle shaped and formed their lives. Neither dirt nor beasts were willing to freely give up their treasures to feed Doug and Dora's family, nor any others. It took some doing. "You bet," Albertans would say!

It took, also, a sense of humour displayed by that farm couple and their families. Walking the path shaded by trees to their farm house on the home quarter, the hoot of an owl first greeted us, and at the door, the croak of a frog, both imitations of the real thing.

Not only did every tree on that farm, planted by Doug and Dora, and the ponds they kept filled, comfort them, but they were rewarded for their efforts. They sheltered birds and creatures of all descriptions in the heat of summer and cold of winter.

Without deliberately doing so, they had unintentionally created a wonderful bird sanctuary, a pleasure to visit. You could hear a bird orchestra on awaking, knowing full well that the sound meant turf wars and relief for some creatures who had survived to hear the flapping of owls' wings through the night. Great Horned owls had moved, uninvited into Doug and Dora's yard. Two or three generations of them in fact, in time helped keep down the rodent population. The owls enjoyed their menus, not being fussy eaters; for baby duck feathers and rabbit ears didn't spoil their appetites. There in Marose's trees, baby owls clung, hopped from branch to branch, blinking and testing wings and shyly chirping. Their parents' heads turned on corkscrew necks, allowing them to pay close attention to their brood, and, it seemed, to attend to Doug and Dora's welfare. For one day, a rabbit whizzed by Dora's head and dropped at her feet from the sky. Was that a gesture of paying the rent, or a free will offering, a bomb or merely a fumble?

Geese who chose not to commute South in winter also honoured Doug and Dora with their presence, using the yard as a toilet. Once, one even laid a giant egg on a shed roof. Thus those pets not only shared outdoor living space with the Maroses on a voluntary basis, but they also provided help and entertainment. Such birds of a feather can be tolerated. They can even be accepted and enjoyed.

However, one other specie of a bird, pests, as one farmer put it, were a pain (you know where) causing pheasants to rush into his yard to flee oncoming eager hunters. Men with disregard for property often charged into yards, blindly firing at practically anything that moved. If farmers didn't have to fear for their lives and those of their wives and kids, they did for their land and crops, as hunters' four by fours barged through fields, causing open wounds left long to fester. However, some sportsmen did care, were careful, and found that they had an open invitation to hunt and share the hospitality of the farmers and ranchers. The municipality had both visiting types, the raiders and the welcomed guests

Raiders

Farm folk like Doug and Dora knew about the raiders. They, like bandit racoons, came in many different forms to challenge and cause uneasiness among those who sought peace through work. Mennonite families who had moved to Mexico years ago were returning to Canada to work, to improve their lot, and perhaps either to stay or to return to Mexico. Among them was a disabled couple nearby, whose boys were out of control, shouting, shooting, hurling abuse at anyone in their way. They harassed and intimidated. Even the police, whom they cursed at, could do little to lower Doug and Dora's anxiety. I had spoken to the Mexican Mennonite minister about those teens. However, he too could only note that there were good and bad among all peoples. I agreed. Months later I was heartened to find that one of the older boys had sought pledges from me and others in Taber for a good cause. He planned to roller blade almost to Alberta's northern border. He obviously had a social conscience, unlike his siblings. That young man verified my faith in humankind.

Lesley and I had visited Ross's Buffalo farm, first to buy buffalo burgers, and later to show Lesley's English cousins around. We were always greeted kindly, and once driven out among the buffalo while Len, the owner, explained their attributes, making them easy stock to raise. As long as they were left alone to give birth and weren't given antibiotics or growth hormones, they usually stayed healthy, and were a good source of lean meat. However, they did have one shortcoming of which the Maroses bore the brunt. When stampeded, for whatever reason, they charged blindly ahead as destructively as a tornado. One day they tore through Maroses' barbed wire and shredded corral fences. Snorting and churning up the ground with their black hooves, they evaded the best efforts of those who dashed about to bring order out of chaos. It was days before the Maroses sent those delinquent buffalo home, and peace reigned.

I soon learned, from talking to farmers, that peace is often short lived. They say that good fences make good neighbors. Nevertheless, when fences get knocked down, not only by buffalo, but by people and cattle, then a man's patience reaches the breaking point. That often happened when a senile old man's cattle, short of feed, broke through into Marose's pasture. Other cattle even found a way of sidling along on either side of Texas gates to avoid breaking their legs on crossing to greener grass. Were they dumb, or shrewd? I wasn't sure. A patient farm woman put me straight on that. Lesley and I once saw cattle casually hoofing down a road. We drove into the woman's yard to ask if they were hers. We were thinking someone had left the gate open. She didn't seem surprised or bothered about her cattle's adventurous ways. I learned that an opening in a line of fence didn't necessarily mean someone didn't shut a gate.

Responses to creatures' behavior varied. There were traps for racoons that raided chicken houses, and barns for cats. Town folk dropped many of those feline domestic animals off. That annoyed farmers! I remember when Lesley and I lived on 52nd St., in Taber across the lane from a lady with five cats. Her cats became our preoccupation. The game began with cats winning claws down. We tried gooey stuff on our fences, moth balls and black pepper in our flower beds, and finally, a cage-like trap. Cats, I caught; scratches I got, and when I took the cats back to the owner, they kept coming back. The bylaw officer said, with traps you have to let all the people up and down the block know your intention, even then they could sue you. Where town gardeners tried to rid themselves of cats, Dora and Doug accepted the ongoing, uninvited, unannounced arrival of orphan cats and kittens. Dora even now and then gave a cat or two a squirt of milk after feeding a bottle-fed calf.

Rescuing

When calving time came around, ranchers got very little sleep, checking the cows every three hours or so. Sometimes a cow in agony needed the help of a rancher or vet, especially when giving birth to a Charlois-Herford cross. Sometimes that meant pulling that calf, levering it out, and sometimes it meant a dead mother cow, leaving her calf to be bottle-fed, or adopted by another willing mother. Many a rancher like Doug and Dora would sometimes find an orphan calf, almost frozen to death, out in the pasture. They would bring it indoors, thaw it out in a hot tub, and bottle feed it a special artificial milk. Thus, they showed love for one of God's creatures, and a need to make up for the loss of a good mother cow. Then with luck a mother cow, perhaps one that had lost a twin, might be found to take over the arduous feeding schedule.

Oh the joys of calving time. Oh also the pain of being knocked about and boarded by an inconsiderate cow. Sons of the hard-working Maroses felt the pain of cracked ribs, and often the agony of carelessly stepping cows. The necessity of having bulls around kept persons on their toes. For instance, a new bull, facing one or more old timers, would cause a thunderous crashing about in the pens till it was determined who was top bull. Then reluctant peace seemed to prevail for a while. It never failed to amaze me, as someone not farm bred, that what seemed a peaceful existence back on the ranch or farm, was far from it!

Those who feed us, and often go unrecognized for the fine job they do under adverse conditions, are in the front line doing battle with unpredictable weather, markets, and many of God's creatures who share their space. Dora and Doug might be considered examples of the many persons in the municipality that willingly fit that mold.

I hunch that couples and others with kids who have grown up on the farm, took the edge off the uneasiness about what could happen by injecting some fun into the unknown. Halloween offered that opportunity most years. Doug and Dora knew their kids and grandchildren would cook up an offering of outdoor surprises, for they had never let them down yet. During the dark of night they filled their elders' farm truck cabs with paper and what-have-you, and wrapped toilet paper around them. They also installed hideous creatures outside their elders' windows, lit up to scare. Had Doug been one to swap can-you-top-this-one stories over coffee with cronies, he and they no doubt could have topped the youngsters' shenanigans. For in their youth on Halloween night, full size tractors peered down from the tops of buildings. Backhouses were tipped, with or without occupants, and new uses were found for hay bales

I quickly learned by listening and watching that it takes imagination, creativity, a sense of self reliance and survival instinct to ranch and farm. That set of strengths seems inherent in kids growing up on the farm. Even when they have left those familiar surroundings, venturing forth into concrete jungles to work, or strange bush country to hunt or fish, they found their way, well equipped by their upbringing. Scott, Dora and Doug's grandson, showed that to be so when lost in northern Saskatchewan bush, proving wrong the idea of the "home-grown hay seed back-on-the-farm."

Others Farming and Ranching

It's nothing new to say that farming or ranching was a gamble. It would overwhelm town and city folk, like me. Farm folk, though, took it in stride. They braved the wind and dust, weeds, and lack of water. They drove the gravel and mud ruts. They skidded and slid their pick-up trucks on winter roads to town to fill water tanks, get mail and groceries. They moved wheels, sometimes scratching up money for costly irrigation pivots to beg the land to produce to pay the bills. They confronted each challenge repeatedly. To keep their spirits up, they remembered the way it was to what it is now.

Charlie, a church-going faithful oldtimer remembered his dad's inventions, and spoke of his own. They came about out of necessity to confront the limitations of farm machinery of the day, and to get water where needed. Still, it took even more than mechanical ingenuity. It took political will. Charlie did battle with many government departments, fisheries included, to dam off a stream on his property. His experience resembled another inventive soul's, Mr. Leth, who went toe to toe with the government to validate his own ingenious use of wind power on his farm. One bright survivor once said,

"It took a heap of thinking to make it all work. Nevertheless, damn it all, I'm still here!"

As I learned more about the toughness of the farmer and rancher, I also saw a kinder, gentler side. Roy Reti and Geri drove all the way to Winnipeg to bring back an old horse that their daughter once owned. The Manitoba owner was going to send the old fellow "down the road." Roy and Geri, real softies, pastured the "old boy" to live out his day's content in retirement.

Roy too, retired, but unlike the break that he gave his daughter's old friend, went the second mile as he always had, driving to meetings, and planning, all to champion the cause of local owner-operated rural electrification. He and others continued to weave in, around, and through the bird's nest of government bureaucracy, dealing often with the stubbornness of persons who lacked interpersonal skills. Roy had those skills in abundance, as did another Roy, a church member and Town Councillor. I had no doubt that, like some others, those two men's upbringing and continual contributions to their church instilled in them that strong sense of what was right and what was wrong.

Knox, as a corporate body, didn't make public pronouncements. Nor was it noisy like a "mighty army," doing battle with evil. Still, the Knox church family members did go out into the local community and beyond to witness through individual action. Oh so true! "Action is eloquence."

There were also the likes of Kay and Ann, who proved that action often spoke louder than words. One could take the Knox Church photo directory and see page after page of persons who could drive a tractor, bake a pie, hoe a garden, and prove their worth with ease and unselfish devotion to their church and community.

Despite the efforts of those in the agri-business to succeed with much at stake, not all went well. Failure wasn't foreign. During high interest times some farm families discovered, too late, that they had over extended themselves and went bankrupt, losing family farms where parents and grandparents had proudly raised their kids. Despite the grieving that must have eaten away at them, their know-how was marketable, and they found employment at the sugar factory, cannery, potato plants and elsewhere. Some farmers in their fifties found it just didn't pay, so sold out and took early retirement.

Many drylanders, though, said that they were in it for the long haul. They always looked forward to planting, despite the challenges. They confronted head-on the impact of low grain prices, dry years, fast flow elevators' demands, and a litany of costs: crop spray, fertilizer, pesticides, trucking grain, costs without end.

I once asked, why not think small and simplify? The answer was twofold. When it comes to crops, take away the additives and you've got nothing but dead particles of dirt; take away the idea of more and bigger machinery, and you're on the edge. Still, there is a catch. Go for big equipment and monster tractors to pull it, and you're so far in debt that worry works you prematurely into your grave. Despite the success of irrigation and contracts, the processing plant operators told the farmer what to grow, how much, when to put it in, and take it off. Where, before, the cynic could say he owed his soul to the bank, now, if in the bean, pea, beet, or corn business, he also may owe his soul to the food processors.

Having heard all this from the men and women who ranch and farm, I sensed, that to succeed today, they practically have to be horticulturists, engineers, mechanics, accountants, amateur vets, and much more.

19   A Joys and Sorrows Church

It is within this context, and that which surrounds the oil business, that Knox United Church found itself dependent for its finances. Nevertheless, far more important, it is in this context that the Knox people's hopes, dreams, and aspirations were planted.

Thus in getting on board with the Knox church family, I found I had to try to understand the track on which their personal freight was carried.

Church Life

Bricks and cement don't make a church family, but buildings such as Knox's do symbolize the extreme effort made by farmers, ranchers, oil men and Taberites. They saw the need to broadcast God's presence among them in a visible way. Presbyterians and Methodists, separately and then together, in 1922 as a Union Church made it happen on the corner of 50th and 50th across from Confederation Park. Methodists left their building and carried their documents and symbols of worship over to the Presbyterians' bigger brick building. Years later the Methodist's white wooden church became a recreation hall for Knox. There it stood next door till bought by the Lutherans and moved. Still later it became the Elks Hall, and in the year 2,000 was moved out in the country to become a Kanadier's (Mexican Mennonite) church.

The old Presbyterian building, with an attached 1950's brick and mortar sanctuary and lower hall, continued offering a high profile presence. The inhabitants' goal included a good friendly diet of worship along with other church family nurturing. When I first entered that sanctuary at the beginning of my ministry at Knox, I felt something was amiss. I saw that the bare walls, heavy coloured glass windows, and almost bare communion table set a sombre tone. The worshipers' response to the ambiance of the place might have been,

"So we're here, now what's on the menu." Eventually the space came to life when it was appreciated, not only for its visual impact, but also for its value as a memorial. It was then that it became an expression of unselfish giving.

The Sanctuary

Each coloured window's brass plaque in "memory of," included the donor families' names: real people, with their own stories that had given meaning to their lives. Searching out their stories brought them back to life in the minds of those who viewed those windows.

The candles, Christ candle, the two on the communion table, and the candelabra, were all in memory of a Chinese Canadian, a German Canadian, a Japanese Canadian and others. They were remembered for giving so much of themselves to their church family, and to their community. The communion table and neighboring spaces were no longer bare. Banners created by Laura hung on the walls and colourfully symbolized great truths carried throughout history by the church. The banners' symbols and others, blended the sensory with thoughts to enhance the worship experience.

When people connect thoughts with symbols and appreciate the lives connected with them, then pew cushions or the absence of them, flickering of light from intruding fans, or other objects foreign to prayer cannot distract from worship of God.

Yet it is true that some persons who had lost loved ones and had funeral services in Knox church sanctuary, couldn't bear to attend again. In their minds, they sometimes relived the pain of loss when sitting in the pews. Thus, they turned away from the greatest source of comfort. On the other hand, others, like Yo and family, who painfully mourned young Ted's sudden tragic death in a cannery accident, didn't forsake their church home. Instead they gave candles and a Bible stand, and continued to worship, faithfully following the example of other devote Christians. I felt many found hope in worship.

People of all ages contributed to preparing and leading in weekly worship. I once heard a person who had joined the worship team say,

"If people only knew of what-all was involved, they'd appreciate more what's being done."

That comment hinted of the inevitability of "burn out," and that persons need a break before putting their hands, hearts, and minds back at it. Learning what's involved might cause others to spell off those who needed a break.

That also evokes the question, did most of the Knox people know about such things as the patched together sound system. Doug kept it limping along by stitching and weaving bits and pieces together in a most mysterious way. He willingly donated his time, as he has done for many years, to keep things going. Sometimes he did so to make up for a well-meaning minister's curiosity. One day I discovered in my tower study a strange bird's nest of wires in the wall. I encouraged an active member to cut a few wires. To my chagrin, I discovered that I had silenced the tower carillon. Fortunately, Doug, as always, somehow made it right.

The carillon played taped music through a late model tape deck, left over from a garage sale. Doug recorded a tape from a CD sold to the church by a funeral home music supplier. It included a Christmas carol, played every Sunday. No one commented! Theologically it had validity which I thought would encourage comment.

Thank goodness, educating the troops wasn't only my job. Dora, chair of the Worship Committee and Vestry person, quietly and patiently taught both children and adults to carry the Bible, light candles, read scripture, and serve communion. She also willingly phoned to recruit readers and ushers, which few wanted to do for fear of rejection.

Each Sunday, we both waited as the clock's second hand reached out for eleven, wondering if anyone would attend, since the pews would often be begging for people. Then, at the last minute we would breathe easier, seeing people, including ushers and readers streaming in. Those sudden appearances of people to fill empty pews reminded me of our Alberta Chinooks.

The Approach

Children also breezed into church, like breaths of fresh air. Unlike many denominations, Sunday school happened at the same time as worship. Many young moms took a turn about teaching Sunday school. Before the children went to their classes, they met with me for "Children's Time." That proved entertaining for the adults, and full of surprises for me. We never knew what would come out of the children's mouths in answer to my questions. I remembered that old saying, don't ask when you know the answer, for we know children offer the unexpected. A teacher asked a child,

"Do you know who God is?" The child answered,
"God is the man who saved the queen."
Even when I stuck to my script, with little sincere

eyes peering at me intently, a little child would suddenly interrupt with,

"I got a new toy for my birthday. Do you want to know what it is?"

Right there and then I had lost the children's attention, and suggested that we say a little prayer and sing the children's hymn. I learned that preparing Children's Time is the toughest task, and one to leave open to spontaneity and God's Spirit.

The Word

Nothing was left to chance when a person in the congregation was to read. The prescribed lectionary lessons were prepared for delivery and then shared at the appropriate time in the service. The care and attention given to the readings constantly reminded me before I even delivered the sermon, of how onerous was the task of interpreting scripture that wasn't to be taken lightly. Over the years I had tried to develop a personal style of preaching. At first I read my sermons, then preached from notes, and finally in the last few years took the plunge and preached without manuscript or notes. That allowed me to connect directly with the congregation through eye contact and free use of body language that came naturally. At the seminary I learned that one could preach many different kinds of sermons: ethical, prophetic, evangelistic, devotional, healing, expository, textual, narrative, thematic, doctrinal or sacramental, or a combination of these forms.

Several years after leaving the seminary I found ways to prepare and deliver those sermon types by using a memory tool. I was never good at rote learning, but found I could commit the contents of a fifteen to a twenty-minute sermon to memory using this approach. I'd do some research, gather the bits and pieces up into a full manuscript, pick out thought blocks. Then, using a Star of David shape, I'd place single words on the points and sides of that star to remind me of each thought block in sequence. I then felt ready after picturing that star and single words in my mind before the worship service.

Yet, despite how well I thought I was prepared, I would often do a postmortem on the way home, or later, listen to the service tape. Lesley, my best friend, was also my best sermon critic. When I asked how it went, she would tactfully make valid suggestions. She seldom volunteered comment unless I asked for it. She once pointed out that, despite not having notes before me, I gave the impression, as one other person in the pews thought, that I had crib notes by my feet since I often bowed my head while talking. It took me awhile to overcome that habit, and also not lose my train of thought so readily, especially when preaching over the crying of infants, the socializing of preteen girls and boys, the screeching of hearing aids, and the coming and goings of people walking in or out of the sanctuary, all accepted as church family behavior.

One thing I never did get quite right though, was wearing a stole (scarf) around my neck. I had to admit to the senior choir before our prayer and entry, that my appearance seemed to look as if I had thrown my gown and stole in the air and run under them, letting them fall where they may on my shoulders. During preaching my restless arms and hands, what some called semaphore signaling, made my stole slip, causing me to look frazzled. Sometimes it even dragged on the floor. After the service, when I was eager to gain feedback from the sermon, someone would say,

"You know I was sure itching to get up and straighten you out,"

"You mean about what I said?"

"No, about how messy you looked."

Finally, Phoebe helped me out by becoming my official dresser before service. Eventually she stuck velcro on my coloured stoles which I often changed to coincide with the colors of the church year.

The Response

Following "God's Word," read and preached, came the "Response to God," which included the offering. I had a deathly fear of forgetting to announce that, having sometimes missed it. For the whole idea of an offering had implications connected with why people attend church. It caused me to ask one person,

"You come to church to worship?"

"Kind of." "You come to church to hear me?"

"Huh?" "You come to church to do what?"

"To pay my dues."

I hope he hadn't meant paying dues as one pays a membership fee to belong to a lodge, fraternity, or club.

Money was only one of God's gifts given to respond to God. Time and talent were others. So, in coming to church we gave thanks to God, celebrated God's presence, heard God's Word and responded.

The Sacraments

Offering a communion service meant preparation, and handling mundane things of life: a loaf of homemade bread made by a devoted woman, bread crumbs, a squeegee bottle to help fill plastic cups with grape juice, trays to serve from, candles, cloths, and time, lots of time. That seems sacrilegious to speak so of the Sacrament of Holy Communion. Nevertheless, a liturgy which followed the preparation meant the works of the people, and at Knox it meant that many persons, farmers, tradespeople, bankers, clerks, office workers, and homemakers, all participated, taking a turn about. That included delivering Communion Invitation cards to persons identifying with Knox, informing them of the communion date.

In the early days elders took attendance via returned communion cards at the service. An attendance Record book was still around, a reminder of another era in Knox's history. Then, they did not allow women to serve communion, men elders only, and where neither children, nor those who hadn't made peace with their neighbor, nor had a clear conscience, could partake.

I used a simplified version of the traditional communion service, believing it would have greater impact than a more complex one. The Worship Committee also made it easier for all to partake, giving an open invitation to anyone who believed in Jesus Christ, without judging their attendance record or public behavior. Times had changed!

The worship committee considered using a version of the old style in tincture method ("dunk and dip") communion service. Though not served at the rail, people came to the front to receive bread dipped into a chalice containing grape juice instead of having the elements delivered to them in the pews. Many of the "old folks " couldn't easily navigate to the front, some others felt conspicuous standing in line, and so most preferred communion in the pew.

Sometimes bits of bread fell off trays onto the floor. That also happened at a Conference worship service where they ordained new ministers. The wax paper between the stacked trays caused bits of bread to stick to them. Like scattering crumbs for birds, some bits fell at the feet of the Conference President. Rather than draw attention to what happened, the president and servers carried on, tramping a few fallen bread bits underfoot. That wasn't a sin, since in the United Church, the act of Communion, like Baptism, is a symbolic act, a visible sign of an invisible truth. The elements in and of themselves are not sacred, as they are in the Roman Catholic Church. Nor has the minister the power to change the bread and grape juice into the body and blood of Christ in some mystical way. Despite the perceived difference in meaning, the Knox people did look upon Communion with reverence.

Baptism Requests and Preparation

Often Jo Ann, the church secretary, would get a call, hearing a voice that she didn't recognize saying, "I'm new in town, how can I get my kid done?"

292

Another phone call,

"I want my child christened, but I haven't been in church for ages."

Still another,

"You are baptizing my friend's child in your church, can I have mine done at the same time?"

Some asked,

"How much does it cost for a baptism?"

We answered, "No charge for sacraments."

Others asked,

"Can we have it done at home?"

The answer was "No private baptisms," since the worshiping congregation also make vows at baptisms.

Often young mothers, after I agreed to baptize their children, asked if we could baptize them, too. Many grandmothers called, or dropped around to talk to me about wanting their grandson or granddaughter baptized, and then added,

"But my daughter isn't married, or her friend, the father of the baby is away or cannot be found. Will that make a difference?"

People did come feeling a great need to have their children baptized for many reasons. Once I had a call from a mother whose child was attending the R.C. school. She said,

"His class was to be confirmed, but since he wasn't R.C., nor was he baptized, he would feel left out."

Neither mother nor son had attended any church recently. However, since she was so anxious about helping her child, I agreed to meet with her. She never showed up.

The rule was that at least one parent or guardian must be a member of the United Church of Canada, or must have a sponsor in good standing. Thus, the Worship Committee and I had our work cut out for us to decide how to deal with each unique request. That required an interview with the parents or guardians, followed by a mini rehearsal, prior to the baptism.

Sometimes the parent or guardians of the child or children lived in another part of the country. Then the fun began. That meant talking to the parents, checking the United Church Year Book to find names of churches near where the couple were living, and having the couple agree to the idea of me sending a letter to the minister of their choice. It would say that the baptism took place and why, and asks the minister to contact the parents to encourage their involvement in his or her congregation. We called that "Baptism by proxy."

The Baptism

Parents arrived early for church. A Knox member introduced the couple to the congregation. During the service, just before the Baptism, the father, parent or guardian lit a candle that was on the communion table above a banner bearing the child's name. After reading the rite of Baptism, I baptized, using the ancient Trinitarian formula,

"I baptize you in the name of the Father, Son, and Holy Spirit." Then I marked an invisible cross on the child's forehead, denoting Christ's ownership over that person.

Surprises

Sometimes things did happen that gained laughs

or groans. Shouts from a toddler during the baptism triggered laughter.

"He is getting all wet mommy."

"I want to splash too."

Then there was the toddler who dipped his hand in the baptism font and splashed about while the minister read the introduction to baptism. One wandering toddler hopped about, up and down the steps during Baptism, totally oblivious to the drama of the event. During baptism, babies often took a liking to my glasses, yanking them to half mast. I hesitated to hold some infants, so tiny, so fragile. However, I did; just as I held little souls that looked ordained to become football linemen. Some squirmed. Some wiggled, and others wailed while their little hands reached out for their moms. One cannot forget either, youngsters beyond toddler age. Should I have picked them up, or have them stand?

Soon after baptism services, I found satisfaction in signing the baptism record book. For one or more had just joined the church family. Years ago the church records were the only evidence that a child officially existed. To this day, calls come to church offices, from some elderly seeking proof of age from baptism records in order to apply for old age pension benefits. Sometimes we got requests for copies of baptism certificates from persons wishing to marry in the RC church. I felt good about the RC church finally recognizing our United Church baptisms.

I also felt good that some effort was made to follow up on baptized children. For many years, as Cradle Roll secretary, Bernice kept track of the baptized children. She contacted their parents or guardians by sending birthday cards till their children were old enough to attend Sunday School.

Music
Music is well said to be the speech of angels 1

A new model hymn book at last! Unlike the old, the "Voices United" contained both hymns, psalms and some readings, leaving the old books abundant and redundant. The question was, what to do with the old ones? Book burning seemed sacrilegious, and recycling by shredding, abhorrent. So the question remained partially unanswered.

Yet, books don't make God's Word live. People filled with the Holy Spirit do. Besides the people in the pews who stepped forward to help lead, Knox was blessed with a faithful crew. They were dedicated to the job of making worship meaningful, enhancing the worth and joy of the hour. Orla, the organist, coaxed the organ to play properly despite its idiosyncracies. She pampered it, all very necessary since some of its innards were a mystery. The builders refused to give copies of the schematics to the church for others to keep the organ in good repair. Despite its sensitivity, Orla accompanied the choir well. Darrell, the music and choir director, was an accomplished singer, well versed in everything from New Orleans black gospel and blues, to contemporary and opera. He used humour and a blast of energy to raise the choir's level of output and gain the singers' respect. That rag tag of choir members often even surprised themselves.

For some years Bettejean did the same with the bell choir. It was amazing how the players kept their composure and concentration while handling several bells. I never lost my fascination with bell choirs, nor with the dedicated seniors who, through sheer will power, made it to choir. Phoebe displayed that kind of dedication. Others followed her example, faithfully turning out each Thursday evening and Sunday morning to offer an anthem and lead the congregation in singing the hymns. Some members, as age dictated, like Theora could barely make it up and down the few steps to share their ministry of music. But sheer stubborn determination prevailed.

The choir fascinated me. Persons jelled to form an identity and a tight group within a larger community, the body of worshipers. The members, along with their spouses and other family members, drew on their own and others' resources to make things happen. Years ago the Senior choir took over the traditional Irish Stew dinner from the Scouts. People took home the ingredients to cook, and bring back to fill the stew pots and serve droves of people from Taber and surrounding area. The Senior choir members were determined to "get em all fed," including takeouts. They proved their zeal that one March Stew Dinner night when Linda, JoAnn and another drove their 4x4s, and slogged knee deep through snow to deliver stew dinners to shut-ins.

Knox church family not only had seniors responding to the need and challenge to participate fully. Children and youth also worked hard and had fun. The Minis and Angels formed and led by Barb, replaced the Kids for Christ choir, a brain child of Mark's. The excitement that Mark generated as an accomplished pianist and motivator, and the skills that Barb showed as flutist, and artist, raised the height of interest of all ages in Taber and district, supporters and recipients of enthusiastic young blood.

Barb's and Mark's choirs had contrasting characteristics, just as do ministers who come and go over the years. Mark's choir was a mixed bag of kids from the congregation, other denominations, and off the street with no church affiliation. Their music was as large and loud as the huge number that sang out with consistent gusto. In contrast, Barb's choir consisted mostly of children from Knox families, and Sunday School attenders. They often sang more sedately in the presence of their mascot, a fine-looking angel doll, a gift to the church from the angels and minis. Two sculpted doves also appeared when the young choirs sang at Baptism services.

For some time the congregation would respond to the youth choir's songs with applause. I and others felt clapping suggested children were there to perform rather than lead in worship. Performance, I'm sure wasn't their intent! Opinions were divided. Some felt clapping was appropriate to encourage the children and to show appreciation for coming. Others felt, as I did, that, if that were valid, then it would follow that soloists, the senior choir, and others who lead, should also be applauded. I tried, with the support of the choir leaders, to suggest that singing in the service was an appropriate response to the gifts that God has given. If anyone deserved applause, it should be God. The senior choir director suggested that if the worshipers shouted a resounding AMEN! that would suffice after any ministries of music. So that is what most did from then on, except a few who threw in a clap or two.

No matter how much we may seek identity and independence as a church apart from the secular world, the outside world impinges. Choir choral contributions are dependent on song and hymn writers. Churches should pay authors for their work, for the hymn writers rent it out. They don't give away. Thus, all should stick to sheet music copyrighting laws. Yet, people still infringe, revealing a perennial problem in churches. The enthusiasm to express God's gifts freely, unencumbered by secular influences, still existed. Companies do try on behalf of artists to address the problem by collecting copyrights to licence churches to use music. Worship leaders at Knox tried to avoid making unauthorized copies of music, and looked seriously at using licensing companies.

When it all came together well, the sermon, the scripture readings, prayers, hymns, and anthems, worshipers usually got a good diet of worship. Though it was only after the service that I would often find out how it went. Sometimes disappointments did rob the worship of its effectiveness. Often the sound system didn't work. Persons would say,

"I never heard a word of the sermon." or,

"Parts of it were muffled." or,

"The readers didn't speak into the mikes." or,

"The candle lighter or ushers didn't come in on cue."

Twice I even forgot to turn off my wireless mike, and so shared unedited conversation with worshipers rising from their seats after I had given the benediction from the narthex. That reminded me of the minister who left his wireless mike on while in the washroom. The odd time, persons also have told me that the tape of the service for shut-ins was sometimes blank, often because I pushed a wrong button on the recorder. Frustrating!

I gained one consolation. After the worship service, Dora organized Cup and Conversation in which she, ushers and greeters, UCW, and midweek groups brought and served goodies. All were welcomed. Regrettably, few newcomers took up the invitation given during the announcement times. It takes a bit of courage for most people to walk into a room to meet new people unless someone provides an escort and introduces them. However, Knox members did try to help people feel welcomed.

Many seniors couldn't get to church, let alone to Cup and Conversation after church. They were living in the hospital continuing care or in senior lodges. So Dick, singing and playing his harmonica, Gordon and Shannon singing and strumming a guitar, Orla on piano, and I would lead in worship. Often Dora, Bula and a few other members would move around to enhance the comfort level of those gathered. Those senior home residents, a few in wheel chairs, some without, others with oxygen tanks, tried to be as attentive as possible. Still sometimes they fell asleep.

At Clearview Lodge a couple of caged canaries sang along with us as we shared good old gospel hymns. At Continuing Care, many seniors were suffering various states of dementia. They didn't really seem aware of our presence. Yet they weren't excluded from worship nor from other events. With the effort of Lori, heading the recreation department, they were exposed to stimulation to avoid sensory deprivation. One resident, a dear Dutch lady, Jake's mother, when asked, would sweetly sing solos, bringing tears to the eyes of many present. It must have been tough for the staff in those care homes when she died. For together they were family

Remember now thy Creator in the days of thy youth: Or ever the evil days come, And the years draw nigh . . . And the dust returns to the earth, As it was, And the spirit returns unto God Who gave it. 2

Funerals

Some people are troubled when a loved one says, "I don't want anything, no funeral, no bun fight (reception after), just get it over with."

Persons forget that the funeral or memorial service is for the living. I have heard it said that a funeral service had these purposes:

A time to thank God for all that's been good in the life lived. An occasion for praising God, for knowledge of sins forgiven and promises fulfilled, and hope for everlasting life, a time when those in the church strengthen one another, a time for Thanksgiving, declaring the great Christian message, a time for farewells, and a time to help the bereaved begin their inevitable grief work.

When conducting funerals, I kept those thoughts in mind. Yet, that didn't inoculate me from extraordinary challenges. I did gain support from many who understood what I was going through when I helped bereaved families. After a service of someone I knew well, or when I had dealt with a tragic death, I appreciated it when I'd hear, "That must have been a tough one for you!"

Most people, especially ministers like me, can recall very painful times. At the funeral home I met with one young couple who wished to have a still- born baby baptized, and a graveside service. Another time, parents wanted a funeral for their toddler. Violent, or tragic road accidents causing unnecessary death also evoked feelings of both sorrow and anger, especially when young persons died suddenly. Often those, unlike hospital deaths, gave no time for loved ones and friends to say goodbye. Then there is also the lingering pain of parents, whose children go before they do.

Yet, the need to face reality is essential, including the wilderness experience that the minister and funeral director lead one through, hopefully with sensitivity and understanding. At least that's the idea. Though, often, unforseen needs surface, that call for extraordinary responses. A father, his wife, and son ended up in a tangled car wreck in the ditch, having been hit head-on. His wife and son survived. He died. His close friends arranged the funeral at Knox. Because of his background, the request was that a

Greek Orthodox priest should share in the service. I agreed, and it happened. Both the priest and I tried to satisfy each other's way of doing things. I felt good about the fact that, not only did we satisfy the needs of the mourners, but also showed fellowship in Christ. The Knox people, as usual, were empathetic and revealed a genuine honest tolerance of others' faiths. That was most reassuring!

People not familiar with the United Church's expressed needs were less tolerant, even when they heard that there were limits in what we could do. For instance, several bereaved families wanted taped music of popular vocalists that were far from sacred. Some wanted to use their own sound dubbing equipment that accompanied singers who seemed to be there to perform. True, there were others who were sensitive to the sacred tone required. Still, one never knew till the service began what to expect, which was a bit stressful. Once, though, I just couldn't resist when a family made a very unusual request which I accommodated. The deceased vowed that his pallbearers would recess out to the tune "It's a Long Way to Tipperary." He had a fascinating sense of humour as a Japanese Canadian!

Sometimes the oddest thing happened. Two candles were lit on the communion table. At the end of one service, just as I gave the benediction, one went out on its own, leaving the other lit, almost suggesting the husband had now gone for sure, leaving his widow represented by the remaining lit candle.

Knox did accept memorabilia for display in the

sanctuary or narthex if it related to the life of the deceased. To my surprise, families sometimes went almost over board in what they brought in, or had the funeral director display. Saddles, cowboy hats, lariats, hobby items, photos appeared with some regularity to enhance flower arrangements. One day, the most striking object greeted my eyes when I walked through the sanctuary before the service. Proudly displayed was a huge stuffed fish, reminding me of a massive weathervane. Comment after? "Inappropriate!"

As Knox's minister my theme was to accommodate! That I tried to do. In doing so, I found value in the use of the services of the local funeral home. But a family representative of the bereaved wanted a do-it-your-self funeral. Though he wasn't familiar with the neighboring town's cemetery, he insisted on arranging, on his own, to have the grave dug and opened. When we arrived, we drove and walked around searching for that grave. Shouts of, "Maybe it's here!" "No, I think it's over here," broke the silence of the cemetery. Most disconcerting! Finally someone directed us over to it. Then, the person who made the arrangements, went on and on to explain away the mishap.

I felt hurt one other time. Rather than follow protocol and have the family meet the Knox minister to discuss the funeral service, an out-of-town family, not connected with Knox, decided they would have their own minister of a different denomination officiate at the service of their loved one at Knox. They expressed their intention through a funeral director via the telephone. I hesitated agree, suggesting they might want to have the service in the church where their minister was the pastor, or in one of his denomination. They were very put off!

One family member expressed the strong opinion that the deceased had a right to be buried through any church that he wanted. The upshot of it all was that they held the service in the funeral home where they made the arrangements, conducted by their pastor, whom I had never met. The service was packed, practically spilling over onto the parking lot. I learned a lesson, to always make a point, even go out of my way to talk directly to the family. Had I done that, they might have addressed the need for a bigger building for the service. For I recalled the words of one who said

I shall utter what I believe today,
even if it contradicts all I said yesterday. 3

Every minister has his or her own little preferences. I always had a need to open the door of the funeral coach just before the pallbearers placed the coffin in the coach. Once a new intern undertaker almost beat me to the punch, letting go of the coach door with the most curious look on his face.

That same kind of look sometimes appeared on the faces of those who stayed for receptions and lunches served by the UCW following the services. It was my duty to get people's attention and say Grace. I would ring a bell similar to a school bell. Eventually all eyes would turn my way. I had felt a little awkward thinking maybe I should hide the bell behind my back. Despite those awkward moments, I appreciated that engraved bell as one of my retirement gifts, knowing that the congregation laced the presentation with a bit of humour.

Pathos, sadness, and quiet humour surfaced, also, when a middle-aged athlete died suddenly. Her daughters felt strongly about the need to have a memorial service at Knox. Their mother was not only a keep fit person, but also did fine crafts, and made wine. When I heard about the latter while meeting with the family, I said, for fun, that I would be interested in a taste of her wine. After the service I carried the cremain's urn by the table displaying some of their loved one's crafts, and near the table I saw a bottle of wine, for me!

Weddings

Young men and women who had been in the wedding parties of couples married in Knox, would return to be married themselves. Those in the wedding parties represented an interesting cross-section of the community. There were professionals, oil men, process plant workers, and even bull riders and cow girls who rode the range and had much in common. Most of the women were employed, a few still finishing off high school or college. Some young men were doing the same. Often couples had their own children in the wedding parties, who ranged in age from infants to toddlers to pre teens.

Preparation

After many years working alone in preparing and conducting weddings, I found I was becoming jaded, and less patient with what I called cosmetics, along with the various feelings, opinions, and expectations of members of families involved. Since much of it didn't really relate to worship, I decided to create a team approach that involved three persons and myself. Jo Ann, Heather, and Marjo. They were kind enough to play key roles. Jo Ann, church secretary, fielded telephone calls and questions from people who dropped into the office. Brides-to-be gave and got information. Then Jo Ann referred them to Heather who explained the process leading up to the wedding, including the required counseling using a preparation workbook. The couples, having met with Heather, then went away, did their homework guided by the workbook. Marjo then went over their work with them; Then they met with me. The couple and I would cover some material in more depth, talk about the wedding and their vows. Later, often the evening before the wedding, Heather would usually conduct the rehearsal.

Despite all that work, I found the preparation didn't improve my marriage batting averages. Couples still kept coming to be married at Knox and others would divorce.

Pre marriage Counseling

During my counseling session with the couple, if I felt that their marriage would be a disaster, I would try to tell them so, knowing that they were going to get married anyway. Before couples met up with our team and the preparation process, some seemed to give a lot of attention to the logistics of the wedding, and little to the meaning of Christian marriage. I was a bit surprised that many couples during the pre marriage counseling sessions, hesitated, and needed help even in dealing with this question,

"What do you see in this man/woman that you want to spend the rest of your life with him/her?"

Answers varied from,

"He's cute and fun to be with" to

"He/she is good to me, dependable, and trustworthy." Many couples had been married before and had been living together. That seemed to be the norm with very few who had not already cohabited.
Different Denominations

Young men and women who wished to be married at Knox often came from different church denominational backgrounds.

Sometimes I found emotions running high when parents didn't approve of a marriage, but the couples were going ahead anyway. In one instance a man who grew up in the JW's went along with the U.C. girl's wishes to wed at Knox. He did that despite his mother's strong objections. She found out also that, in the ring exchange, her son would also be including these words, "I give you this ring in the name of the Father, the Son, and the Holy Spirit." The son interpreted that so she could save face. She attended the service. When the bride or groom came from an RC family, I substituted "Holy Ghost" for "Holy Spirit" which made some feel a bit more at home.

Some couples didn't have that problem. They had no strong ties with Knox. Often they assumed they could bring along their own pastor to officiate. Then it wasn't the bride or groom, nor their families taken aback. It was the Knox minister and congregation

308

who felt "used." In the end, many of those couples decided to go elsewhere.

Drop Outs:

When several couples had "booked the church," received their homework, and found out what was involved in preparing for the marriage, they canceled, sometimes without letting us know. I did hear that some couples decided they weren't compatible, even at that late stage in the game. Others decided to have their wedding performed by marriage commissioners. Still others headed south to Reno or somewhere similar.

Cosmetics and Special Requests

Those who did so may not have felt as satisfied as those who married at Knox. For Knox brides and grooms, though their wishes were not always okayed, at least they felt that we had heard them. Yet, at times some of their requests seemed a bit far fetched. For instance: one bride wanted her two big pet dogs to accompany her down the aisle.

Both Heather, the wedding hostess, and I have had to hold our breath at times wondering how young ring bearers and flower girls, some still toddlers, would behave. We have found, apart from being cute and photogenic, they were often all over the yard. Some never had a clue what it was all about. Many en route down the aisle dove for a pew into their mother or grandmother's arms.

Unforeseen Happenings

Taber weddings have certainly been interesting, and many brides and grooms were very exciting to know. One groom, an American marine, arrived minutes before the service bleeding profusely from his chin after an attack on his whiskers. Heather dashed over to my house to get a styptic pencil from Lesley. That solved that problem. The contents of Heather's survival kit, as wedding hostess, increased as the wedding parties' surprises grew more numerous. They convinced me of the value of a good wedding hostess like Heather! Though, no matter how capable we felt, having everything presumably under control, patience was still the name of the game

Irritations:

Brides or grooms would sometimes arrive late. Often the guests, knowing the service started at two, arrived at two, just as the bride was coming down the aisle. Weddings varied in size from the "full meal deal" where a rehearsal resembled a complicated football play, to simplicity at its best. Wedding party size had no bearing on the inventory of irritations. There were many: blinding flash cameras, the odd zealous amateur photographer "in one's face," giggling bridesmaids urged on by the old gag "Help" printed on the bottom of the kneeling groom's shoes during the wedding prayer. Despite all the interesting distractions, Knox did have many good weddings during my eight years there.

Joys of "Good Weddings"

Those were the times when couples and families focused on the main reason for a "church" wedding. In planning, when counseled, and during the rehearsal, the wedding couples felt supported. Parents, families, and friends honoured their wishes.

310

Many voices had counseled the couple at first, but ultimately in the "good wedding" they met the couple's wants when in consultation with the minister. Like previous Knox ministers, I was blessed with a congregation that gave the minister the freedom to develop meaningful Christian marriage preparation and wedding protocol. Heather and I found that those couples who had a history of church participation usually had a good wedding. Some others could have used their first wedding ceremony as a rehearsal for a future Christian one.

Special Worship Services

Knox Church kept many worship traditions alive, such as the White Gift Service. Usually it was without added excitement of two small kids crawling under the pews from back to front, with a few startled people lifting their legs as those kids slid under the pews. Later in December came the CGIT Vesper candle light service, and Christmas Eve Services 7:30 and 11. Following those, people worshiped at the Journey to the Light Service which began the New Year. It offered a time when persons lit votive candles in memory of their deceased loved ones. In the spring, during the Good Friday "Tenebrae" service Gordon and Martin carried the cross down the aisle. Then came the Easter day service with the handbells joining with other choirs. All those brought attendance surges and words of appreciation. Like other dowager churches, Knox's brick walls and dominant tower, were not barriers to entry, but symbols of stability, and a place for all during the mountain peaks in people's lives, baptisms, weddings, funerals, and more.

Pastoral Care

Years ago I read a book written by an English Anglican vicar who told how he organized his visiting so that he gave almost everyone equal attention. He did this by mapping out his parish by street blocks, and then visiting each neighborhood in turn. A similar system existed at Knox. The church Board had assigned "Elders" to neighbourhoods or rural areas, each with several families to care for, deliver communion cards to, and report any family concerns to the minister.

Thus each elder had what we called a "District." That systematic care program existed for many years. But when I arrived at Knox it had all but vanished. The need still existed though. The Board endorsed the forming of a team to create a new program. Linda, a local druggist, who knew the Taber people well, and how the town was laid out; Mary, who had an incredible facility in remembering names and peoples' circumstances: Jo-Ann, church secretary, and some others including me, set it up. It was called "Neighborhood Reps." The work resulted in a program similar to Elders' Districts. Persons volunteered, were assigned districts, and given a guide to follow.

The intention was that every person who identified with Knox would be contacted four times a year at least. They would receive information, be invited to communion, and have the opportunity to let the minister know, through the district reps, their concerns and interests. The minister then would respond. This program worked until, as always, people got involved in other things, or got discouraged by responses to their visits or phone calls, and quit. That left the program too short of reps. for it to continue.

While visiting a church in Calgary, I picked up a pamphlet describing a telephone tree where, again, persons volunteered to reach others under their care by phone. Then in turn, the phoned would call others on their list. Through a fanning out process all persons would be contacted, and kept on board about what was happening in their church. They would hear of opportunities available to them to participate. The "Connectors" who had made the calls would also pass on any comments, concerns, or requests to the minister, who again would respond.

The failure of both those programs wasn't the fault of anyone, but it revealed a disturbing fact. People, especially young families, tired and programmed out, spread themselves too thin in an attempt to be responsible parents and citizens. Thus, long term commitments such as required by care programs were out of the question. At times I felt the best that we could do was to respond to needs, rather than to go out looking for the hurting; continue also to rely on UCW members who visited faithfully, and try to raise church family members' awareness of those on the prayer list.

Home Visits

For the first few years in Taber, I visited by appointment most of the families identifying with Knox. I recall that years ago, people felt okay about the minister dropping by their home unexpectedly. No longer did that seem acceptable. So I followed a pattern set by Arji, the minister before me. Jo-Ann made the appointments. Later Marjo did. She marked Family record cards "visit," or "no visit" as expressed by those whom she called. In the process, we found those who were actively committed to Knox, and those who merely wanted to identify with the church family.

Unlike in cities, many town residents had no visible house numbers. At first I would set out seeking a home for a night call, only to end up stumbling around in the dark, peering at doorways, and risking arrest as a prowler. I eventually got smart and drove around to locate homes in the daytime before I made the evening visits. Live and learn!

Counseling

After many years I became convinced that most active church people didn't see the minister in the role of a counselor. Having had some training in counseling, I became a bit disappointed that Knox members seldom called upon me to provide that part of my ministry. Perhaps, people were reluctant about parking their vehicles on a week day in front of the church for fear of what others might think, especially if they were not known to do so on a regular basis. No doubt they were as fearful as those who showed up for worship after a prolonged absence. Many, especially older folk, seemed to prefer sharing their concerns over the phone, or tried to make an appointment for me to see them in their homes. Often they wouldn't get to talk to JoAnn, church secretary, or me over the phone. We were out of the office, or the line was busy. Knox went to voice mail but, as with the previous tape machine inviting persons to leave a message, older Knox members usually just hung up.

I often felt that many seniors gave in or gave up without much fight when attempting to express their feelings and concerns, rather than follow the suggestion of the writer who said

> Don't go gentle into that good night,
> Old age should burn and rave at close of day;
> Rage, rage against the dying of the light.   4

I found that people who were at their wits-end, and had no connections with Knox, would make appointments to see me. They did so despite having to leave a message, or they would just drop in out of the blue for help, unlike most regular church attenders. I felt that those people who came did have me at a disadvantage in that often I didn't know them, but they presumably saw me as one whom they could trust, since Knox endorsed my credibility. In the early years of my ministry, I gave everyone the benefit of the doubt. In later years, I often felt uneasy unless JoAnn the secretary, or another church person was in the building for fear of being accused of inappropriate behavior. For that reason I left my study door open and had an escape route for the visitor or myself. Placing my desk against the wall rather than me sitting behind it, also helped avoid an authoritative stance, and allowed that psychological seven feet between myself and my visitor.

Life is for each man, a solitary cell whose walls are mirrors. 5

AA and Alanon members came in numbers. I respected them and their program and made myself available to do 5th step work with them. They, hopefully, left the troublesome part of their history behind, and in return, I kept in touch with reality. That helped prevent me from lingering in my ivory tower. I felt good that those people who struggled with life, trusted me. Had I not seen confidentiality as critical I would have been dead in the water.

I found that, like AA and Alanon, persons with no direct contact with Knox would come seeking help or direction: the single parent out of food; the transient wanting a meal or two, a hotel room, a bus ticket, or gas. Once, a young man in his late teens wanted to know what the UC church believed. He had been shopping around for a faith and had sampled many churches. My first reaction when he introduced himself with a quirky name, was to say to myself, "Oh well, that's a new approach." However, it wasn't long before he convinced me of his sincerity. I found him to be a breath of fresh air. Yet, there was no quick fix for him as a searcher, I found the best I could do was to make referrals for him and others. I felt the ultimate answer would be to have a storefront centre set-up. There, all church denominations and helping agencies could offer a 24-hour service to answer the multiplicity of needs expressed. Taber community spirit was no doubt up to such a task.

Hospital Visits

I was grateful to Mary for her sense of responsibility, and to a few other persons who called me to the hospital bedside of the dying. Yo and family called me to George's bedside for prayer, Larry and Karen to Jack's, and I think of others who did the same, like many dedicated hospital staff. People didn't always let us know when they, their loved ones or friends were going into a hospital. I walked by many hospital rooms. Some church members saw me pass by and wondered why I hadn't dropped in to see them. They didn't realize that a government "Privacy Act" muzzled many who could tell ministers who were in hospital. The Regional hospital chaplain tried to protect the patients from-well meaning persons who felt they had a captive audience in hospital beds to proselytize. Still, he did seek to have a part-time chaplain supervise visiting Taber clergy volunteers.

Despite all efforts, it was still hard to stomach one premise put forward by some hospital administrators. I heard that they believed, by limiting total free access to hospital patient lists only to paid staff, (even if the stipend was only one dollar a month), patients' privacy would be protected. The theory was that paid hospital staff would be more accountable and responsible in respect to patient privacy.

It was amazing how, when I wore my dog collar while making my own hospital rounds, I had access to most of the hospital, despite the bureaucratic malaise. The backward plastic collar opened more doors than did the plastic name tag, unless the I.D.

tag also included the staff member's role on the medical team. A drawback that the name tag wearer didn't confront was the moment when the clergy collar wearer stepped into a hospital room when the patient might be thinking,

"O my God, I must be at death's door!"

Despite the politics and other intriguing hospital hurdles, I found I never forgot why visiting was a must, that is, to be there for the patients, and not for myself. Though I must say, it wasn't easy to leave my personal baggage outside, to be a non anxious presence, as we say in Interim ministry.

Church Attendance

Attendance at Knox was kept and graphed. It showed a pattern where "low Sundays" began in May, through to August, and ended when school started again. Attendance grew when children were in school. That made me think parents and children viewed church attendance as they did a school year. Sunday sports also cut into church attendance, especially during the hockey, baseball and soccer seasons. Eventually many children and teens, no longer thrilled with the idea of attending church or Sunday school, stopped coming. It was then that their parents also dropped out. But parents often did volunteer to lead when their children and youth were busy in midweek groups. If not worshiping, at least they were tied into the life and work of the church. Though when children were drawn away by school or social activities, or to hang out as teens, their parents also seemed to drift away. They had "been there, done that church thing."

Lack of consistent church attendance evoked the question: What do many other church denominations have going for them that keep people connected and active? I hunch each had something uniquely related to its cultural background, or faith stance. The RCs go regularly to church out of necessity to receive the sacraments. Perhaps some Reform and Lutherans went also to maintain a sense of belonging ethnically, having German or Dutch roots. Perhaps the evangelicals went to celebrate their joy in being reborn again and for the "buzz" that they got from lively theatrical entertaining music. Possibly the LDS and JW's went to maintain their unique identity and to charge up the troops to go out and gain more converts. Knox Church had none of these built-in inherent motivators, making it harder work for clergy and committed members to hold it together. Yet, one thing it did have going for it, was the fact that young families wanted Sunday school for their children, and older folks, who had remained faithful, wanted "church" for their grandchildren. Still, many felt sad that their adult children didn't attend, nor commit to "church."

Christian Education

I was heartened that a small group of faithful enthusiasts put their heart and souls into attending to the education needs of Knox children and youth. They also made it fun, using one CE committee member's words, "CE meetings are a "Hoot."

The committee endorsed a curriculum called "The Whole People of God." It dealt with the same lectionary as that used in adult worship. In that way the parents who worshiped could go home and talk to their children about the scripture lesson contents for any particular Sunday. Thus, their children were well exposed to the depth and breadth of the Bible.

Leadership and Youth

Despite our efforts to step up our care program, at a church Board meeting, some young adults complained. They said that they and others were not getting the attention they needed via contacts with the church. The critique of our program frustrated some Board members and me. After hearing from them, we wondered how we could make it better. I left the meeting having a sense that those critiquing were busy people, but not keen on coming half way by increasing their involvement in leadership roles. I had often heard that Knox had nothing to offer young people. I had trouble with that comment for two reasons. First, my understanding of the church by definition is that it consists of the people of God. That is to say, it also includes young folks. They, too, are the church! I didn't believe that they are called to be entertained by the middle-aged or seniors in the church. Instead, I felt they were to nurture and be nurtured. I understood that those who critiqued the church started from the premise that the church was to operate within the consumers' society, as merely another provider of goods and services. I felt that was wrong! Still, I could then and now understand how people might think that way in a wealthy province, such as Alberta. Yet, I did feel supported, as did others who tried to care, when someone said, what I have heard often,

"Well, you cannot please all the people all the time."

Though that didn't lower the frustration level. What worked better for me was to hear and believe that we're not necessarily called to be successful, but faithful!

Mid Week Groups

Many who look in from outside Knox might have missed seeing the energy expended by kids and teens caught up in organized action. Carol, Lesley and Donna inspired the CGIT girls, helping them with their Vesper services. Eighty-year-old Jeanette resuscitated the Explorers group, refusing to let it die, and recruited Teresa who faithfully led for six years. The Gregus girls, Teresa and Roxie displayed dedication, like so many. Such creativity! They followed many whose voices echoed over the years within the church's brick walls.

Knox leaders were a gutsy bunch. Kay led Messengers. Despite her "bionic" knees, she, along with Kari, matched the girls' short attention span with mind-body Christian centered activities, crafts, and sleep-overs with smells of bacon, pancakes, and maple syrup.

Oh, the tales told after Manitoba CGIT camps, the girls at the lectern preparing scripture, the candle lighting, the small hands grasping big offering plates, the questions, oh the questions!

"How come dinosaurs aren't mentioned in the Bible?"

"What does epiphany mean?"

Those memories surfaced as I'd leaned over my desk preparing for Sunday, hearing girls shouts and laughter, giggles and thumps on the stairs.

So too, the Beavers, Cubs, Scouts with many parent leaders filled the building and the gym, the old church sanctuary, with unique worship: the celebration of youth, sinew, bone, bird-like limbs in motion, sweat-rubbed kerchiefs, badge sashes set aside, all to free bodies for play, and leaders' hand signals often calling all that to a halt. Throughout many of their evening meetings I'd hear playful crashing about, base fiddle-like voices and responding high-pitched fiddle-shouts, then long silences, followed again by more music to my ears.

Many, both leaders and boys were RC or from other churches. That didn't matter. Knox's generosity might have been represented by a lawn sign stating, "For All Parents and Youth, compliments of Knox Outreach." The leaders Jody, Pat, the lady clerk from 7-11 down the street, the parents from across town were also very generous. They all gave of their time for their kids, yes, but also for so many others whose parents dropped them off. Then there were Harry, Rob, Barry, and others like them whose years in Scouting were silently marked by the many stickers on the 5th Taber Scouts Canada Charter.

Over the years the grand old Knox structure of brick, boards and glass stood proud despite the expected scuffed floors, bruised walls, and plugged toilets of playful kids. In all that time the injuries it sustained were very few, compared with public buildings. No graffiti on the inviting white washrooms walls, incredible! Only once a phone call incident. Some youths phoned random numbers from a church phone and spewed out obscene language. One recipient called me and raked me over the coals, saying, rightfully so,

"I didn't expect such filth from the church!"

There was always a remedy. The culprits were identified, admonished, and they apologized. A church member moved the phone from down the hall to a more public spot in the kitchen. The move proved more convenient. It just goes to show "If given a lemon make lemonade," a motto Knox members demonstrated well in dealing with a difficult building.

They also showed me something else: determination by young parents can make things happen in the church, despite the heavy load of parenting, homemaking, work, and having to keep their own kids healthy. The shooting at Myers school, where one teen was killed, brought home to two parents, Lori and Susan, the need "to draw closer to the kids in the church," to support, encourage, and instill Christian values. So they, with the support and involvement of other parents, formed a youth group without any help from me. The group engaged in many "we mean business" ventures to learn and to do. They raised funds to attend a youth rally in Edmonton. They made 400 apple pies on an assembly line as one of their projects. One parent, a hunter, a fisherman, and tough oil man, scooped out the pie filling. One strong farmer parent crimped pie crust toppings. Sisters, brothers, and other friends battled it out with mechanical apple peelers in many races laced with laughter and teasing. Youth turned work into play, and mothers, as always, kept it all rolling along, dipping in wherever needed.

Memories tumble together, like looking through a Kaleidoscope. In one's mind's eye I saw colourful people doing meaningful things. Some projects succeeded. Others such as Bible studies didn't. Yet successes abounded: fund raising for a new metal roof, a bequest to help it along, CGIT bike-a-thons and another bike-a-thon fund raiser to Grassy Lake. Linda, who once rode across Canada, organized and bubbled over with smiles and energy, encouraging us to press on. Young and old wheeled their way east, including brothers Blaine and Blake, their little legs pushing and burning up the miles on their tiny two wheelers.

Membership
We are not Christ's because we belong to the church,
but we are of the church because we belong to Christ 6

Soon after settling in at Knox, I dug into the office safe. I pulled out some black-bound, official looking books and put aside the wedding, baptism, and funeral records. Flipping through the brittle pages of the "Historical Roll," I found it only to be a list of names in alphabetical order. Names were crossed out, some lists rewritten, an amazing maze to get lost in while trying to count the number of current members. I had seen this remarkable honest effort before, in other towns, to keep track of who were members of the congregation. I felt it worth the effort to make the records reflect reality. On many important matters, members had voting rights. Adherents didn't. Members could serve on all church committees. Adherents could not serve on Worship and CE committees. Members had other rights that Adherents didn't.

Having also read back into the Board and annual meeting minutes, and attended several Board meetings, I found that the Board members agonized repeatedly over the issue of setting fees for weddings. A tempest in a tea cup continued to spill over when people thought members and their families should not have to pay for the use of the church facilities. But often the comment was,

" We don't even know who is and who isn't a member!"

Taking the bull by the horns, Mary, JoAnn, the Membership Committee, Bob, Pat and I attacked the problem. Two years later, after bending the ear of many on the phone and in person, sorting, licking stamps, typing and retyping, and computer entries, victory at last! Knox chronological historical roll, index to the roll, computer printouts, and roster eagerly awaited constant updates to keep the Knox church family records current. Now we knew for sure who were members.

People began to get the message that Knox took membership seriously. Several long time attenders and leaders found that it was okay to make it publically known that after all those years, they had not joined the church. Those fine persons weren't expected to attend membership classes, something I hunch many feared. Nor did they have to come forward alone to profess their faith publically, since a whole raft of them had agreed to "join." It was a very moving experience for me to see them state before their children and grandchildren what they already knew, and others assumed, that they did belong, having worked with their head, heart, and hand over many years, and voted with their feet. It was now official!

So many memories and so many members have passed through the doors of Knox church. More than a thousand names are listed in the historical roll, alive and deceased. True, some have left over the human sexuality issue, but many have remained, and others have come, their names and faces appearing in the church photo directories.

They were wrapped up in the human condition common to us all. Though what happens to us may differ, our responses may vary, but conditions are much the same. That causes one to ask, what responses to life's happenings motivate persons to choose to invest something of themselves in a church such as Knox. Is it curiosity, loneliness, fear, a feeling of emptiness, despair, hope, a need to belong? Perhaps it's all of these things and more. I've heard it said that it depends on what gender a person is, whether one risks getting involved or not.

Some say men will come if they have something physical to do, whereas women, being more social by nature, will have an edge on men when it comes to enjoying church. Whatever the reason, men and women are active at Knox!

It may not matter how many, or how few men and

women there are proportionately, but rather, how active each group is, and how secure they are in their faith. For that's what would help them to hold fast when buffeted by the storms of controversy that rise up now and then to challenge the church family. Knox church family had weathered many controversies, and adopted the necessary dig-in-one's heels stance that farmers and ranchers often took to survive.

Over and over, Knox continued to witness in Taber. Sometimes a person was forced to take a stand with a church family to lean again the storm. When differing with the then-moderator's view about who Jesus Christ is, I asked the editor of the Taber Times to print my strong view that Jesus is God, contrary to that moderator's opinion. It seemed to calm the waters somewhat, and few, if any, left Knox. In fact people continued to drop in and often stayed.

We set up a way of helping them to integrate into the church family. Our efforts also included those who had, somewhere along the way, already identified with Knox. The system to integrate new-comers came about after much effort was made to focus on the attendance of those listed on the church roster. At first we gave attention to the casuals and dropouts with the view of reactivating them, but to no avail. So we decided to give attention to the faithful and committed. The thought was that the active would bring new persons into the church. I, for one, got tired of trying to follow up on the many baptized and wedded who, after their big day, seldom ever returned to worship. In fact, when phoning some

newly-weds, I found that they were surprised at my call to find out how they were doing. Often, on hanging up, my feeling was that many cared less.
Controversial Issues: Property

> If we want things to stay as they are, things
> will have to change. 8

That feeling of indifference didn't fill the air when it came to people trying to grapple with issues thrown their way. Just as in every family, different opinions rage on. So Knox was no different! Someone or some group would do something. Others would object, and the fur would fly. A few persons wanted to sell stuff in the narthex before or after worship. "No way!"

"Okay, during cup and conversation in the gym?"

"Let's raffle off a quilt or sell tickets for a draw."

"All right, we won't. That's gambling, frowned upon in the United Church."

I recall that sometimes, to act first, and let the chips fall where they may, was better than seeing nothing happen. That was well illustrated by the saga of the ceiling. Visitors often rave about the fine wooden ceiling in Knox's sanctuary. A prominent member on the church Board decided, after a lot of non-productive talk, that a new ceiling was in order. He risked all, on his own, without any real thought where the money would come from, by arranging with a local contractor for it to happen. It did, and people were happy with the results. He allegedly broke every rule in the book in so far as church decision-making procedures were concerned, including not consulting the church trustees in charge of real property, or Presbytery, the ultimate authority on such big ticket items. No matter, the church family was pleased with the man who took the initiative and got the job done.

Now, it would have been risky for me to try a stunt like that. That was clear to me after I offered a suggestion in the church newsletter that some property, owned by the church, be sold. I learned that would just open old wounds. Knox owned a chunk of property next to its parking lot and right next to a home. The lawn and trees, which beautified and enhanced the church and the neighbour's home, took a lot of care. In fact, in my view, the church caretaker was mowing the lawn and attending to the trees for the benefit of the neighbour.

A previous minister was alleged to have suggested removing the trees and grass to extend the church parking lot. That idea didn't fly. Nor did my suggestion. Though, most likely the neighbor would have wanted first bid on it, in which case he, rather than our caretaker, would have looked after it, and thus helped enhance the church landscape. Then the shoe would have been on the other foot. Since the church was strapped for cash to make major repairs on the building, I thought that was the answer. But it wasn't, from the point of view of some who still smouldered over the sale years ago of the manse. Selling another piece of church property would be like removing a little bit more of the stump of an amputee, causing one to wonder where would it all end.

The sale of a manse had always been a bone of

contention in church families. It was no different at Knox. Some who were bitter thought the church "sold it for a song." It apparently did go for a low dollar by today's standards. Still at the time "reason prevailed." The minister had said that he didn't want to live in a house next to the church, to be bothered by transients. He needed some equity in a house down the line when he retired. Too, many members were tired of keeping a demanding building in repair. Still, despite those reasons, a few members of the church board resigned, and some others continued to regret that decision to this day.

Years went by, and new issues surfaced. One minister generated an interest in moving a few walls about and adding an extension to offer more visible office space, accessible to off the street business. Long hours of struggle resulted in a plan put forward by an architect, and costs assessed. Then it didn't happen. Those who were keen on the project had the wind taken out of their sails. The killing of that project no doubt left many eager members conveying the message,

"No, more, we're not out of here, but don't ask us to do anything again!"

Like a garden perennial, another issue surfaced called "wheel chair accessibility." Many have stood together peering at the stairs at either end of the lower hall, trying to picture in their minds, how a ramp would work. When they renovated the old part of the church basement, they included a wheelchair-accessible washroom, but no way to get down to it, apart from lugging people in wheel chairs, or carrying them down the stairs into the lower hall. In combing through the old Board minutes, I found evidence that the problem was tackled once before. Someone donated an improvised wheelchair lift, only to find it was rejected after it didn't meet all government safety codes. Unfinished business still caused the concerned to ask and respond.

"How come that church has one and we don't?"

"Well, we have handicapped parking signs and spaces. That's a start!"

Lingering in the shadows was another potentially contentious issue. But a solution was found. The old part of the building, once a free standing Presbyterian church, now a gym above, and Sunday school rooms below, started showing a need of more than a face lift. The decision was made. Rather than demolish that part of the church and rebuild, a bunch of the dedicated went at the scrungy basement tooth and nail. They sledge hammered stubborn chunks of concrete into submission, stripped away and replaced mildewed wall board, replaced crumbling lead pipe, installed new plumbing and used gallons of paint. When workers completed the job, surprise! They had boarded in a ceiling smoke detector that beeped pitifully for months hoping that someone would find and liberate it. A retired toilet became an ornament in the furnace room, but overall a miraculous transformation had occurred, and the grumbling was stilled, for the time being at least.

That do-for-now approach, nickel and dimed to death, make do, patch it, splice it, twist it, tie it, (just like using bailing twine and hay wire on the farm), was another fellow's approach. That guy took the bull by the horns on more than one occasion, whether asked to or not. He climbed, and practically crawled on his hands and knees to fix lighting in the dizzying heights of the sanctuary rafters, painted, hammered, crunched, whatever it took to keep things in shape, including a weird sound system. He unselfishly and willingly did what he thought had to be done his way, and thus arose the expression, "Let Doug do it," or "Doug did it!" In every church I've been, I've found a Doug, and I reluctantly had to admit, there was some kind of eccentric angel in disguise.

People like Doug B, who seemed not to question who owned the title of the church property, are few and far between. Many heard that the property is in the name of the United Church of Canada, rather than owned by the rugged Albertans whose families built and maintain it. They wondered why, especially when a happening caused rumbling that they might have to give something up that they have worked so hard to keep. There was some talk that, to avoid the threat of bankruptcy faced by many church denominations over the alleged Indian residential school abuse of students' claims, the church corporate might have to liquidate some of its assets, including some owned by individual congregations. News like that generated a "What's the use!" attitude among some who had invested heart and soul into keeping buildings from crumbling. For some, nothing seemed secure. Thus, when perennial intrusions raised their ugly heads, the only thing that kept people hanging in there to fight them off was grit and sheer stubbornness, like clinging to the back of a bucking bull.

Oh, there were many intrusions! Basements flooded, toilets flooded, and odd stinks attacked noses from who knows where? Water pipes burst, and not even the town knew where some led, since the long-gone retired town engineer allegedly had kept the locations in his head rather than on paper. The tower roof also leaked, and, for what seemed forever, evaded all diagnosticians until Willy found the answer. Mice took up housekeeping as bonafide church mice, and after the Irish Stew dinner thieves broke, in expecting a big haul of cash. Yet, sad to say, some kidnaped cherished silverware was never recovered.

The sanctuary fan's blades, as they turned crossing between the ceiling lights and the floor, created flickering light that defied all, including Doug and Martin's corrective efforts. Thus, there were so many interesting distractions that could, if one let them, shove a church off track.

UCW (United Church Women)

One group at Knox that wasn't easily distracted from fulfilling its purpose was the United Church Women (The UCW). The women belonged to several units. They pitched in to raise funds to help keep the church afloat, along with offering spiritual and social life to its members. As members got older, some units retired, while a young women's group picked up some of the slack. The Sunday bulletin notices throughout the year listed dates and times for rummage sales, teas and bazaars, meals served at teachers' dinners, hospital volunteer help, help at the thrift store, donations to non profit appeals, to training centres, and theological colleges. The men and the minister could only feel wistful that their efforts could in no way match those of the women.

Fellowship

The church families needed to have fun. That meant heads needed to get together to shake the bushes for ideas. A family dance went nowhere, though the lonely organizers enjoyed their event. But other ideas again got moms, dads, and kids in motion. Near Christmas time, tissue paper, wooden bird house parts, pine cones, ribbon, such stuff that crafts are made of, got the glue gun, scissors, and hammers and nail treatment. Happy accidents, fun creations, hair and hands sprinkled with sparkles; all came together. Kids and adults created Christmas decorations and displays, and new homes for birds next spring. Food and hay rides and Christmas carols followed. Other together-times included monthly men's breakfasts, with speakers, pancakes, sausages and jokes. Family fun did find a place at Knox.

Finance

The joy of giving wasn't only in putting something on the offering plate, sending a cheque or making a pledge. We found joy also in fund-raising events; full of fellowship, times when sweat, aching arms and backs, joined with jokes, kidding, and laughter. All that made annual fall suppers really something else! It wasn't only because of the fellowship, but also because of the great feeling of seeing the whole community dig in to help, the old and young, farmers, ranchers, and town folk.

Fund-raising from suppers and the great silent auction didn't completely stop the worry over needed money. One or two weeks were set aside for people to make pledges. Rather than go door to door, two by two, using the old approach of telling people what their church was up to, and what it had on the go, the finance committee sent letters of appeal with the same message to all who identified with Knox. Persons were also encouraged to arrange with their banks or credit unions to have givings sent from their banks directly to the United Church of Canada who, in turn, would then credit the local church. That helped pay the bills in the summer months when many weren't in church to put money on the offering plates. The program was called "PAR " (Preauthorized Remittance).

I always felt the finance committee and treasurer had to have nerves of steel to keep the church out of the red. That wasn't the reason, though, why I stayed clear of finance, and the church secretary's score keeping role. I made a point of never knowing what people gave, for fear that it would affect the way I worked with them and their pastoral needs.

My only shadowing of finance had to do with the promotion of the United Church Mission and Service Fund. I encouraged the monthly minute for mission where lay persons read from the lectern a description of a project somewhere in the world where M and S funds were well used. I, and many others, were happy. For, despite the congregation's motion on the books not to make up the short fall in individual givings to M and S to meet a target set by Presbytery, individuals' givings always almost matched what Presbytery called for. That money could not be held back to cover local expenses.

Lee, then Geri, and Harry, along with others on the finance committee, did a thankless job where often, only when the books were in the red, did persons raise their heads to question spending. The only relief for the committee was that they didn't have to give final approval to the paying of the bills. That was done at the monthly Board meetings. I felt a little remiss in not continuing to emphasize the idea of promoting projects and then encouraging persons to respond, not only with money (very necessary stuff), but also with sweat equity.

Outreach

I was grateful that Knox gave the OK for my secretary and me to give meal chits of five dollars and fifty cents each to persons who came, saying that they hadn't eaten for some time, and could we help? Since we never gave cash, nor kept it around in the office, that band-aid response served as one outreach to the needy. The odd time persons would become belligerent when I refused to give them money, bus tickets, or gas. Once a man, tanked up on alcohol, said,

"Well, I can always beat you up." I suggested the police might be interested in that. He left promptly, empty handed. I heard later that he and his lady friend were picked up for shop lifting at the nearby convenience store across from the social services office. I always felt responsible for those who came, in the sense that I didn't want them to intimidate or prevail upon the generosity of worshipers coming or leaving the church. Once, I walked a young man through the park across the street, heard the life story he wanted to give me, about his jail time, and hard luck. I felt I'd heard it all before, concluding that to survive on the street, persons like that man, needed a line and persona to hide behind, to get a fix, whether it be drugs, alcohol, attention, or what have you.

Unlike handouts, one of the effective outreach ministries for Knox was providing space to non profit self help groups such as Alateen, AA, and Tops (take off pounds sensibly). The only drawback was that, sometimes, an outside group would gradually spill over into other spaces needed by church programs, or bump up against them. When I first arrived at Knox, I took the liberty of asking the Tops group, who had their weigh scale and other paraphernalia stored in the choir room, to move it into the lower hall nursery. I appreciated their positive response. But I finally learned as the minister that it's best not to be involved with building bookings, or space allocation. I learned it was better to leave that to the church secretary or the caretaker. I'm glad I did. The odd time a group or two would be asked to move to another space just for a particular evening. Sometimes people responded to such requests unpleasantly. It was even more a sensitive issue if a member of the congregation happened to be a member of the outside group. Distancing myself, I was able to act more effectively in a pastoral role to calm the water. Though that didn't always work.

Knox facilities did offer a useful venue for performing groups, especially on the lower hall stage. For four years, once a month, singers, instrumentalists, and cowboy poets stood on that stage and shared their talents. The best thing about it was that persons of any, or no denomination, or faith stance were welcomed to give it their all, providing that they didn't do any heavy duty testimonies or offer altar calls. Conversions weren't the name of the game. The goals were good fellowship, fun, and opportunities for old and young to try out their talents in public, maybe for the first time. John and Edna, Shelly and her sister, and for a time, John's gospel singers, held forth as the anchor group. Other persons came and went; that was the whole idea of it. Performers didn't audition, they just dropped in, wrote down what they wanted to do, sing, play, or recite. Just before we started, I shuffled the papers, putting them in the order that people would perform to give variety, and it happened! The rules were simple. Content had to be western gospel, folk music or family stuff. Slick, slushy love themes weren't welcomed. Occasionally such did creep in, as did some unpolished stuff irritating to the ears. Still, that wasn't discouraged, for usually over several months the presentations improved, and the public cable TV would sometimes cover the events, adding to the fun.

Communications

The key to growth and what's been coined as "community building" centered in letting people know what was going on, and how they could fit into that scheme of things. To help make that happen, the church family used message boxes, and pew cards so people could identify themselves and their interests. New families and visitors often used the cards as a first contact to make themselves known to the minister and other active members. Old timers, who finally overcame their uneasiness in sticking their neck out to volunteer, also used the cards. Interchangeable signs, John and Russ's creation, were wrapped around the corner tree to broadcast upcoming events. Drivers, nosing up to any of the four corners on 50th and 50th could get a gander of what was up at Knox. People reading the Sunday bulletin insert and newsletter also got the latest. But often "suggestions for consideration," fell flat. Bible study and growth group offerings got few bites, hardly even a nibble. I learned in talking to a colleague that, he, too, found a lack of interest in study groups.

I envied pastors in evangelical churches, and JW's who had zealous "Christians" keen on Bible study. I recall counseling one rural mother who had a rough upbringing and rocky marriage. Her home visiting JW hairdresser was "bringing her into the fold." The person convinced that young woman that UCs don't study the Bible like JWs do. When the young woman told me that, I responded by giving her material spelling out what UC and JWs believed. She left for the JW's. I became convinced that, lacking stability in her life, she sought someone or some group who would tell her what to believe, and do so in black and white terms.

Oh, the cross we UCs bear in working with greys, rather than prescriptive messages. We dare to challenge persons to struggle with their faith rather than create intellectual and spiritual cripples. That's Knox's way.

Knox did have some material unique to its church family: a mission statement identifying "who we are;" a brief list of suggestions on "when to call a minister;" a constitution spelling out the process on how decisions are made, and what the committees do; and a member's handbook. All that was well and good, but unless the people exposed to that stuff were in the right frame of mind to look at it and work with it, no sales pitch got to them. All the pictures of Jesus hanging on the walls throughout the church building didn't really do the trick either, neither did the unread notices on the many bulletin boards. The only way that I accepted the reality of that communication dilemma was to accept the advice, Do all you can, then leave it up to God.

Official Board

Leaving it up to God to ultimately turn people toward the Creator of it all was one thing, but it was another to help a church congregation like Knox to do God's work. It took a body of decision makers. At Knox, that was the Official Board. Unfortunately, over the years, fewer people showed up for Board meetings. It got to the point where the Board, normally made up of more than thirty people, ended up to be about the size of the executive. I tried planting a seed suggesting what some churches and Presbyteries had done. They faced up to reality, and restructured so that, rather than a large body made up of all the various committee members, they formed an active executive. Whenever the executive identified a project, informed by the congregation at quarterly meetings, it would set up a task force. When the job was done that group would disband, and others formed as need be. So, instead of having ongoing committees, with the exception of Worship, CE, Finance, and the Trustees, there would be a body of decision makers keen on getting the job done and not so vulnerable to burn out and drop out.

One person gave this reason why he dropped out. He claimed that the Board often rehashed what committees decided, often becoming a committee of the whole. That happened when Property or Finance matters surfaced at Board meetings. Despite the many reasons given for a new structure, the idea for a change got "no takers." Maybe the old guard, made up of devoted hard workers, now tired, wouldn't buy into the idea because years ago, they had worked their hearts out to change from a Session, Stewards structure to a Unified Board made up of many ongoing committees. Perhaps they just couldn't see their way to chuck it, after having invested so much of themselves in it, even if it wasn't working.

A new decision-making model might have given the congregation more time and energy to focus on the mission of the church beyond its doors, put more effort into "building community,"and benefit more often from resource people and speakers. That, of course, could still happen if the church family took a

big step to rely on the elected executive members to
do the housekeeping, and then report the results of
their efforts to quarterly congregational meetings.

Although I got the idea that the restructuring
wouldn't fly, I did feel some seeds were planted in
the form of a Board Policy Manual. I felt that before
this was compiled, decision makers, especially those
with long service records in the church, carried Knox's
church policies around in their heads, powered by
experience. Like computers, they were consulted
about what was on their cerebral tapes. The problem
with that was that eventually those persons faded out
of the picture. New Board members came and went,
and each time, the new comers often rehashed policy
to "reinvent the wheel." True, in time, policies need
to be revisited to see if they still fit the situation, but
at least there was now a starting point, that is, the
policies spelled out in the Board Policy Manual.
Thanks to Carol and Charlotte and Jo Ann copies
were finally in the hands of Knox decision makers.

Near the end of my tenure at Knox, inspired by the
Interim Ministry course that I had completed, I read
through the Knox historical material, Board minutes,
and whatever I could get my hands on to make a
"Time Line." That showed where the church family
had been, the highs and the lows, the losses, and the
gains. It also identified some of the ghostly issues
and decisions that smoldered in the memories of still
active church members , that coloured their views,
attitudes, and opinions, and influenced their
decisions. I had hoped that enough interest would
have been generated that, when I displayed it to the

Board and congregation, we could have grappled with what it all meant. However, that didn't happen.

Office and Study

When I first arrived at Knox, something got my attention right away. Climbing umpteen stairs to the church secretary's tower office and crossing the threshold, I found myself standing in a few square feet surrounded by a huge desk, file cabinet, photocopier, and typewriter stand. Jo Ann sat amidst it all. She had succeeded a series of secretaries over the years. Carol, her mother, Jeanette, and Mary also had worked in those cramped quarters. Having seen the minister's big office off the main floor lounge, it didn't make much sense to me to see a crammed-in secretary greeting elderly persons, who climbed to the tower office on church business. So I negotiated a trade with JoAnn with the approval of the Board chair. She would have my office. I would have hers.

I found the space uplifting and even fascinating. For a couple of years I saw two pigeons perched just outside my window cooing, no doubt with admiration for each other. Opening the door to reveal a ladder leading to where the bell hung I noted, a yellowed, brittle sign reading,

"Boys are not allowed up in the tower to shoot pigeons." signed, Rev. Kennedy

There might have been one reason for that rule. I heard that, back then, the tower floor was knee deep in pigeon droppings.

In the corner by the window was a square, metal gas heater of another era, and in various locations along the room's baseboards, crawling up the walls, were mysterious wires leading to who knows where. It appeared, like other older churches, Knox, not only had its traditions, but it also had a structure decorated with many interesting innovations of unknown origin or purpose. There was always someone around though, who knew of someone, who knew what that something or other was for. The trick was to find that person who knew.

JoAnn faced the same problem. People dropped in and out of the main floor general office, and often, in her absence, left things behind as if she ran a warehouse. Often people never retrieved those items. In time stored financial records, boxes of paper for recycling, and other residual from projects, and unclaimed lost items did indeed transform her office into a bit of a warehouse. That didn't help much as she wrestled with the peculiarities of the photocopier to produce Sunday bulletins, prepare financial statements to put in the message boxes, produce an annual report, and do all that and more, with constant interruptions.

I found it incredible that she was able to keep her composure, and show an immense amount of patience for about ten years. What's more, she did that, working for "many bosses," all at the same time. Perhaps she was able to "keep her cool" because she wasn't expected to make policy decisions. For, according to church protocol, she was to pass the buck to those on the Board required to make tough decisions. I was relieved that neither was I to set policy.

South Alberta Presbytery

That was also so true when it came to my work in Presbytery. Since ministers are members of Presbytery, they are required to serve on committees. While at Knox I briefly chaired two Presbytery Committees, first Stewardship, and then Oversight. The former included soliciting responses from congregations, having asked each what they were prepared to budget for the Mission and Service Fund, a job that was like pulling teeth. The Oversight Committee job meant recruiting Presbytery members to band together in teams to do the mandatory visits to congregations to find out how they were doing, and to address any problems that they might have. All that was done following prescribed protocol. Recruiting wasn't fun. I had the choice of grumbling, cajoling, or just passing a paper around the Presbytery meeting tables and assumed people would accept their responsibility and sign up. To my pleasant surprise, they usually did. Within three or four months persons visited the selected sites for that year and reported back to the Oversight committee. That wasn't an easy task since South Alberta Presbytery extended from Medicine Hat to the Crows Nest, from Milk River to beyond Foremost, to Lethbridge including Fort McLeod and Granum, and extending north to Brooks and Empress,

I did enjoy when I was chairperson participating in Covenanting services of ministers newly called to congregations. That was when the minister, the congregation, and Presbytery agreed together to support each other in a common ministry, and the minister agreed to be subject to the discipline of

Presbytery.

Chairing Presbytery was really something else! From my point of view the clergy seemed to be doing most of the talking, reporting for table group discussions, and putting forth motions, whereas the lay delegates were supportive of motions put forward by the clergy. I felt that, because Presbytery met during the week when most employed lay people, including students, were at work, that a disproportionate number of delegates were retired folk, thus not ensuring representation of a cross section of the Presbytery population.

There seemed to be ongoing tension between the need for fellowship and doing the business of the church. It appeared that some Presbytery reps. came mainly for fellowship, and others, like me, to get the business done. I saw Presbytery as mainly the Court of the Church.

As Chair I also found building the agenda with the executive prior to a meeting was a challenge . I felt uncomfortable with the style of chairing meetings that seemed to be expected, so I was relieved when I finished my term. On the upside, I did appreciate the past chair attending meetings in Edmonton and Calgary when I wasn't fit to travel while dealing with an eye problem. I also found it heartening that so many excellent ordinands (recent grads of theological seminaries) had been called to congregations in the Presbytery, especially to those down on their heels, or requiring a strong presence.

Among them were two scholars, and one who, because of his height was eyed as a good prospect for an LDS basketball team. It felt good, also, to know that all three other ministers whom I had supervised when they did their required internship, were making significant contributions in full time accountable order of ministry. Their personal stories were fascinating to hear. There were so many, but one in particular stands out for me.

Prior to entering a seminary, Bruce hiked all over the middle east, Europe and England, working for wages or room and board as he went. That's nothing new of course. But his novel approach aroused my interest. In Israel he worked on a Kibbutz. There, to relieve boredom, he and a friend decide to start a club. They called it the "Red Shoe Laces." Anyone who belonged could wear red shoe laces. Many who saw their laces became curious, asking "What's up." They were told, and then wanted to join.

"But what do you do?"

"Oh, nothing, we just wear red shoelaces."

Well, somehow the word got out about the red shoe lace club, beyond the Kibbutz, beyond Israel, as far as Europe suggesting that possibly a subversive organization was on the loose. Our minister friend was astonished at how a fun idea to relieve boredom had got so out of hand. Yet at the same time he shared with me the humour of it all. He also once worked in a pub in England. When asked what he knew about English beer and spirits, he said, "Oh nothing." He must have had a lot of guts to field the requests of serious drinkers who, by their accents and his responses could spot an intruder. But they didn't mind! On my friend went. When he got back to

347

Vancouver, he recalled those incidents, including one where he was thrown in jail in the far east for a border crossing infraction.

My fascination with this character didn't stop there, having heard of his Gulliver-like journey and safe return home. For that talented fellow also turned out to be an Elvis Presley impersonator, and a good one, one who didn't burden himself down with a lot of rhinestone-covered costumes or other props. One of his many contributions to the life of the community in which the church had settled him, was staging a massive Elvis Presley event. Impersonators came from far and wide to literally invade that small town and draw enthusiastic crowds to all of the performances. Besides raising funds for the church, his effort offered an opportunity for the town residents to pull closer together, sharpen their identity, and renew pride in their accomplishments.

I won't forget that fellow, not only for his drive, but for his ability to tell children's stories standing on his head, a feat so marveled at, that youngsters would often time him to see if he broke his last record.

One might suppose that each Presbyter (reps to Presbytery) from every congregation takes pride in his or her church family, town, or municipality's accomplishments, projects or victories over adversity. One year, a clergy couple encouraged their congregation to visit with some Christians in Africa, and the Africans would in turn visit Southern Alberta. The couple gained the support of Presbytery and it did happen, thus enlightening, not only their own congregation, but many others who heard what Christians in another country were dealing with.

Not all of Presbyteries' agendas focused on such people-centred projects. The presbytery sometimes received letters that demanded a lot of scratching of heads to figure out what to do. A farmer wrote that he'd been plowing and seeding around an old country church grave yard for years. He had had enough and wanted to know who owned it and should pay taxes on the land that he couldn't use. He was willing to care for it, if it was deeded to him, but right then, whoever owned it wasn't looking after it, and that bothered him.

Then there was the very small congregation that summer students had served for years. Since it had a delegate to Presbytery, it was assumed that it had the powers given to pastoral charges, but was it a Pastoral Charge, or was it a Mission field? Some said, "Who cares!" Well, apparently Presbytery did. For, if it was a mission field, ministers would be appointed by Presbytery and a committee would oversee the life and work of that congregation. If it was a Pastoral charge, then the presence of a voting delegate from that charge would be in order; and on the discussions went. We had laboured over what to do about a little church in the middle of nowhere, with one or two small families of ranchers represented on the membership list who just wanted to get on with being a church.

Now, some retired ministers, free on Sundays, and others in institutional work, felt for these orphan church families, or those who just couldn't find a minister. Some traveled about, filling in on Sundays. But a few not only did that, but acted like "Lone Rangers," marrying, baptizing, often without consulting with, or gaining an invitation or permission from the incumbent ministers where the events took place. Finally measures were taken, endorsed by the courts of the church to put a stop to that. Ministers had to be on staff, or be invited by a church Board to perform the sacraments, weddings, and funerals in the precincts of a pastoral charge. Once that happened, a visiting minister could get a letter of permission from the province's church office to perform weddings that he or she had booked. That seemed to make sense to me, but I found it sad that it had to be legislated. It almost tempted me to praise the good old days when integrity and empathy won the day. What's been happening to our church and society? Is our church merely a reflection of society, or should society be a reflection of the church? I struggle with that question.

Local Churches and Denominations

The Taber Ministerial, made up of the various church denominations helped us to appreciate each other as parts of the Body of Christ. Perhaps it also made us even a little more tolerant of each other. But sadly it had a flaw. LDS and JW's were excluded because they didn't subscribe to the Apostles Creed and/or the Trinity which were the common denominators that qualified a minister for membership.

I must admit that I had real problems with the theology of those two "outsiders." Yet the LDS, who represented a big percentage of Taber and the municipality population was a group that wanted to cooperate with other churches, unlike the JW's. So I suggested to members of the ministerial that we encourage the formation of an interfaith group, where all faith stances might be represented. But I had no takers. I sensed suspicion haunted the group, thinking that those two "sheep stealers" as some called them, would have a field day if let loose on "their flocks."

Taber churches seemed to be divided into camps, the LDS in one, the Evangelicals, Pentecostals, and Anglicans, and Christian Reform in other, the Lutherans, Roman Catholics and United in yet still another, and the Canadian Reform, Seventh Day Adventists, and JW's hanging out on their own.

I hunched some of the sense of division among the denominations may have had something to do with the individual beliefs and temperaments of the clergy in some churches, rather than the congregations. In some others, which were often populated by one ethnic group or another, and where there were large family enclaves, church elders might have discouraged their clergy from "fraternizing with those others." Yet again, it might be that clergy or the people of different denominations were just too busy with their own people to find time for more collegiality.

What I did find out for sure is that, when ministers went out of their way to rub shoulders with other clergy, a greater appreciation of each other's gifts, interests and concerns surfaced, and learning took place. I found out from the Rev. Chuck Daisley that the strange tower on the RC church was shaped to resemble a grain elevator to honour the work of farmers. I learned that the Rev. Dale gave flying balloon instructions, that Pastor Nick had an extraordinary knowledge of the Bible; that Rev. Linden was very much a church historian, and that Father Andy was a gourmet cook, and allegedly owned a big Lincoln and car wash in Calgary.

Learning these things, and more, about my brothers in Christ, I realized they were fascinating people to know. Yet still, I had problems when some of them dug in their heels over such things as refusing to see their congregations participate in the Kiwanis Music Festivals because they were held in the LDS Stake House. In the end, Knox choirs participated in both the Ministerial-sponsored Christmas Carol services at the Christian Reform Church, and also at the Kiwanis Carol Festivals. Unfortunately, because of so few ministerial church choirs participating, the Kiwanis Carol Festival became highly represented by LDS choirs from the four wards in Taber.

It seemed to me that different church denominations went about their own way without much give or take, or for that matter, checking to see how their activities would impact on others. Knox was the recipient of that lack of touching bases one Sunday when one of the evangelical churches decided to have a service practically outside Knox's front door just when our worship service was to begin. At Confederation Park just across from Knox, using a public address system and a loud band, they carried on with their event, seemingly totally oblivious to how that affected our service. If I hadn't known about that church and the good work it did in the community, and if I hadn't known how fine a Christian the pastor of that church was, I would have blown my top. However, I learned that I didn't need to express my displeasure, for the long time residents of Taber, many of whom were related to each, but with feet in different churches, had a quiet way of dealing with such matters. They didn't need my two-cents worth.

Sometimes, keeping silent seemed best, something hard for clergy to do. I believe that some members of the ministerial found that keeping opinions to themselves was a must. For, unlike UC clergy whose bishop is, in a sense, Presbytery, they answered to the local elders. That set-up unfortunately led to the loss of tenure of several pastors during my time in Taber. Many of those were put in the position to walk in a mine field of political intrigue, strewn with the emotional debris of infighting among families. I was fortunate to be able, by the nature of our UC church policy, to avoid that path.

Although I felt reasonably secure, I believed some of our members were not, in the sense that there were door knockers out gunning for them, using tactics which I felt were often unethical, and certainly not Christian. In one instance, a couple of LDS missionaries attempted to convert a confused woman member of our congregation. I was concerned because I had seen before zealous types going after persons when they were most vulnerable. The member came to me all confused and upset because she didn't want to alienate her good friend who was LDS, and who had introduced her to the missionaries. I listened to her, and over a period of a few meetings shared what the United Church believed, and what I understood the LDS believed. I explored with her what she was going to get and what she would be giving up and left her to decide, even though she wanted to be told what to do. That was an especially sensitive issue since in no way was her husband going to join the LDS church. She stayed UC but wanted to be baptized again. I suggested a rededication service. She appreciated that.

It seems so easy to get caught up in the intriguing web of church politics and what may seem as esoteric theology, that one loses touch with reality beyond the doors of the church. Most ministers today try not to isolate themselves from life beyond Sunday worship and insular thinking. I, having come into full time accountable ministry later in life, felt I definitely still had my eyes open to observe what was going on in town and country from the point of a non-clergy person.

20   Taber Town and Traffic

Town Life:

I found a kaleidoscope of fascinating characters, not only in the church, but also in town and businesses, on acreages, ranches and farms, so many down to earth persons, the salt of the earth. Each who had his or her own unique personality and slant on life, took in town events.

Henry and Jean, "Mrs. and Mr. Museum," though getting on in years, drove the loose gravel to town practically daily to nurse along the local museum or orientation center. Jean, also a local historian, wrote a couple of books that you'll find in most nearby rural homes.

Miss Kathleen Rowley, now deceased, and no doubt with her Lord, often spoke about the importance of a person's name being in the "Lamb's book of life." She wrapped and decorated almost anything, including picture frames, with aluminum foil. She often told of hitchhiking across the country as a missionary for Jesus. I heard that, after growing up in Taber, when there were mud streets and "Tin Lizzies" (cars), she left, arriving back years later, a forgotten lady, only to be rediscovered sitting in the bitter cold on the front steps of Knox church. People, who remembered her and her parents years ago, looked after her needs, finding her food and lodging. Thereafter, she trudged to church every Sunday, insisting on witnessing, or giving her testimony if I just hinted that I was open for additional announcements from the congregation. Miss Rowley allegedly had a well off, caring family somewhere, but she was a very proud, independent lady, who wanted to go her own way, and she did!

The aging Anderson sisters, who were inseparable, lived in their old family home. Molly, who had been a successful agent with TCA when they flew the Lougheeds, was called home by "daddy" to care for her bedridden mother and her sisters. "Daddy" owned and operated Anderson's Clothing Store where the girls worked off and on. The family had a cottage at Waterton Lake. Molly remembered dancing to the music of Mart Kenney and his orchestra. She remembered the famous jockey, Johnny Longden, when he was just a boy riding down the back lane. A couple of the sisters, their faces withered, spoke using expressions long out of use, coming from their teenage days.

Visiting them in their big rambling house made me think that time had stood still for them. Betty had a sweetheart that she had corresponded with for years. Ann loved to bet on the horses, and play the VLTs, and garden. Marion, the oldest lived across the street and loved cats. Before he died, her husband Roy drove her across that street for the "girls" afternoon tea, served in the veranda in the summer, at precisely the same time each afternoon. Their deceased mother and father were Irish, and in preparation for Molly's funeral, I learned her mother had played and performed in music halls in Ireland. I thumbed through a stack of sheet music yellow and crisp with age. Some of it had been her mother's. It was Molly's and her sisters wish to have Irish music played and sung at Molly's funeral, and no doubt it was her wish that her sisters be cared for, as that had been her life's calling to please "daddy."

Beyond where Anderson's family home sat, straight north of the sugar factory, across from the old Hungarian Hall, now the Seventh Day Adventist church, once lived "old" John Reti. Now there was a man of many talents! He had farmed and scratched a living from a bit of land. Before that he raised and herded sheep, gaining a reputation as a fine stock man. His son followed his dad's footsteps and once raised sheep. John's neighbour's respected him for his know-how and his stewardship of the land. He was also known for his zeal as a collector. While digging into the old garbage dump for antique bottles, he hauled out three Medical School diplomas that years ago hung on the wall of Dr. Hamman's office. A school was named after the old doctor. One of those diplomas eventually found a place on the school wall.

John once had a kind of museum in his house on the home quarter. One of the rooms in that humble home became a shrine in memory of his dead wife. Her combs, hair brushes, jewelry, pictures, a lamp, all were displayed almost as she had left them. That remained just so until years later John had a huge garage and yard sale. Walking around John's yard, with people descending from their vehicles, reminded me of an old National Film Board movie, a flashback into the past, and a scramble by many for nostalgia. John's memories were encased in things he once cherished, but left for a future with his lady friend and her family. He replaced his "antiques," some which he offered for sale at Parkside Manor, (the senior drop in centre)with new interests .

I recall John surprising me when I stood as Legion chaplain to help initiate new Legion members and saw him, well into his eighties, marching forward alongside his new companion. What a man! Bone and sinew, as if he was held together with hay wire. He, of strong Hungarian stock, could squeeze out a tune on a concertina, do magic tricks, and dance. When others were covered with sweat and practically crawling off the dance floor, he was still stepping lively. I felt a little sad when John left Knox, where he'd been for years, to attend the RC church with his lady friend. Yet, why not?

Taber was blessed with many unique characters like John. Mr. Petrie, the "bike man" was another. CBC once featured him on its TV. series, "On the Road Again," a program that celebrated unique and eccentric Canadians from across our vast country. He came from New Brunswick with his wife to work on a railway section gang. His back gave out, so he was left to pick up odd jobs here and there. He figured everything out in his head, inventing useful things like a wheel chair lift for his crippled son. He repaired bikes, created things of his own invention, bedstead bikes, bikes that humped along like running buffalo, and the biggest bike ever, along with other weird contraptions. He and his boys would ride them along parade routes in many towns and cities, leaving crowds marveling at his ingenuity. He impressed me too, not only for his parading and mechanical skills, but also for his collection of vintage bicycles which could have been another town tourist attraction if housed prominently. But lacking travel money needed to continue parading, and no support from the town or other sponsors, no doubt by now, rust has invaded the bodies of his bikes.

Though, for years, neither he nor his wife was able

358

to read or write, he still was able to match the best minds in problem solving. Once a University prof challenged his engineering class to build a bike that had many wheels that would rotate in unison, powered by two standard bike wheels. Apart from those two, the other wheels were not to touch the ground as the bike moved forward. Mr. Petrie said, "I can do that!" Where the students failed, Petrie succeeded. He had the many wheels positioned and in motion in a rainbow-like arc above the bar of the bike.

Despite that man's demonstrated genius, rather than be recognized as a public treasure, as one might be in Japan, he continued to eke out a mere existence, unselfishly repairing bikes and wheelchairs, improvising some to meet users' unique needs, and yet, always remaining true to himself.

Like old John Reti, he refused to stagnate. You could see him, with his white Santa Claus beard, shock of white hair, and baseball cap rambling along with his cheerful wife toward the adult learning center. They were going to learn to read! And they did!

The Local Press ("The Taber Times") also had living treasures: two men who once owned the newspaper, really did a job for the local people. They, as owners, had an investment in the community that went beyond merely satisfying the absentee shareholders. Rather than building the paper around advertisements and filling the spaces that were left for stories, often not of the local scene, they may have leaned toward doing it the other way around.

Local interests allegedly came first, advertisements followed to fill in the spaces.

It might have been true, also, back then, that the local resident reporters chose Taber as home. The two owners, no doubt, as town residents, having a greater stake in the community, demonstrated that by joining in with others to support worthy causes.

Many small rural churches have seen excellent ministers come and soon go at the first chance to get a "bigger and better church," or live in a larger center. So, after the two men sold out, it seemed, that happened also in Taber with editors and reporters. The only consolation was that the local manager had a commitment to the community. So, though subject to the policies from on high, she was sensitive enough to shape the paper so at least the readers could live with the changes within the limits of the dictates of outsiders' policies. That paper's manager even once asked the public for ideas to make the paper better. She got them, and did what she could. Simple things like the "Fridge News," listing upcoming events, dates and locations, helped, since there was no other really visible outdoor public notice board in town.

Community Causes and Controversies:
Persons picked up on a litany of local issues from the Taber Times, off the street and from coffee shop talk:

Arts and Crafts Association building extension. Some artists left.

Residents debate the new condo location and the loss of some ball diamonds and a tennis court. Some players were unhappy!

A few seniors mad over the relocation of one tennis court near the senior drop in said, "They ain't going to use our washrooms!"

Some residents wanted more stop signs, especially across from the furniture stores. One top town official replied,

"I don't agree, and how come I wasn't in on the decision."

Many residents were in the dark over a police chief's firing.

Pro-Life, and crusade against pornography group, very alive.

No Smoking bylaw anywhere children are present, debated.

No police dog anymore,

But the public raised funds to get it and "we need it!"

No pawn brokers allowed in town.

On it went with Town Council in the batting box, hitting some, and striking out on others.

Down Town Taber

A town like Taber was dependent for its image on the make up of its down town, just as a church is dependent in part for its image on the shape of its property. A thriving business section with well-kept buildings entices visitors to return, and new residents to come and stay. That being a given, how did Taber stack up?

Looking at the town of Taber is like looking into a vehicle rear view mirror. When I thought back to what I saw downtown, I found clues and examples of how businesses work with buildings and land to get the "biggest bang for the buck." I concluded church denominations, like other institutions, or corporate bodies follow these same patterns in other towns and cities. Take these for example:

Reusing like the Hermit Crab:

Anyone who has lived in the town for many years has seen buildings used and reused for different things. A bowling alley became a funeral home, a movie theater, a dance studio. A harness shop became a florist's shop and sports store. A butcher shop became a book store, and CG Confectionary became Panagopoulos (another "Pizzeria), and on it goes, not unlike in other communities, with school houses becoming homes, and churches becoming granaries. The process reminded me of what the Hermit Crab does. Not having made a shell of its own, it finds a vacated one to occupy. The only difference is, it gets it rent free.

The Need for More Elbow Room:

As Taber grew, so also did the need for more police services. No longer was Taber a "one horse town." Yet the Police Service's cramped quarters gave that idea to the public. The work space, dispatching equipment, interview rooms, cells and more, offered little to ensure efficiency. Still, the staff did deliver, working out of a building that seemed to hold hands with two other inadequate facilities, the library and the retired court house across from the Post Office. There was talk of having the police move into the Post Office building since Canada Post had farmed much of the postal business out to the local drugstore, and deliverers on contract. That idea was found wanting, just as rescuing the old court house as a heritage building was a non starter. The verdict?

Relocate the police station down in the Industrial section. Someone asked, "Will that mean another empty building?" The answer? "Not necessarily. Maybe they could punch a hole through the library into the police station."

Like musical chairs, as businesses and services started bursting at the seams, they often found a bigger building, with the previous occupant moving into a yet a larger one. When the dust had settled, and the shifting around had ceased, the one without usually left Taber, or built an even bigger building. Exceptions to that game existed. The Food Store owners took over the IGA leaving a long established business location. Eventually an accounting firm bought it, tore the guts out of it to make offices.

Stuck with a White Elephant:

Creating a new identity for a grocery store took money, something not everybody had. The owner of a another store sold his stock, but couldn't sell his building. Like a taxi meter that kept running, the taxes on the building kept increasing. Stuck with a "white elephant," the only thing he could do was restock with something different in a town that seemed to have everything. Could he make a go of it selling health promotion stuff and bottled water? I wondered.

One Stop Shopping:

Picture this: For shoppers' convenience, some businesses with something in common related to life and death. Starting on the corner across from the swimming pool, a funeral home, next door a medical clinic, just around the corner, a chiropractor, and next to that, a florists. Then across the street from the medical clinic, a church, and across from it a real estate office. And if you get hungry while helping yourself or someone else move on, there's an A & W next to the florists.

Not in My Back Yard:

A convenience store across from Knox went out of business. There was some talk of the building becoming a liquor store, a competing business. God forbid! A sigh of relief resounded as if from the church's carillon. A dentist bought the building, very appropriate, since getting people to church was somewhat like pulling teeth.

Success Formula:

The dentist's new location was a plum, in that it almost satisfied the four musts for a successful business. A needed product, high visibility at the town's center of gravity, the corner of 50th and 50th. The other two necessary ingredients, parking and marketing seemed sufficient, since it was a fast flow operation. Empty parking spaces happened as fast as two dentist chairs emptied and were refilled. That was not unlike McDonald's, the new kid in town, near the new Safeway. It seemed to me to offer uncomfortable chairs to help people inhale their burgers and "keep 'em moving." Unlike McDonalds that had to hard sell a common piece of ground beef, the dentist's advertising came by word of mouth.

However, what the dentist didn't have to face, the businesses on the main drag that sold merchandise, did. Parking was a problem. Yet, some business people, rather than parking away from the main drag on the parking lot behind the Dairy Queen "hogged" the convenient customer spots on the main drag. That invited feathers to fly, especially if a business rival parked in front of the competition's store for the day. It appeared downtown Taber was showing signs that it would become like a small strip mall in a city, full of lawyers, accountants, and other paper-pushing businesses that neither relied on tons of parking, nor feared competition from Lethbridge.

Lack of Consumer Loyalty:

Taber, like all small towns, turned itself upside down with "Midnight Madness" and other common gimmicks to encourage people to shop locally. Still, that admirable effort seemed doom to failure. For the only way to stop the Cosco shoppers, apart from blocking off the new paved twinned lanes to Lethbridge, would be to provide the shoppers with cheap entertainment, and answer one big beef: that is that many Taber business owners won't or can't go out of their way to give the same or better service than the Lethbridge competition.

Competing Similar Businesses:

Two Taber furniture stores were located kitty corner from each other. "Isn't that terrible," some said? Yet, one who knew the business said, "No," human nature will prevail! The shopper will go from one to the other, seeking a bargain. Both stores will benefit, Two are better than one to draw customers, offering choices to compete with Lethbridge. Unfortunately, one store did go under by trying to sell the top of the line, high-priced stuff, offered in Lethbridge. Yet, the old low price, general store bread and butter, off the shelf items still appealed to the farmers struggling to make ends meet.

Mr. Dress Up Times:

False store fronts still hid many run-down buildings, a reminder that you can't make a silk purse from a sow's ear. Roofs leaked, businesses moved in and out when leases ended and weren't renewed. One needed only to walk the back alleys downtown and count the number of buildings that even face lifts wouldn't cure. The irony of it all was that Taber, unlike many towns, didn't seem to go out of its way to honour heritage buildings. Yet many wrecks with no historical value were gussied up to disguise decay.

The Old Country Look:

One Taber builder from Holland showed a respect for integrity in workmanship. One could walk the main drag and recognize his buildings and face lifts. The facades had an old country appearance that evoked stability, longevity, and integrity, such as the drug store eating annex, a secondhand store building, the Christian store, and others. Unfortunately not all owners saw things his way.

Absentee Landlords and Write-Offs:

As in many small towns, some building owners lived away from Taber, so they didn't have the same emotional attachment to the town as did the local residents. Some others used their businesses as tax writeoffs. In some cases a spouse operated the store, while the real bread winner worked elsewhere. That often showed in the lack of desire to work with others to improve the downtown, either by having a common theme, or improving the condition of the buildings.

Hey, What About Me Signs:

Popping up around town on vacant lots and elsewhere, like flowers and weeds, were portable signs with day glow letters advertising bold events, but also businesses in trouble. Many revealed a desperate last minute effort to save something before going under. One could measure the health of the Taber economy by the size, condition and nature of the signs.

Bud, Bloom, Flower and Seed:

Often a dream became an idea, which became a proposal, that blossomed into a business that went to seed, and was blown in the wind. Some businesses called franchises blew into town. They choked out many home-growns, causing the weeding out process to continue unchecked. Some businesses just began to die on the vine. The Cameo, on the main drag, one of the first general stores, thrived for years. Now shelves are bare. Dusty tobacco pipes hang on yellow frayed cardboard racks. Glass cases displaying tobacconist's stock of the fifties and sixties now are seldom opened. Robert sat behind the counter, keeping vigil where once his brother Norman kept him company. He died, leaving Robert to sell lottery tickets, a few newspapers, magazines, and pocket books. The old timers that once dropped in are dropping out, leaving that fine, quiet gentleman with his memories and an unknown future while he seemed to watch the world go by.

Demolished Dreams:

Where Taber says goodbye to a few fading businesses, it also said goodbye to bulldozed landmarks, the old fire hall, gone, leaving one old man tearful for he, as a volunteer fireman for years was a driving force in getting it built. Now the land, begging for any enterprising venture or public service building, is idle, like so many other plots, garden space for weeds.

Property that Went Begging:

So businesses came and businesses went, sometimes leaving spaces that nobody could use, either because the floor space was too big, and thus too expensive, or the cost of reclaiming the land was out of sight.

Driving through the Taber core one sees what, on the surface, look like great locations! The secret why those parcels of land are not snapped up by eager potential buyers, and why they turn their noses up at them is found beneath the ground. " Oh hell," many have wailed, "Well, wouldn't you know it!" Defunct gas stations defiling the land. "You'd have dig all that dirt up, move it, clean it, and fill the holes up again. The cost wouldn't be worth the effort." So what looked like prime property by the old Taber Times building, the piece across from A&W, and others, went begging for attention with no takers.

People have worked with buildings and land to reach desired ends for themselves and for the town. The ways and means are the same when it comes to churches. It is worthwhile to take each example and compare it with how churches and congregations work with building and property. I hunch one will see the similarities. A person may also see in Taber a heartening phenomena.

The Neglected Are Now Getting the Whole Meal Deal!

Where the Taber "better off" North-siders once enjoyed the lion's share of shopping and services; where once the South-siders had to cross the highway and tracks to get a little of their share, the shoe is now on the other foot. A lot of the action is now on the south side of the highway, with the former downtown a little down on its heels.

Now within walking distance, the South-siders can shop at a huge Safeway, "pig out" at McDonalds, or dine out at respectable eating spots, and visit a couple of convenient stores that also serve gas.

Burning Issues

Talk also went on in the bars, coffee shops, Chamber of Commerce, and town council meetings about the burning issues of the day, but also how to promote Taber and really put it on the map. What did Taber have to entice visitors to come and "have a look ?" Taber got the giant corn stalk that the Kiwanians worked so hard at raising funds to have it stand proudly by the swimming pool. The trouble was, it looked so real, and what? No golden cobs? It was hardly noticeable. Well, there is the big rock with the plaque attached honouring the pioneers, placed by the LDS, but what about the many other ethnic groups that contributed to life of the community? There is the Taber sugar beet logo. But what about the corn, shouldn't it also be on that logo to represent Taber? And how come there aren't any bumper stickers, or the like, for visitors to stick on their vehicles, showing they have visited Taber?"

On coffee row, at the tables in many watering holes, such stuff was tossed about, mingled with contents from the "Alberta Report" and the "Calgary Sun." Sometimes, persons with other local issues also elbowed their way into the conversation.

The town drinking water reservoir on the south side becomes a worthwhile chew. Geese swam in it and crapped in it; should the guy that's been shooting to scare them off be allowed to get back at it?

Then, what about that business of having to pay when you take stuff out to the dump(the land fill), what one called the "Taber Mall." The "Mall?" Sure, you can get good stuff out there, pay a few bucks, and you've got, you name it, windows, doors, computer parts, bikes. They tried to recycle just about everything they could. Hearing that, my thoughts went back to the Frobisher Bay dump where a local RCMP member found enough parts to build a skidoo. At the Taber dump I once saw one young kid engaged in a less exotic project. He sat digging into a mess of scrungy juice boxes that he planned to turn in, like pop bottles, for money.

The Legion

Many of the coffee row regulars were alive and active during the war years. Some served, others were required to stay home because, as farmers, they were carrying out an essential service.

Some felt, as seniors, that society had little use for them anymore. Still others looked forward to at least one day in the year when they again, as Legion members, would be looked upon, not as discards, but as persons deserving respect.

As comrades in the Legion they clung to the past to honour the dead and promote the cause of Peace! That was achieved, not so much in brick and mortar, but in the blood coursing through the veins of the surviving vets, who roused their aching bones from soft sofas to stand erect as funeral honour guard, to march in the Remembrance day parade, to sell their poppies, and visit the old folks homes. Ray Evanson, a vet, and prominent LDS member, and I, served as chaplains.

I replaced the retired Anglican priest, the Rev. Chuck Daisley, who was a popular veteran. He had been a good acquaintance, having been one of the first persons to greet me on arriving in Taber. He had brought comfort to many of the troops throughout Europe, and saw the parachutes fall from the sky with food for the starving Dutch. Back home, he visited the sick, the dying, and from the prayer book led worship and administered the sacraments. Then, his dear wife, Zetta, saw her eighty-year-old husband, such a gentle giant of a man, gradually slip away. He got broadsided by a truck as he tried crossing the highway from the north to the south side. His car was a write-off, and he, his body, broken beyond repair, lingered, for weeks, then died. His chaplain colleague and dear friend, Father Christmas, conducted his service. Both he and Zetta, who died a couple of years later, will be missed, Chuck for his stories, and jokes, and empathy; Zetta, for what she brought of herself to family, her church, and to the Arts and Crafts Society. where she shared her talent as a painter of china.

Each year, fewer and fewer of the old gang were left to sit around the table at Taco Time where Chuck had held court. Each year, fewer and fewer of the old vets gathered around the Legion lounge tables to relive their own personal horrors of war. During the year the few vets who were left joined with associate members to problem solve. What to do about the loss of income from motel VLT machines? How does the Legion persuade the Town to take ownership of the cenotaph to cover expenses? The "soldier" needed a going over and the foundation was crumbling. Will Harding still beat the bass drum to march from the cenotaph to the civic center? What about Ray's idea for the Remembrance day service? It's a good one. No more string of dignitaries giving little speeches, instead, honour the vets one year, widows another, the women who served in the war still another year, and another time the women who "kept the home fire burning" when their sweethearts were across the pond.

Then, hey, what about that "damn" tape recorder? We just can't seem to get it right when we play the Last Post. It played either something other than the Last Post, petered out completely, or someone forgot to put a tape in the player. What do we do about our Youth Hall where Air Cadets meet? The upkeep is crippling us, and the town doesn't want it. The bus, what are we going to do about that? It's on its last legs, somewhat like most of us. And who will fill the

chairs? We're running out of executive material. Ernie
is gone, Norman is gone, other good leaders too,
and do you remember... another good soldier, gone.
In fact, very few vets are left to chair committees. And
just look at the Ladies Auxiliary, lots of them have
passed on, too, or are too crippled to work; still
others aren't getting any younger, and some are on
their way out. The Mayor and former police chief
Harley did his bit, others too, but now...? So the talk
went on through the years over a beer or two as one
problem after another staggered into view

Education & Youth

It's all that the young can do for the old, to shock them and
keep them up to date.   1

As grandparents, the Legion members were
concerned about what was happening to their
grandchildren in the schools. Most of the children
were doing okay. But some just couldn't hack W.R.
Meyer's or St. Mary's high schools. Many late teens,
who had been out a while in the hard cruel world,
wanted to get back. Some had babies. Some had
jobs . Hugh Harding, working for the school division,
ran an alternate learning centre above the post office
to serve the needs of those persons. It was called
ACE Place. Going there was meant to be like going to
work at a regular job. The product the students
produced, was credits they earned toward grades.
They had to be really hungry to get what the centre
offered, but the hours were flexible, and the learning
contracts that they made, reasonable. Having been
screened to qualify for entrance, they had a good

chance of succeeding, and many did.

School Division's programers said, "Things are a lot different today." Still "seniors" remembered parts of the scene years back, when Connie Russell, Ruth Fisher, Ruth Mueller, and principal Bill Broadfoot, among others, gave their all to ensure the kids got to know up from down. Long after they retired, issues came to light formulated as questions that they wouldn't have even thought about back then.

Do LDS Myers students get school credit for courses they take at the LDS seminary across the street from Myers?

Should there be a Christian chaplain at Myers, such as the University of Lethbridge, and the Community College have?

Should Christian Education be offered in the public school system?

How best can the school system serve the Mexican Mennonites (The "Kanadiers? ")

How can the system best prepare youth for the work force, especially for one who, working in a fast food outlet asked,

"Watch wan tete?"

No matter what one might think of the youth today, one thing is for sure, the Taber and country kids had a tough row to hoe. Unless they were going to inherit the family farm or ranch and wanted to labour that way, which it seems that not many wanted to do, then it had to be university, or community college and then some, or bust! Perhaps flipping hamburgers would be enough to cause them to want something better, something that would have them not only serve themselves, but serve the real needs of others.

I know that the Taber caring community spirit was such that the youth, if open to it, could be sensitized to the less fortunate's needs and, see ways to help. That might put them in a frame of mind to choose vocations where helping others was the main thing. For, staring them in the face, was care put into action. Individuals so moved by persons suffering unexpected costly tragedies had advertised the needs and put on benefit fund raisers such as auctions and garage sales and dinners. Appeals for Help posters and newspaper items often caught the eye of the public, and despite the number of appeals, people still gave.

They gave generously also to the hospital telethons. I felt, with all the money the Alberta government rakes in through gambling and oil revenues, it could more than cover the cost of the equipment that the telethon was trying to raise. Perhaps all the talent, time, and energy could be directed toward other worthy causes that would make the donors and performers feel just as good about their contributions.

Two other projects that raised the interest of Taber's caring for the needy were meals on wheels, and the newly-opened food bank. Projects like those also heightened the emotions , especially if one sector of the community, who wanted to help, was denied access. The whole community had ownership of meals on wheels with an army of volunteers from churches, service clubs, and others.

But the food bank, initiated in part by church members whose ministers belong to the local ministerial, allegedly excluded LDS people from its Board of Directors. The LDS folk had, as always, gently shrugged off the rebuff, and opened their Lethbridge cannery to help fill the food bank shelves, and continued to work hard as volunteers. Many non-LDS were put off that their neighbors weren't given a chance to have some say on how the food bank would be run. It seemed that some against more LDS involvement were fearful that, powerful as they were, the LDS would take over the project, a fear perhaps not totally unfounded, given the LDS's aggressive recruiting methods, and strong organization of committed workers.

Taber certainly offered intriguing town politics. Yet, on the other hand, it offered a gentler side, memories of nostalgic scenes of boys nudging cows home for milking along back lanes; of wooden side walks, muddy streets churned up by model T's and A's, loaded with family in town for the Saturday night show or dance.

The scenes were transformed. You might still see a truck pull up beside another, the drivers leaning out of their windows to swap stories or talk business. You might see a tractor splutter by, but more than likely, you heard the rumbling of 4 by 4's, the roar of oil patch trucks, or police car sirens, and get a sniff of the sugar factory.

One might even think that we humans have the whole place to ourselves. But, if God's other creatures could talk, they'd say, "Don't kid yourself, we're here too!"

That was true! Blue Jays hid gifts of peanuts under leaves. One Jay even squawked like a rusty old clothes line. Once an Owl perched motionless on a 52nd St. tree for hours, causing a phone call to the Coaldale Birds of Prey sanctuary. Hawks swooped down from their babies' nests, forcing park pedestrians to duck. Golf course rabbits hopped about. Centennial Park crows scolded people passing by, and cats, candidates for traps, sprayed and pooped in gardens. In some ways those creatures could humble humans, who could never conquer the birds and animals desires, despite the town's joining the high tech world.

I couldn't help but feel that, despite our distancing ourselves from nature's arena by building and busyness, we still weren't, in essence, much different from fur and feather creatures. Just a dab of paint, smear of glue, bit of metal, and an inclination to do stuff to avoid boredom, only that separated us.

Just think of all the paraphernalia and places that occupied conversations around town: the new golf club house, the swimming pool and early bird swims, the weight room and Randy Spark's drug free power lift meets, the tennis court, the Ken McDonald park's new soccer pitches and ball diamonds, the curling club, the two hockey rinks and yes, the Lion's concession, Sunday Sports, the annual fair, Cornfest, The Heritage Inn Suds room and VLTs, and bus tours to the Regina Casino, the Fish and Game Club derbies, camping at the municipal park, much of it to keep all amused, called community amenities.

Then there were the garage sales. With the oil patch and other less settled industries, many came, bought houses, accumulated, and then left, giving the garage sale addicts, like myself, great pickings. I call it recycling. I believe that since there's been enough junk produced in the world already, there needn't be more. It will go quite far if its just spread around like jam on bread. The funny thing is, sometimes the urge to buy causes one to see something one just has to have because it looks familiar. You buy it, get it home, and then your spouse says,

"Well, that's lived here before!"

People who looked over other people's stuff sometimes commented,

"You know with all this stuff I've picked up at garage sales, I should have one of my own to get rid of it."

The garage sale fanatics could have given "wanna be" sellers some do's and don'ts for having a "good" garage sale. But before they try having one they'd be wise to check with the town office to determine if a permit to sell was needed, and what the rules were for posting signs. People got very upset over garage sales when they weren't aware of the ins and outs of the business. A scarred power pole riddled with nail and tack holes on Taber"s corner of 50th and 50th, suffered the indignity of displaying Garage and Yard Sale Signs. One day, the bylaw officer ("Bylaw Bob") had enough. He tore the signs down and searched out the owners. That didn't deter the sign posters. Soon signs like mushrooms sprouted up on Knox church's lawn. Again Bylaw Bob did his duty. Once, I happened to be walking out of the yard of one surprised yard sale vendor, just as Bylaw Bob tore up in his truck and hopped out with a smile waving the vendor's sign. His polite sharing of information regarding the sign, the need for a permit (which the vendor lady didn't have) triggered an indignant,

"I'm new in town. I had no idea, a permit?! Never needed one in the last town I was in!"

Not too long after, again, Bylaw Bob caught a character in the act of stapling a sign to the well-riddled post. The character responded with a barrage of unprintables, threatening the officer with a law suit for stealing his private property. Bylaw Bob had already removed a scattering of those character's signs from around town. The silly saga didn't end. Time passed, then lo and behold, the undeterred fellow stuck another of his signs in the church lawn. Again I saw a repeat performance of the pole drama with the same players. Later, I got a call on my cell phone.

"You're the minister at that church?"

"Yes," Then I got an ear full.

"Some woman answered your church phone and said I could do that! What the hell are you guys playing at." More abuse, then,

"I hate this town, it's not worth a...! I'm goin get the H...out of this crappy town!"

What could I say? That ended the exchange.

Perhaps, minor remedies might help people with short fuses maintain their composure and protect their bruised egos. Community outdoor bulletin boards, instead of posts that canines use to stake out their territory, might do the trick.

Bad actors can be most entertaining, as I'm sure I have been, when also acting childishly. Fortunately there are others, residents of Taber and municipality, who were far more entertaining in an uplifting way. There were so many gifted people: among the many that blessed Taber were those whom I knew from the Western Gospel Hour, singers, Bonny, Deb, Barb, Shelly, Jake, Dick and poets Lois and Gerry, and others. Those folk represented several extended families , who, among others, tilled the soil, served the public, and offered a population base that ensured stability and continuity. Others came to join those families, arriving as an aftermath of WW11's devastation.

Lesley and I got to know many of those folks, heard their stories, and were moved by their demonstrated patience, and courage. Stepping off the trains in Taber with their cardboard suit cases, and bundles of bedding, they faced an unknown future. Soon they knew. The picture became clear: drafty crowded shacks, water-filled ditches, canvas dams, and rubber boots; kids and adults hoeing and topping sugar beets, and the beginning of crippling backs for many.

Those who designed and endorsed the rising sun and sugar beet emblem on Taber's flag could be congratulated for intentionally or otherwise replicating the traditional Japanese rising sun emblem. For in doing so they have, and rightly so, symbolized hope, and also the great contribution that the Japanese Canadians had made to the community. That might not have happened. Those Canadians could have simmered in cauldrons of hatred for the injustice they suffered. But that wasn't to be. Bob, a successful potato farmer remembers his dad, whose thriving BC lumber business was stolen, from him, saying, " Holding on to hate won't get you anywhere. We'll start over."

They did, and like many, not only those of Japanese ancestry, but the Chinese, Dutch, Czechs, Hungarians, Italians, and so many more, sweated, toiled, saved, and succeeded. Their good names grace the pages of the telephone book. One would assume success would cause them to cling to the hard earned fruits of their labors. But, to the contrary, they gave, often quietly, without drawing attention to themselves.

If all our misfortunes were laid in one common heap, whence everyone must take an equal portion, most people would be contented to take their own and depart.   2

Every year, the people of Dutch ancestry faithfully show up in great numbers on November 11 and reverently placed a wreath at the war memorial in appreciate for what Canadians did in fighting and dying to liberate Holland. War has brought people of many different ethnic backgrounds together to help make Taber what it is. It's ironical and tragic that it took conflict to make that happen. It's equally as tragic that town and country families still suffer sudden terrible losses, and have to come to terms with their pain, and begin again. Yet

Unless we believe that God renews creation every day, our prayers grow habitual and tedious   3

Tragic Taber Happenings and the Police
Shattered glass, ruptured steel, and mangled bodies, bullet wounds, and fearful victims of break-ins and theft spell tragedy and loss in blood and tears. The RCMP and Taber Police Service's men and women coped with that and struggled to deal with their own feelings. That's not all that I found that they lived with. There were debates about whether Taber should forsake their Police Service and contract with the RCMP. In contrast to such serious political ranglings was the heavy load of paper work, and the phone calls that police fielded that just showed the patience required, not only to maintain the right, but to educate the public. It wasn't unusual for the officers to get calls where they just needed to convey a little assurance that all was really okay, and not to sweat it. Once a woman, highway driving, said that she was very concerned about a horse that she saw in a field rolling on its back with its feet flaying away. The officer explained, without being condescending, that's just what horses do, not to worry.
Like airline pilots, the police lived with thousands of hours of sheer boredom, and moments of sheer terror. I had once been given the impression that the South Alberta RCMP detachment, working around Taber and beyond, was one of the most peaceful in all Alberta. I learned otherwise, as did so many who were greatly impacted by certain tragic events affecting them personally, or their families or friends.

Eileen McCoy, a clerk at Macs store was shot and killed. The Rev. Dale Lang's son, Jason, was shot to death at his school. As a member of Victim's Services I drove Jason's brother from the high school to the hospital where Dale broke the news to him of his brother's death. Dale and his wife Dianne, surrounded by caring Christians, went on from there to show incredible courage, drawing strength from Jesus Christ. They ministered to others in their grief, including the other boy who was shot, the young shooter's mother, and the students and the teachers of Jason's school. Dale and Diane did that while accommodating the needs of the Press that was on a feeding frenzy.

Despite their grief, the couple worshiped with the students and staff, officials, and the public in the school gym, and later stood to offer prayers at the spot where their son was killed, to "Take back the school." Rather than blame God, they pleaded thereafter across Canada for all to care for others, not to tease or put down those who don't fit in, like the lost youngster who did the shooting.

God is subtle, but he is not malicious   4

Before the Langs demonstrated their strength of character and Christian witness, shortly after the shooting, Victim's Service workers mingled in the school gym, along with crisis counselors, and other care givers, including the police, to be there for the students, teachers, and parents. The majority of devastated youth and grown ups were clearly in a state of shock. They were open to what the care givers could offer, but most were trying to avoid the press. The response of the whole Taber community seemed different from the USA Columbine school shooting tragedy. The Taber folk went home, closed their doors, and dealt with their grief in private as much as they could.

Then and in other incidents, I did what I could, as did Celia and Sharon, two strong, experienced Advocates, and other good workers, to carry out the goals of Victim Services: to provide "Support, Information, and Referral to victims of crime and/or misfortune."

The local RCMP and the Taber Police Service and staff provided the necessary information and work space, and helped with contacts to make Victim Services workable for my colleagues and me. During the training provided by Barb and Phil's crew, I soon realized that confidentiality was of utmost importance, and second, that we were not to counsel, but, through active listening and empathy, point the way to where the victims could find help. Third, to leave it to the victims to decide whether they wanted to go that route. The operative question to victims was, "What do you want to do?"

I found the experience to be one where my eyes were opened even more to the terrible circumstances that people found themselves in, often feeling trapped. It's unfortunate that, though the helping agencies' resources are there, often victims either don't know about them, or hesitate to turn to them. Many "streetwise" people believed that they knew how, but sadly some used the resources in a non productive way that often got them nowhere, certainly not out of what kept them captive, which often came from within themselves.

Tragic Road Accidents

I found in many families, there were innocent victims of road terror. Mary was one, who helped save her own life by fighting the urge to pass out after a teenager's monster 4x4 truck crashed and crushed the driver side of her small car. The driver allegedly failed to yield, claiming he was driving into the sun. Mary's face required some reconstructive surgery. That kid's carelessness turned her life upside down, and no amount of legal financial settlement would ever make it totally right again.

Mary's life was saved, Kortney's wasn't. That little girl perished when another teenager, allegedly under the influence of alcohol, driving a water truck, failed to slow and stop when a row of drivers ahead of him did so. They had seen a signal to slow down and stop for construction ahead. The mental anguish suffered by her parents, family and friends was overwhelming. Something good, though, did rise out of that horrible scene. Kortney's aunt, driven by anger began a chapter of MADD (Mother's Against Drunk Driving) which, in a short time, had members from across southern Alberta. MADD received the support of police and businesses. Kortney's mother had said that she didn't want her child's life and death to be without meaning.

The adding of another lane between Taber and Lethbridge did, no doubt, help cut down the number of killings. Before, not only Kortney died unnecessarily, but also Steve who died in a roll over in which his wife and son were passengers. They survived, but his wife, already ill, died a year or so later, leaving their teenage son to cope. The young mother with her child in the car, who hit them had somehow been distracted before she slammed into them. She and her child lived on.

Death doesn't always raise its ugly head though. Fender benders top the statistics. Sometimes a hit is ignored by the driver. Once an absent minded old chap backed out of the Taber post office parking spot just as a neighboring truck driver was starting his engine. The old boy crunched the neighbor's fender. Then he immediately drove off, with the dented car's driver in pursuit. Flagging the old fellow down, the driver rolled down his window and said,

"Do you know what you've done to my truck?"

"No."   "Well, look!"

"Gee," the old fellow said, "I just thought I'd run over a big rock on my farm."

21 Beyond CornFest, A New Beginning

Personal Challenges

The problems I personally faced weren't anywhere near as devastating or annoying as those others have confronted. The only similarity between mine and many suffering from crash of steel and shattering glass, were detached retinas. There was the need to continue to live with the after effects of the initial happening. It seems our human condition is such that there is so much beyond our control. Cataracts begin to cloud our vision as we age. Hopefully our maturing as adults develops faster than the cataracts or other eroding health problems, so that we can handle that stuff as grown ups. Ministering is a great way to rapidly reach that maturity. For a person called to pay more attention to the needs of others than to self, doesn't really have much time to worry about the aches and pains that come with aging. But there does come a time, I soon discovered, when a person reaches that "retirement" age and needs to think seriously about where to live, and on what, and how.

Preparing

The four stages of man are infancy, childhood, adolescence, and obsolescence.   1

Nuts to that cynical view! Life's more than that. I have always believed that there are three ages, chronological, mental, and spiritual. A person can be physically old, and yet be bright mentally, and/or spiritually. Creeky joints, and bowed backs don't mean the end. Living and learning need not stop when leaning into the winds of change, unless persons prefer to flop over, brain-dead, prematurely. I find, at this stage in the game, it's good to look to the past, not to mourn the regrets, but in revisiting, retrieve what is worth reusing

What you become accustomed to do in your youth, you

do in your old age. 2

While looking at the positive side of that thought capsule, we move on. Lesley and I, not that conversant with Alberta, used some of our holidays for a few years to check out towns throughout Alberta, as possible places to settle in. It wouldn't be fair to my successor or the Taber Knox church family for me to hang around there after eight years. A new minister needs the undivided attention of the congregation, and the church family needs his. So we hunted and ended up making a short list of Strathmore, Stettler, and Claresholm. After continually gravitating back to Claresholm, we finally said that's it. The close-knit town with its history, lots of variety and mix of people, the medical facilities, indoor swimming pool, close vicinity to Calgary and Lethbridge, and a good view of prairie and Porcupine Hills, sold us on the town. For Lesley, not happy with mountains, expressed this view

> Oh give me land, lots of land under starry skies
> above, DON'T FENCE ME IN   3

In our last year at Taber we began looking at what was available to purchase on our limited income. We had already sold our bungalow on 52nd St. in Taber, and moved into a condo apartment(rented) which was really too rich for our pocketbook, and didn't suit our lifestyle. So our options whittled down to low cost housing or a mobile. Often, clergy are familiar with these circumstances, having lived in manses without building up enough equity to have a substantial

388

down payment for a house. In Claresholm, we found
that many persons living in Calgary were able to sell
their homes for two or three hundred thousand
dollars, move to Claresholm, buy a home, and bank
the rest. It seemed that helped to escalate housing
prices. With that happening, we were happy to have
found a mobile home which we began to buy and
live in.

I felt satisfied, since ever on my mind was the fact
that, for me
    A house is a machine for living in.　　4

There after, we commuted to Taber for almost a
year. Thanks to many friends who opened their
homes to us, we were able to sleep-over two or three
times a week or when road conditions were bad.

Other caring persons helped us move from the
condo to the mobile. Marilyn, our Claresholm realtor,
owned a U Haul truck of unknown vintage, and with
the help of Marjo, my Knox church colleague and one
other, we rattled our way empty to Taber and back,
loaded with what we hadn't given away to the
Salvation Army.

Commuting

Throughout the fall, winter, and spring we usually
drove to and from Taber in our van through Granum,
by Nobleford, through Picture Butte, and Coaldale.
Nasty weather sometimes caused us to pass through
Lethbridge. On our usual ride we waved to donkeys,
ponies, cows, and llamas. Lesley loved such
creatures. She was one who would cheer for the
calves and bulls at the rodeo, rather than for the

riders and ropers. It would be a job for me to try to persuade her to join me over at the Claresholm agriplex, within walking distance of our new home. Just about every weekend horse trailers circled the building, a sign that people and cattle were at play. When I first arrived in Claresholm, I hauled out my cowboy hat that I had bought at a garage sale. I put it on, looked in the mirror, and decided that just wasn't my style. To each his own!

My Adopted Style of Ministry
In the twenty-two years that I've been an ordained minister in the United Church of Canada, I'd seen a lot of changes. I look back at my ministry in tandem with the Taber church family's ministry and found it seemed to unfold this way:

The Beginning
At first I did a lot of "wearing out the shoe leather" as one of my mentors once said. I tried to visit each household. I joined a few clubs, associations, and organizations. Then I set up some trial balloons, throwing out a few ideas for the church members to chew on, spit out, or digest. Some ideas did become realities. Others went plop. I tried to offer Bible studies and courses to use my teaching background. Very few showed an interest.

The Middle Years:
If in the past few years you haven't discarded a major opinion and acquired a new one investigate, see if you're not growing senile.   5

During those years, I tried to develop a few more

skills, first, to become a supervisor of theological school interns. That required a supervision course, and attending an interpersonal dynamics lab which just about turned me upside down and inside out. The lab helped me see how I came across as a person while interrelating with others. It hit me even harder that

> Everything that irritates us about others can lead us to an understanding of ourselves.   6

So, even at my age, I learned a lot about myself. Then I continued stretching by training as an Interim Minister, something I might use after leaving Knox, to prepare a congregation for a new minister somewhere. The training called for reflection and practice. In the middle years I tried to grow personally. But I also worked to do a decent job ministering to the four hundred or so church family members. As I aged, I wanted to stay current and not foist myself on the congregation as one without anything to offer. I believe that's the feeling of many ministers in the last years of their formal ministry where the danger is to merely tread water.

Remembering these words, I responded to the public notice, Victim Service Advocates Wanted.

> No man can discharge his debt to God, but he can make regular payments on it.   7

I appreciated the congregation's willingness for me to continue to reach out in the community. After taking the training as a Victim Services Advocate in

Taber, I soon discovered another side of Taber, or any town, for that matter, that placed a heavy burden on care givers and the cared for. It's amazing how people can be so hard on themselves and on each other. They seem to work very hard at doing that.

The End part of Ministry at Knox

I continued to offer a ministry of Word, Sacrament and Pastoral Care to which I was called. But I gradually dropped involvement in many groups, and organizations including Victim Services. Commuting and ministry at Knox consumed all my extra time and energy. During that time I did continue to try to improve my preaching skills and keep up with hospital calls and my Legion chaplaincy. In all my ministries, I stuck to one motto and one ultimate goal:

We are not called to be successful, but faithful.

And the goal: to encourage the church family to work on four garden patches that are the marks of a church: Worship, Pastoral Care, Christian Education, and Outreach , while always putting forward the invitation found in the Bible in Matthew 11:28.

To help the Knox leaders , I was grateful that they gave me time to develop and leave behind some documented reference material. I believe that was needed, being convinced that the ownership of the congregation belongs to them under Jesus Christ, the head of the church family.

The opportunity was there also, in the last few months of ministry at Knox, to introduce the Five Developmental Tasks that I learned about in Interim Ministry, to help prepare the way for the new minister.

In summary: to rediscover the rich history of Knox, to connect more with Presbytery, to anticipate leadership changes, and consider new ones, to discover a new identity, and to see some new directions for Knox ministry.

The last task, a hard one, was for the congregation to let go, and to pray that when Lesley and I had gone from the scene, people wouldn't say,

"Well, that's not the way that Ken or Lesley would do it."

This always reminded me of a scene in James Herriot's books, "All Creatures Great and Small," where an old duffer who was visiting a farmer having a cow attended to, breathing down the new vet's neck saying ad nauseam,

"That's not the way Mr. so and so would do it."

In contrast to that, I echo this view

The man who believes that he can live without others is mistaken; and the man who thinks other can live without him is more mistaken.   8

I have confidence in the integrity of the Knox church family, and any church family, for that matter, that no new minister would have to be subjected to that experience. With that in mind Lesley and I left Knox to begin a new direction in our lives and ministry, that we will share together.

Postscript

The Jonah person I have been, found a new direction. Sooner or later that surely happens to each one of us.

> " I feel the winds of God today, today my sail I lift,
> Though heavy oft with drenching spray, and torn
> with many a rift;
> If hope but light the water's crest,
> And Christ my bark will use,
> I'll seek the sea at His behest,
> And brave another cruise."

References Cited

Ch.1.1   Catcher in the Rye (1951) ch. 1 J.D.
          Salinger 1919-
Ch.1.2   John Masefield 1878-1967 Ballads and
          Poems (1910)
Ch.3.1   Author unknown
Ch.3.2   Rhoda Morgenstern
Ch.3.3   Gilmor's Album, CBC Radio, Canada
Ch.4.1   David P. Gardner
Ch.5.1   Milne, A.A. 1882-1956
          Winnie-the- Pooh(1926) ch.6
Ch.5.2   Catholic Digest Aug 1960 p 102 E.
          Roosevelt 1882-62
Ch 5.3   Life of Don Quixote and Sancho pt 1.
Ch.5.4   Bishop J. Taylor Smith
Ch 6.1   C. Jung, Memories, Dreams, Reflections   1962 ch 9
Ch 6.2.   Henry C. Link From a 78 rec, lyric &music
Ch.6.3   Longfellow Henry Wadsworth
Ch 6.5   Albert Einstein
Ch.7.1   Stephen Spender 1909- Poems (1933) no.17
Ch.8.1   Mitchell, W.O. Who Has Seen the Wind,
          Conversation with W.O. Moose Jaw Library
          March 21, 1981
Ch.8.2   Kris Kristofferson 1936- and Fred Foster
          Me and Bobby McGee (1969 song)
Ch.8.3   Robinson, Carson & Pleasant a record
          Valley Boys, Life Gets Tee-Jus, Don't It.
          from Song, Lyricist and Music
Ch 9.1   Shakespeare, All the World's a Stage,
Ch.9.2   Unknown
Ch 9.3   Kornhauser, Arthur W. How To Study
          U. of Chicago Press, & U. of Toronto, 1937 Ch 9.4
          Author unknown Poem,
Ch 9.4   Unknown House That Jack Built in Old English,
Ch 9.5   Sartre, Being and Nothingness (1943) pt.4, ch 2
Ch 10.1   Unknown
Ch 11.1   Metropolitan Life (1978) p 101
Ch 11.2   Carlyle, Thomas
Ch 11.3   Schulberg. Budd 1914- On the Waterfront

	(1954) film spoken by Marlon Brando
Ch 11.4	Jung,Carl Gustav (1875-61)Memories. Dreams and Reflections
Ch 11	Crassweller, Ken Let Ookpiks Fly Trafford Press Victoria, BC 2004
Ch.12.1	Frost Robert
Ch.12.2	Thompson Francis 1859-1907 Poems 1913 vol 1.'Hound of Heaven' pt.1
Ch.12.3	Russell Bertrand 1872-1970 Sceptic Essays (1928) Dreams and Facts
Ch.12.4	Holmes Oliver Wendell
Ch.12.5	Unamuno Miguel de 1864-1937 Poe'sias 1907) Salmo II
Ch.12.6	Steinbeck John 1902-1968 Grapes of Wrath (1939) ch 14
Ch.12.7	Elliot T.S. The Rock (1934) pt. 1
Ch.12.8	Garibaldi
Ch.12.9	Schutte, Dan S.J song by Lines from Isaiah 6, Pub 1981
Ch.13.1	Address at Queen's Hall, London, 16 July 1917 in Times 17 July 1917 Maude Royden 1876- 1956
Ch.13 .2	Skinner, B.F
Ch 14 .1	Shelley, Percy B. 1792-1822 Ozymandias of Egypt
Ch.14.2	Bible, Matthew 7:3-5
Ch 14.3	Longfellow, Henry Wadsworth
Ch 14.4	Plain Tales from the Hills 1888 On the Strength of a Likeness"
Ch.14.5	Lennon, John 1940-1980 and Mcartney, Paul 1942-Yesterday 1965 song
Ch.14.6	Nash, Ogden 1902-1971 Good Intentions (1942) 'Sampson Agnostic'
Ch.14.7	Bierce, Ambrose
Ch.14.8	Author Unknown
Ch.14.9	Tennyson, Alfred, Lord
Ch.14.10	Thompson, Francis Poems (1913) 'Hound of Heaven' pt 4
Ch.15.1	Schumacher E.F. 1911-1977 Ch 4.2
Ch 15.2	Cecil Richard
Ch.15.3	Talmud Ta'anith 7b

396

Ch 16: 1   Penn, William
Ch.16 .2   Disraeli, Benjamin
Ch.16 .3   Thoreau Henry David
Ch.17.1   Sterne
Ch.17.2   Sheen, Bishop Fulton J
Ch.17 .3   Confucius
Ch 17.4   How to Survive the Loss of a Love
Ch 17. 5   "Johnny Appleseed"
Ch.17.6   Wheatley, Melvin E
Ch.17.7   Terence 190-159 B.C.
Ch.17.8   Shakespeare, William
Ch.19.1   Carlyle, Thomas
Ch.19.2   Bible. Ecclesiastes 12:1-14
Ch.19.3   Phillips, Wendell
Ch.19.4   Thomas, Dylan 1914-1953,
            Collected Poems (1952)
            'Do Not Go Gently Into that Good Night'
Ch.19.5   O'Neil, Eugene, Lazarus Laughed
            (1927) act 2, sc.2
Ch.19.6   Forsyth, P.T
Ch.19.7   Lampedusa, Giuseppe di 1896-57
            The Leopard 1957   p.33
Ch.19.8   Unknown
Ch.20.1   Shaw, George Bernard 1836-1950,
            Fanny's First Play 1914) "Introduction"
Ch 20.2   Socrates
Ch.20.3   Tov, Baal Shem
Ch.20.4   Einstein, Albert 1879-1955,May 9, 192 "Einstein"
            (1974) ch 14, Princeton University
Ch.21.1   Linklater, Art 1912-
            A Child's Garden of Misinformation   1965 ch 8
Ch.21.2   Unknown
Ch.21.3   Porter, Cole 1891-1964 song film,
            Hollywood Canteen, 1934
Ch.21.4   Le Corbusier 1887-1965
            Towards an Architecture 1923 p.9
Ch.21.5   Burgess, Gelett
Ch.21.6   Jung, Carl
Ch 21.7   Smith, Roy L Ch.21.8   Hasidic saying

Glossary

A.L.S A wasting disease where the body functions gradually shut down and ultimately leads to death.

AA Alcoholic Anonymous

ACE Place An alternate school offering flexible study arrangements on a contractual basis with students seeking to gain high school credits.

Alanon a support group for those who live with alcoholics

Alateen, a support group for children and youth who live with alcoholics

Alberta Report a magazine with a particular political and theological slant reflecting the editors views.

Amnesty International a world wide organization that works to free political prisoners by writing letters to those with the power to free the captives.

aneurysm the swelling of an artery caused by blood pressure connected with an injury or disease.

antibiotics drugs that attacks micro organisms

Atonement, at-one-ment ie: becoming one with God, eg: through confession, forgiveness, reconciliation

B Ed Bachelor of Education Degree.

beaters beat-up, big cars, usually driven by the youth.

blue grass gig events where blue grass music is played.

Boys Brigade A group older than scouts that had for its theme ,from Luke 2:52 And Jesus increased in wisdom, and stature, and in favour with God and man.

burn out a mental condition, work or parenting related, symptoms: physical and mental fatigue, an inability to make decisions. Often suffers from depression.

carillon a sound and speaker system broadcasting music from the church tower.

Catechist a non clergy person assigned to teach Christian ideas.

CCF "Cooperative Commonwealth Federation" became the **NDP**. ie:New Democratic political party.

CE Christian Education

CGIT Canadian Girls In Training, a non denomination girls church group

Charolais beef cattle breed, big, white, often crossed with Herefords.

Chinooks warm winds create sudden thaws during winter months in Alberta.

Christmas Bureau groups supported by most churches and many

398

other help agencies to provide hampers of food and toys once a year.

clinical psychology relates to diagnostic treatment of mental illness

Cornfest an annual Taber celebration and fair.

Depression, Great the time in history when the economies of the world collapsed leaving a big percentage of the world's population unemployed and facing bankruptcy, and or starvation. A great disparity existed between the rich and the poor.

draft dodgers Persons who escaped to Canada to avoid war service

FAS Fetal Alcohol Syndrome.

5th step work One of the 12 steps AAs, Alanon, Alateen do to maintain sobriety

4H Club for boys and girls in rural areas. Aim: improve methods of agriculture, home economics, promote good citizenship. Name: ie: fourfold purpose of improving head, heart, hands, health.

Fujiama Mt.(Fuji) sacred mountain, highest point in Japan.

Gestetner a copy machine that uses typed stencils on inked drum.

growth hormone a substance formed in certain body parts, enters blood stream to influences organs' workings.

Gulliver the hero of Jonathan Swift's Gulliver's travels.

Hereford a beef cattle breed, a red body, white face, white belly.

hippies persons who reject many traditional society customs and beliefs, Believe in freedom of expression, love, fellowship.

hydroponics the growing of plant (eg; marihuana) in water containing the needed nutrients instead of soil.

in tincture communions served using bread and juice where bread is dipped, rather than eaten separate from the juice.

interim A person specially trained to prepare a church for a new Minister, (ie: between ministers)

intern person who serves during a training period prior to fully qualifying.

iron lungs A breathing apparatus used to sustain the life of polio victims

iron-man a person who competes in a grueling number of physical sports of a marathon nature.

issue, the referred to the controversy centred on the **ordination** of self-declared homosexuals

J.W. Jehovah Witness.

Jesus Freaks Christian hippies very enthusiastic about their faith.

Johari Window a model to describe the process of human interaction. It divides personal awareness into 4 different types Known to others, not known to others, known to self, not known to self.

kaleidoscope a tube containing bits of coloured glass and two or more mirrors. As it is turned, it reflects continually Changing patterns.

Kanadiers Mexican Mennonites who returned to Canada

kibbutz. Communal farm in Israel.

L.D.S. Church of Jesus Christ of Latter Day Saints

Lamb's book of life from the Bible, Revelations 13:8.

Last post Music played, to commemorate the war dead.

lectionary List of scripture readings for each Sunday of the year.

lifers persons serving life sentences.

"Lone Rangers" persons who insist on doing things on their own apart from the group often to which they are affiliated

M.S. multiple sclerosis, a brain and spinal cord disease

M&S fund Mission Service Fund of the United Church of Canada.

MA degree Master of Arts Degree.

MADD Mothers Against Drunk Drivers

"Matsqui Miasma" A stench in the Fraser Valley caused by liquid manure on farm land near Matsqui, B.C.

MCC Mennonite Central Committee formed to offer aid in disasters world wide

Mennonites a Christian denomination pacifists and believers in adult baptism, and social justice through collective good works

mission statement a brief, clear statement of a group's purpose and reason for existence.

Mission field locations where the potential for believing Christian communities exist

moderator chief elected officer of the United Church of Canada.

NFB National Film Board.

Normal School Teachers College .

Palliative Care care for the dying .

PCTC Prairie Christian Training Centre operated by the United Church

PFRA Prairie Farm Rehabilitation Act

Pro-Life an anti-abortion movement

RC Roman Catholics.

Religion and Life Award earned by Scouts or Cubs active in church

RRSP Registered Retirement Saving Plan.

Sally Ann Salvation Army.

secular refers to life apart from religion, the opposite of sacred

Seventh Day Adventists a denomination believing the 2nd coming of Christ is soon. Worship is on Saturday.

sour dough A mix of dough and yeast saved and used from one baking to the next.

SQ3R A formula for studying using Question, Read, Recite, Review

Stake House an LDS church composed of several wards (smaller congregations)

Stewardship The responsible care and use of resources .

street rod   A souped up vehicle on a standard chassis and body.

sweet grass   Sweet smelling grasses, when smoldering used by North American Indians in religious ceremonies.

synchronization   When, what two or more persons are thinking happens simultaneously. eg: two people, who had been thinking of each other, plan to be at a certain place, and time; to their surprise, meet without   pre-arrangement. They are said to be on the same wave length, their meeting no mere coincidence ..

Tai-Chi   An oriental form of exercising using slow motions, "emphasising balance, coordination, and effortlessness."

Taylor Johnson Temperament Analysis   a diagnostic tool to determine personality traits

Tenebrae   ancient, Good Friday service of light and darkness

theology   Study of God and how God relates to humankind and the universe.

Tiger Moth,   biplane trainer

Tinker Toys.   wooden wheel-like pieces and round sticks used to construct things. Comes in a cardboard tube.

Tops   Take Off Pounds Sensibly

transients   Persons with no permanent address, passing through town.

Trinitarian formula   God the Father, Son, and Holy Spirit, 3 in 1

Trojan horse   From a Greek legend, a huge wooden horse that soldiers hid in and came out within the walls of their enemy's city. Now it means, persons who identify with a group, gain its trust, for the purpose of making trouble to undermine the members efforts

UBC   University of British Columbia

UC   United Church of Canada

UCW   United Church Women

Unified Board   The policy decision making body in a congregation. Made up of committees with various jobs to do.

Veteran Guards   Veterans of WW1 who volunteered and serviced in the Canadian armed forces in WW2, but too old for combat overseas

VLTs   gambling machines

WAC   Women's Army corps.

White Gift Service   A worship service conducted by the Sunday School where people are encouraged to include in their offering eg; food and toys, traditionally wrapped in white tissue paper for the "needy."

WW   World War

yuppies   socially, economically, upward mobile young adults.

Bibliography

Anderson, Hans Christian,
    "The Ugly Duckling" P 70, Tales
    Grosset & Dunlap Pub.N.Y. 1945
Baden Powell, Lord   1847- 1941
    "Scouting for Boys" 1908
Banks, George, Linnaeus
    "What I Live For"
Beatles, singers, musicians, writers, 1959-1970
    Eg; album "Sgt. Peppers Lonely Heart Club Band
Bible
    Matthew 25:35-40, Book of Job, Psalm 23, 139
Brewin, Gerald
    poem, "A Cattleman's Prayer of Thanksgiving"
Berton Pierre
    "The Comfortable Pew", J.B. Lippincott Pub. 1965
Cervantes ,Miguel de 1547-1616
    Don Quixote de la Mancha   Part 1 1605 part 2 1615
Chapman, John 1774?-1845 teacher
    planter of apple seedlings, "Johnny Appleseed" USA
Chesterton, G.K.
    All Things Considered (1908)
    "On Running After One's Hat"
Church of Jesus Christ of Latter Day Saints (LDS)
    founded by Joseph Smith, 1830
Clemens, Samuel, Langhorne, 1835-1910
    "Mark Twain" (1863-)
    "The Adventures of Huckleberry Finn Publ. 1894
Coleridge, Samuel, Taylor (1772-1834)
    The Rime of the Ancient Mariner
Crassweller, Ken,
    Stress Inducing Outdoor Space in Three
    Arctic Villages as Viewed by Inuit and Kadlunat,
        University of British Columbia 1976
    Let Ookpiks Fly 2003 Trafford Press, Vitoria, BC
Dickinson, Emily
    " Because I could not stop for death..."
Disney, Walt
    "Bambi" (film) released 1942 based on Felix Salten's novel
Francis, James, A
    "One Solitary Life"
Francis, Saint of Assisi

Prayer of: "Lord make me an instrument of your peace..."
Frankl, Victor E.
     Man's Search for Meaning, Washington
  Square Press, Simon and Schuster N.Y. 1963
Frost, Robert
     "The Road Not Taken, 1915, Atlantic Monthly
Goldon, Sir. William 1911-1993
     "The Lord of the Flies" 1954
Gottman, Notarius, Gonso, and Markman
     "A Couples Guide to Communication" Research Press, 1976
Guest, Edgar,A.
     "It Couldn't Be Done"
Hardy, Thomas 1840-1928
     "The Return of the Native" 1878
Haskins, M. Louise
     "And I said to the man who stood at the gate of the year..."
Alfred, Wright 1916-
     "The Lord God Made Them All" Nelson, Canada Ltd, 1981
Howe, Reuel
     Here Is Love, Judson Press, Valley Forge, USA
     Miracle of Dialogue, Seabury, N.Y. 1963
  Mans' Needs, God's Action " 1967
     The Creative Years 1974 " Survival Plus 1974
     Live All Your Life Word Books, Waco, USA .74
Irving, Washington 1783-1859
     "The Legend of Sleepy Hollow" "Ichabod Crane"
Jehovah Witnesses (JWS) founded by Charles Taze, 1872
Kaye, Danny 1913-1987 comedian, singer, dancer, musician,
     Musical, "Hans Christian Anderson".
Kenney, Mart band leader
     "Mart Kenney and His Western Gentlemen" 1981
         Western Producers Prairie Books, Saskatoon, Sask.
Kipling, Rudyard 1865-1936
     poem "If"   "L'Envoi"
Kornhauser, Arthur W.
     "How to Study" The University of Toronto Press 1934, 1937
Lewis, C.S.
     "Mere Christianity" Word Publishers 1987
Longfellow, Henry, Wadsworth poem   "The Day Is Done"
Lovelace, Richard   "Stone walls do not a prison make...."
Luft, Joseph 1960   "Of Human Interaction"
                         Palo Alto CA. National Press.
Milton, Ralph
     "This United Church of Ours" Wood Lake Books

Winfield, B.C. 1991
Mitchell, W.O. 1947-
    "Who Has Seen the Wind"
        MacMillan Company of Canada 1961
Pruyser, Paul W.
    "The Minister As Diagnostician
    Personal Problems in Pastoral Perspective"
    The Westminster Press, Philadelphia 1976
Roethke, Theodore 1908-1963
    The Waking 1955 p.120
Robinson, Carson and Pleasant Valley Boys.
    "Life Gets Tee-Jus Don't it."
Rousseau, Jean Jacques 1712-1778
    "Discourse in the Origin of Inequality Among Mankind"
1755 translated 1761"Naturalism,"
George Santayana, John Dewey.
    Americans 19th-20c
Russell, Bertrand
    Skeptical Essays 1928, Freedom vs Authority in Education
Sartre, John Paul 1905-1980
    Being and Nothingness 1943
Schmidt, Lois
    poems, "I Remember ", "Now and Then", "Farm Accounts"
Shakespeare, William 1564-1616
    "Tomorrow and Tomorrow", From Macbeth
Spence, Hartzell
    "One Foot in Heaven. The Life of a Practical Parson"
    publ. The Military Service Publishing Co. Harrisburg,
Pennsylvania 1945
Sunday Billy 1863-1935, Presbyterian minister
    evangelist, broadcaster
Swift, Johnathon
    "Travels into Several Remote Nations of the World" ie;
"Gulliver's Travels"
Tennyson, Alfred, Lord
    "Morte D'Arthur"
Thompson, Francis 1859-1907
    "The Hound of Heaven" Burns & Oats, London, England Thoreau,
Henry, David 1817-1862
    "Waldon" or "Life In the Woods' ie: "On Waldon Pond, 1854
Wood, Grant 1892-1942, artist
    "American Gothic" Art Institute, Chicago 1930
Ylvisaker, John   (song lyrics) 1985 I was There To Hear Your
                        Burning Cry "..Just more surprise "

The Author

Ken Crassweller: was born in Regina, Saskatchewan, Canada. He. climbed poles for Sask Telephone Company, worked for the Hudson's Bay Co. Fur Trade in northern Saskatchewan and Manitoba, taught Indian and Inuit children in northern Manitoba, Northern Quebec and on Ellesmere Island, Northwest Territories .He once operated a HBC camp trade. Later he served with Industry and Development, of the Federal Government Northern Affairs in Fort Chimo, Quebec, Iqaluit (Frobisher Bay), NWT, and in Ottawa, and with the Gov't. of the NWT, in Yellowknife.

Over those years he traveled the Arctic, sharing in the providing of material, financial and technical assistance to the Inuit (Eskimo) artists, carvers, and crafts people.

He earned a B Ed at the University of British Columbia in Art Education, and an MA, in Community and Regional Planning with an emphasis on Arctic Settlements. He once served as principal of an Indian Band run-school in Northern Sask and also earned a degree from St. Andrew's College in Saskatoon, Sask. After ordination in the United Church of Canada, he served churches in Manitoba; Saskatchewan, British Columbia, and Alberta, Canada. He and his life long married partner are blessed with three adult children.

By the Same Author

Let Ookpiks Fly

He was an adolescent with "itchy feet" who knew only one thing, that is, get out of Regina, go north and hunt, fish, and maybe trap. So he hitchhiked to La Ronge. That began, through the 1950's and '70's, a unique Canadian cluster of experiences; trading with the Hudson's Bay Company, teaching Native and Inuit (Eskimo) children in the High Arctic, discovering an alternative view of Indian Residential Schools; working with Inuit artists and craftspeople, and preparing for work in community and regional planning. This ended with the question, "what now and to what end?" Meet the author and the characters he learned from.

Come away from this, exposed to different perspectives than the conventional ones, having heard from someone like yourself who sought identity, purpose, and spiritual meaning.

ISBN 141202227-4